MORIOR.

MICHAEL KING is New Zealand's leading biographer and historian. He has a doctorate in history from the University of Waikato and an honorary doctorate in literature from Victoria University.

In a career spanning thirty years he has written twenty-eight books, hundreds of contributions to other books and journals, television documentaries, features for newspapers and magazines and radio broadcasts. He has won a wider range of awards for this work than any other New Zealand writer. In the 1970s and 1980s he was the first professional author in New Zealand to specialise in indigenous history. His most recent biography was *Wrestling with the Angel – A Life of Janet Frame*, which has been published internationally.

Dear Sophy,

Happy Birthday and thank you so much again for helping out on Rangatira Island. May this book remind you of the island.

Love, Melanie

By the same author

Moko — Maori Tattooing in the Twentieth Century
Make it News — How to Approach the Media
Te Ao Hurihuri (Ed.)
Tihe Mauri Ora (Ed.)
Te Puea
New Zealand: Its Land and its People
New Zealanders at War
The Collector — A Biography of Andreas Reischek
A Place To Stand — A History of Turangawaewae Marae
New Zealand in Colour
Maori — A Photographic and Social History
Whina — A Biography of Whina Cooper
Apirana Ngata, E Tipu e Rea
Kawe Korero — A Guide to Reporting Maori Activities
Being Pakeha
Auckland (with Eric Taylor)
Death of the Rainbow Warrior
New Zealand (with Eric Taylor)
One of the Boys? (Ed.)
After the War: New Zealand Since 1945
A Land Apart — The Chatham Islands of New Zealand
Pakeha, The Quest for Identity in New Zealand (Ed.)
Hidden Places
The Coromandel
Frank Sargeson, A Life
God's Farthest Outpost — A History of Catholics in New Zealand
Being Pakeha Now
Wrestling with the Angel: A Life of Janet Frame

MORIORI

A PEOPLE REDISCOVERED

MICHAEL KING

VIKING

PENGUIN BOOKS

Penguin Books (NZ) Ltd, cnr Airborne and Rosedale Roads, Albany,
Auckland 1310, New Zealand
Penguin Books Ltd, 27 Wrights Lane, London W8 5TZ, England
Penguin Putnam Inc, 375 Hudson Street, New York, NY 10014, United States
Penguin Books Australia Ltd, 487 Maroondah Highway,
Ringwood, Australia 3134
Penguin Books Canada Ltd, 10 Alcorn Avenue, Toronto,
Ontario, Canada M4V 3B2
Penguin Books (South Africa) Pty Ltd, 5 Watkins Street,
Denver Ext 4, 2094, South Africa
Penguin Books India (P) Ltd, 11, Community Centre, Panchsheel Park,
New Delhi 110 017, India
Penguin Books Ltd, Registered Offices: Harmondsworth, Middlesex, England

First published by Penguin Books (NZ) Ltd 1989
This revised edition published 2000

3 5 7 9 10 8 6 4 2

Copyright © Michael King 1989, 2000

The right of Michael King to be identified as the author of this work in terms of section 96
of the Copyright Act 1994 is hereby asserted.

Designed by Richard King
Typeset by Egan-Reid Ltd
Printed in Hong Kong by Condor Production Ltd

ISBN 0 14 010391 0
www.penguin.com

For
Maui and Jackie
Wilf and Davina
Charlie and Pat

CONTENTS

FOREWORD

Rekohu is the name given to Chatham Island by its indigenous people, the Moriori. It means 'cloudy sky' and refers to the mist which often clings to the land there. Like Rekohu, the Moriori and their history have been engulfed in mists of fiction and mythology since their first encounter with Europeans in the eighteenth century. The purpose of this book is to set aside those fictions and reveal the truth about the Moriori and what happened to them following the island's rediscovery by Lieutenant Broughton in 1791 and the Taranaki Maori invasion of 1835.

The idea of a book about the Moriori evolved over a number of years and is the culmination of a series of events that began with a Television New Zealand documentary on the Moriori screened in 1980. This led to a Moriori reunion in 1983 and the unveiling of a statue in Rekohu on 29 December 1986. It was generally felt by Moriori descendants that insufficient attention had been paid to the Moriori and to their place in the history of New Zealand, and that a book would be the most effective means of communicating to the wider general public the story of Rekohu's original inhabitants. It was agreed that a writer with exemplary qualifications and a keen interest in New Zealand history would be required to undertake the major task of writing such a book.

On the basis of Michael King's established reputation as New Zealand's finest social historian, reinforced by personal observation and discussion, he was invited by descendants of the Moriori to research and write their post-Contact history, using as his sources all written evidence and, wherever possible, personal interviews with people who could provide useful information about the Moriori. For the record, therefore, this book has been written at the request of and in full agreement and cooperation with people of recognised Moriori descent.

Maui Solomon

INTRODUCTION

Throughout my lifetime, the majority of New Zealanders have been confused about who the Moriori were, or whether they even existed. They were the first inhabitants of New Zealand; they were defeated and driven from the mainland by the Maori; they went direct to the Chathams from Polynesia; they are a people whose origins, like those of the Easter Island statues, are mysterious; the last one died in 1933; they never existed; they are alive today.

These contradictory theories, some of them held with the strength of religious conviction by writers of letters to the editor and callers to talkback radio, are all current. They ought not to be. I wrote my first article for the press about 'Moriori myths taught as history' as long ago as 1968; little has changed since then.

When Maui Solomon's letter asking me to write this book arrived late in 1986, it was almost as if I had been anticipating it, though we had never met. I had been keeping a running file on Moriori matters for over two decades; my interest had been further fuelled by conversations with Rhys Richards and David Simmons as much as by the persistence of inaccurate notions in the public mind. After only moderate hesitation I accepted the Moriori invitation to write this book with the active collaboration of Moriori descendants. I did so because I had been asked by those who could be considered the 'proprietors' of Moriori history and traditions; because I was convinced that it was time to clear away the multiple misunderstandings about the Moriori; and because the topic was one I found wholly engaging.

There are many people I need to thank, without whose wholehearted cooperation this book could not have been written.

Firstly, members of the Preece, Solomon and Davis families, especially Bunty Preece, Riwai Preece, Charlie and Pat Preece, Charlie and Cissy Preece, Stella Cotter, Eileen Soanes, Maui and Jackie Solomon, Charlie Solomon, Rose Solomon, Tommy Solomon, Gary Solomon, Denis Solomon, Julie Solomon, Charles Solomon junior, and Wilford and Denise Davis. Secondly, the Chatham Islanders who offered me unlimited recollections and constant refreshment: David and Joyce Holmes, Pat Prendeville, Stephen Barker, Ani Kamo, Father Mark Moesbergen, Rob Chappell, Norman Thomas, Bertha Wilson, Rose Swann, Jane Hough, Bessie Clough and Miria Wills Johnson. Thirdly, those who had done Chathams research before me and generously made available their time and the results of their research: Rhys Richards, Doug Sutton, David Simmons, Roger Green, Bruce McFadgen, Lyndsay Head, Sheila Natusch, Bill Saunders and Television New Zealand, Bill Burt, Phillip Houghton, Ross Clark, Ray Harlow and Miria Wills Johnson.

Lyndsay Head, Douglas Sutton, Rhys Richards, Bill Saunders, Margaret Orbell, K. J. Dennison, Ross Clark and Kendrick Smithyman gave me permission to quote from their copyright material.

Joan Woodward and Michael Purdie of Canterbury Museum, Warwick Wilson of Te Papa, Gordon Maitland of the Auckland Institute and Museum, John Sullivan and Joan McCracken of the Alexander Turnbull Library and Annette Facer of the Hocken Library were all especially helpful in directing me to relevant photographs.

I am indebted also to Ken Scadden and Chris Adam of National Archives; Ron Scarlett, Lyn Williams and Joanne Smith of Canterbury Museum; and Rosemary O'Neill of the Canterbury Public Library. Other valued assistance came from Bill Burt, Hemi Hape, Buddy Mikaere, Kera Brown, Hugh Stringer, Nigel Prickett, Syd Cormack, David and Anita Baucke, Elisabeth Jenkins, Frank Paynter, Joseph Eyles, Paul Lucas, Helen Murdoch, Rie Fletcher and Joseph Romanos.

Acknowledgements to other individuals and publications can be found in the footnotes, source notes and bibliography.

I also record my thanks to the New Zealand Literary Fund for the award of a non-fiction bursary, which gave me the resources to write this book; and to the Tommy Solomon Trust for assistance.

My largest debts, however, are to Maui Solomon, whose knowledge and determination persuaded me to write this book, and whose commitment to his people acted as a stimulant to me when my spirit was flagging; and to David Holmes, Rhys Richards and Douglas Sutton, whose immense erudition about the Moriori is matched by admiration and compassion for them, and who shared fraternal concern for the outcome of this project.

I also record my gratitude to Geoff Walker, my publisher; and to Maria Jungowska, my wife and colleague and source of the best advice I receive.

Some Polynesian words in the text of this book may appear unfamiliar or incorrect to those knowledgeable in Maori; this is because I have used Moriori dialect where appropriate.

Information about Maori activities in the Chathams comes from Maori sources: from Ngati Mutunga living on Chatham Island, from the testimonies of witnesses to the Native Land Court in the nineteenth century, and from oral evidence given to Alexander Shand by Ngati Tama and Ngati Mutunga elders between 1868 and 1900.

Michael King

PROLOGUE

24 March 1933

MANUKAU POINT ON CHATHAM ISLAND FEELS LIKE THE EDGE of the earth. When you stand there facing east, hills rising solidly and comfortingly at your back, the shelf before you narrows to a finger that disappears into a haze of sea spray and fog. There is nothing in front of you but 10,000 kilometres of sub-Antarctic ocean; then the southern coast of Chile.

Manukau also represents the terminus of 5,000 years of Pacific migration and its most distant destination. When settlers eventually reached it, after their ancestors had sailed 12,000 kilometres from the South China Sea to East Polynesia, 3,000 kilometres from Island Polynesia to New Zealand, then a further 870 to the Chathams, they could go no further. There was no additional destination within reach of canoe technology. Those settlers remained and named the promontory 'Only Birds', a recognition of the presence of gulls and petrels that inscribed their winged calligraphy in the air currents over the point and nested in burrows around the land's rim.

By 1933 people had lived at Manukau for at least 400 years. What had sustained them there more than anything else was the seafood. The rock shelf on the south side of the point, accessible in good weather at low tide, was a garden of paua, crayfish, sea urchin and limpets, and a platform from which to fish for greenbone and cod. The trees on the landward side, especially akeake and kopi, provided firewood and shelter from near continuous wind. There was a seal colony close by. And, a few kilometres to the north, the sweep of Hourangi Bay was intermittently dotted with blackfish, small whales driven by unexplained impulses to beach themselves in herds. Inhabitants of Manukau regarded them as gifts of the sea gods and their appearance was often associated with human death.

Only two major features had altered by 1933. The akeake forest was gone, replaced by 720 hectares of sheep-dotted pasture. And the seals had disappeared as a result of ruthless slaughter by Europeans a century before. Otherwise Manukau was largely unchanged. The seabirds still wheeled and cried, the kai moana lay beneath the boiling sea, and the wind blew relentlessly across the peninsula, more noticeable now in the absence of trees. Visitors found the prospect bleak.

There were approximately sixty such visitors on the point on 24 March 1933. They stood in a small cemetery, around half a dozen tombstones, huddling together and stamping their feet for warmth. Low cloud and moisture in the wind promised rain. Before them gaped a hole, three metres deep, three wide and three and a half metres long. It was far too big, even for the bulk of the enormous man they were about to bury. But the gravediggers had resorted to dynamite early in the day, to break through the volcanic rock that lay just below the grassed surface. At 4 p.m. they were still shovelling out shattered basalt and trimming the edges with picks. The onlookers began to speculate that it was too late in the day for a funeral: it would soon be dark.

Shortly before five o'clock the band of Maori workers, led by George Tuuta, another giant, heaved what looked like a black piano case through a hole in the front wall of the solitary homestead, 400 metres up the hill. The coffin, for such it was, was two and a half metres long, one and a quarter wide and a metre deep. The man inside it, who had died five days earlier, was only 1.74 metres in height. But he weighed over 190 kilograms. And this considerable bulk had begun to swell further by the day of the funeral. The coffin was carried to a sledge, covered with a tarpaulin (it had indeed begun to rain) and roped securely. Then two horses hauled it easily down the wet slope. At the bottom, manoeuvres became difficult again. George Tuuta and his pallbearers slipped the coffin off the sledge, grasped it from the base, staggered to the graveside, then slid it across the yawning hole on planks. They passed four ropes underneath, with which eight men would eventually lower the box to the grave floor. Then they stood back to allow two priests and the family — the widow and five children — to approach. Around them mourners closed in, to hear what was said above the noise of the wind and to watch in the failing light.

Because of the approach of darkness, the ministers hurried the prayers: the Reverend John Wilson, tall, thin, pale, precisely spoken, galloped through the Anglican burial service; the Reverend Paniora Te Arahu, vested in purple like a bishop but in fact an Apostle of the Ratana Church, followed with Maori karakia, then led the mourners in the singing of a Ratana hymn. There had been no mention of who the deceased was, other than the insertion of the name Tame in appropriate parts of the ritual; nor of *what* he was. Priests and congregation were nervous about the encroaching gloom: the islanders regarded burial after dark as highly inauspicious.

The ceremony seemed to be over. Most Maori present had said their farewells to the tupapaku in the course of the tangi inside the house which had followed the man's death. They had addressed him directly as he lay inert upon his bed and they had shed tears there, ritually and sincerely, for he had been almost universally loved. Now they stirred impatiently, willing an end to this final act. George Tuuta and his team took the weight of the coffin with the ropes, pulled away the planks, and lowered the deceased to the bottom of the grave. They began to drop the man's personal belongings into the hole, around the coffin and on top of it: clothing and personal effects in leather suitcases, cooking utensils and crockery that he had used, bedding, even the brass bedstead, now dismantled, on which he had lain. This too was customary on the Chathams: these objects were now contaminated by their association with death. As the workers reached for the shovels, some of the women — including the widow — began to keen.

At this point, barely visible in the thickening dusk, a stout, moustached European held up his hand to stop the burial and walked over to the widow. He bent to whisper in her ear and she nodded. The keening stopped and the men with shovels leaned on them and waited. The man, now recognisable as Resident Magistrate Ryan Holmes, walked to the head of the grave. He was wearing a dark suit and waistcoat, with fawn riding pants and black boots. When he began to speak it was with a Northern Irish accent.

Friends. We are gathered here today, as you are all aware, to pay our last tributes and respects to the memory of our departed friend, Tame Horomona Rehe, better known to all of us by the name Tommy Solomon. The passing of our friend as an individual is a matter more of interest and regret than usually associated with the passing away of an ordinary individual . . . It means not only the passing away by death of our late friend, but the passing away of a race of people. It is, therefore, a unique and historic occasion, and one that seldom arises in the history of mankind . . .

. . . [The] deceased was the last surviving Moriori of full blood — a race of people who were the original inhabitants of these islands. Like most people who possess something uncommon, he had come to be regarded by us as something unusual, and we prided ourselves on the fact. Now . . . around this open grave . . . we are conscious that something has happened, and . . . we realise the loss sustained by his death. This large gathering amply suggests the esteem in which he was held by island residents. We all remember his genial expression and love of repartee. He liked sport . . . and always received the result — whether he won or lost — with the same broad smile . . . [He] attracted notice wherever he went, and the press made the most of his periodic visits to the mainland to announce his presence there.

Now he is gone, and the race, as a race, is extinct.

Twilight faded into darkness, a journalist noted subsequently, 'and the dull roar of the ocean breakers echoed along the lonely sandhills as it had echoed before the Moriori came to his new home . . . and as it would continue to echo though he no longer heard its call'.

Within a week a school of blackfish hurled themselves on to Hourangi Beach to the north, as they were reputed to have done when Moriori died in pre-European times and were sat in the sand looking out to sea to draw these mammals ashore.

The noble sentiments expressed by Ryan Holmes and journalist Frank Simpson, repeated by some New Zealand newspapers and magazines, were well meant and sincerely held. But, representing a flow of emotion over judgment, they were not quite accurate. They added further confusion to a public mind already bewildered about who the Moriori were and where they came from.

Holmes was wrong to call them a race: the Moriori were Polynesian like the New Zealand Maori, Tongans, Samoans, Hawaiians and the inhabitants of Easter Island. He was wrong to suggest that, with Solomon's death, the Moriori people had become extinct: descendants of Moriori would continue to identify with that part of their genetic and cultural inheritance in succeeding generations. He was also wrong to imply that Moriori culture died with Tommy Solomon. It would have been more plausible to argue that it had died much earlier, along with the guardians of Moriori language and traditions in the nineteenth century; or that it remained alive in the values and aspirations of Moriori descendants.

But it *is* true that Tame Horomona Rehe, born 7 May 1884, died 19 March 1933, was the last full-blooded descendant of the original inhabitants of the Chatham Islands. And it is also true that four generations of New Zealanders have been taught to vilify Solomon's people, referring to them as a degenerate race, deficient in intelligence and morals, alleging that they were driven out of New Zealand by the racially and intellectually superior Maori, to take final refuge in the Chathams as a pitiful remnant of a primitive and vanquished people.

Nobody in New Zealand — and few elsewhere in the world — has been subjected to group slander as intense and as damaging as that heaped upon the Moriori. They were regarded by many Victorians as the lowest in God's hierarchy of created beings; and by non-Christians as negative proof of the Darwinian precept that only the fit survived. After 1835 Maori colonists despised them, enslaved them for a generation and referred to them contemptuously, in the borrowed currency of racism, as 'black fellas'.

In 1922, eleven years before Tommy Solomon's death, a former Chatham Islander characterised the Moriori as 'fat and greedy . . . [with] enormously swollen, out-curved, glutinously repulsive lips . . . [and] a brute appetite for food and sex and sleep'. Textbooks dismissed them in a few derogatory sentences, comprehensively misleading several generations of New Zealand schoolchildren. In the 1980s another ex-islander described Moriori as 'very degenerate' and 'of low intelligence'. He claimed Tommy Solomon had commandeered 'a good living from the lesser castes and [suffered] an early death through high and lazy living . . . there is, in my opinion, no reason for this kind of soft living to be tolerated . . .'

In the last years of the twentieth century, letters to the editor and contributions to talkback radio revealed that large numbers of New Zealanders still saw the Moriori as a dark-skinned, thick-lipped, wide-nostrilled race who inhabited New Zealand before the Maori and were forced to flee in the face of superior Polynesian enterprise and vitality. At the same time another group, largely Maori, was asserting that the Moriori had never existed, that they were no more than a Pakeha-created myth designed to justify European oppression of the Maori. Both views are equally wrong; and both are legacies of a history that is little known and understood even less.

The 'last Moriori' died in 1933 because the myths that vilified his people had persisted with astonishing potency, convincing even Moriori descendants that that part of their inheritance was of no value and best consigned to oblivion. Sixty years later, however, the Moriori were 'alive' again, and visible. Not because of some miracle of genetic engineering, but because the descendants of Solomon and his kinsmen again saw themselves as 'tchakat henu' — indigenous people and guardians of the mana of Rekohu; and because they had ceased to view their ancestors' unembellished way of life as 'backward' or 'primitive' and recognised it instead as a superbly adapted culture that had allowed survival and security in an otherwise harsh natural environment.

CHAPTER

ONE

Tchakat Moriori

T HE CHATHAMS — FOUR MAIN ISLANDS AND AN OUTLYING GROUP OF
rocks and reefs — constitute the ridge of a submarine mountain known to
geologists as the East Chatham Rise. They break the surface of the Pacific Ocean
870 kilometres east of New Zealand, bisected by the latitude 44° South. This
location and the convergence there of warm currents from the north and cold
water from the south produces the islands' climate and weather: almost incessant
wind (the 'Roaring Forties'), near-constant cloud cover, low sunshine hours, wet
winters and humid summers.

The Moriori had a variety of myths to account for their presence on these islands, the largest of which they referred to as Rekohu — 'misty sky' or 'misty sun'.* The most common recalled an ancestor named Kahu, who sailed the first canoe there from a homeland some remembered as Aotea.** Kahu found the islands in an unsettled state. He joined up disparate fragments and anchored them in what became their permanent positions. He also planted fernroot and kumara. Then, in the East Polynesian tradition of the wide-ranging traveller, he returned to his homeland to report on what he had seen. Three further canoes are said to have followed: *Rangihoua* and *Rangimata* (together), and subsequently *Oropuke*.

Another version of the myth has two autochthonous ancestors created on Chatham Island and in residence when Kahu arrived: Te Aomarama (an ancient Polynesian concept referring both to the dawning of day and to a stage in the unfolding of creation) and Rongomaiwhenua. Their origin is not clear; but the islands are said to have been 'planted' when the first people appeared.

Still another tradition has the peopling of the Chathams originating from Rangiauria, Pitt Island (unsurprising this, given that archaeologists were to find on Pitt what could be the oldest artifacts on the Chathams). These inhabitants were known as the Tuiti.

> How the first pair came is unknown; whether brought by the spirit from above, or created on the mountain . . . They lived upon the top of the mountain, from whence they caught and worshipped the first ray of the morning sun, and bowed in adoration to that luminary as he sank beneath the western wave . . .
>
> One day a youth wandered down to the sea-shore among the birds that lined the rocks, and, seating himself near where a [sea] eagle was perched pluming his wing, they fell into conversation. The eagle complained that he could no longer soar into the high air, by reason of a spell cast over his tribe . . . by the Tuiti . . .
>
> The youth answered that the blood of the honey-eater . . . had cried down to the Creator, and brought down upon the eagle his banishment. The Tuiti warred [with no one]; they fed on fruit and shed no blood: the eagle had banished himself. The king of birds, avoiding the issue, replied that in the great island to the northwest [Rekohu], which his friend had doubtless seen from the mountain, the woods were filled with beautiful birds, and fruit of every colour, hanging over the dark, transparent waters of many lakes . . .
>
> The youth listened to the tempter, and ambition elated his soul; he arose from the rock and asked to be shown the path that led over the water. The eagle, looking at him askance, promised him wings to fly over, provided he would first render an easy service by taking him to the top of the mountain . . . taking the eagle on his wrist, [he at last] ascended the mountain, and in the dark cast him loose . . . All night long the flutter and death-cry of birds smote upon his ear, and, when morning dawned, the song of the mako was mute and the tuis had ceased to mock.
>
> The people assembled in alarm. A child to whom its mother had given fruit fell dead; they gathered about its body in terror. The eagle hovered over them, and uttered his war-cry. The conscience-striken [*sic*] youth confessed. The day was passed in penitence and

---

* Moriori was the name attached to the first inhabitants of the Chathams *after* contact with Europeans and Maori; prior to that they needed no name other than personal and tribal ones. A people long separated from other peoples had no concept of race or culture. It comes from 'tchakat moriori', meaning 'normal' or 'ordinary people', and is the Chathams equivalent of 'maori'. It has also been rendered Mooriori, Maoriori, Maioriori, Mouriuri and Mori-ori. Rekohu was an obvious reference to the frequently hazy atmosphere over the islands. The name applied only to the largest island in the group, which Europeans called Chatham, and Maori, Wharekauri (see page 51).

** It is tempting to follow the example of nineteenth-century scholars such as Alexander Shand and connect Aotea with Aotearoa — one Maori name for New Zealand. But it needs to be stressed that the Moriori had had a generation of contact with Taranaki Maori on the Chathams before these arrival myths were recorded; and that they varied considerably in detail from individual to individual, place to place and tribe to tribe. Further, the expression Aotea was commonly synonymous in Polynesia with 'distant, far away'; it was a concept rather than a place.

sorrow about the body of the child in the lap of its wailing mother . . . The youth wandered by the shore, alone, stung with remorse, and, meeting the eagle, was taught by him to construct the . . . model of all canoes, made in the likeness of a sledge, with a wicker-work of tough creepers, having a false bottom filled with buoyant kelp.

He put to sea with his family, and landed on [Rekohu], which he found, as the eagle had said, uninhabited by man, a continent in size compared to [Rangiauria]; with undulating, fertile plains south and lofty mountains in the north, sparkling with lakes of dark transparent water, and vocal with the song and bright with the plumage of birds. Filled with new joy, he sent back tidings to his kinsmen, and was followed by successive emigrations, until [Rangiauria] was deserted save by a timid few who feared the sea. Thus came about the settlement of [Rekohu]: and to this extent is the tradition of the people.

Early twentieth century writers such as Stephenson Percy Smith and Elsdon Best believed that a chronological history of the Moriori could be constructed from such traditions. They presumed that Moriori mythology embalmed evidence for multiple canoe landfalls and return voyaging to New Zealand, and they tried to calculate the times of arrival from subsequent genealogical information.

This process is now seen as manipulative, presumptuous and of little value. The traditions cited were mytho-poetic stories told to link the uncertainties of the present and future to the measured assurances of the past, to assert identity, to explain natural phenomena and features of Moriori culture. They convey some of the textures of Moriori imaginative life, their 'public dreams', and offer clues as to the manner in which they viewed the world and their place in it. They were not intended to provide — nor did they provide — the objective chronologies and solemn weighing of cause and effect so beloved by Western scholars.

There is the further problem that by the time Moriori stories were recorded, in the latter half of the nineteenth century, the story-tellers had been in contact

The rugged character of much of the Chathams shoreline is apparent in this picture of cliffs on the south coast of Chatham Island.

Burt Collection,
Alexander Turnbull Library

with the Taranaki Maori colonists of the Chathams for more than a generation. Not only had the Moriori language become more 'Maori' in vocabulary and pronunciation, so had Moriori story-telling. It is likely, for example, that mention of Kahu's kumara was a post-Maori elaboration of an earlier Moriori tale. It is possible too that references to canoe landfalls referred to early voyages between Pitt and Chatham Islands. All these qualifications make the shaping of the distant past on mythological foundations a precarious construction.

There was also fierce debate among Victorian scholars about the identity of the Moriori and their place of origin. Arguments were advanced to 'prove' that they were variously negroid, Melanesian, a Melanesian-Polynesian mix, Jewish, Portuguese, and even that they belonged to a race which had peopled the southern oceans from the south and spread from Tierra del Fuego to Tasmania.*

Despite these obfuscations, there is in fact no mystery about who the Moriori are or where they came from. Their language, artifacts and bodily remains show them to have been Polynesian. They came from the Chathams. They were descended from the islands' first and (prior to the nineteenth century) only inhabitants. And they were recognisably Moriori — culturally and physically distinguishable from other Polynesian peoples — by the sixteenth century.

Nor is there any mystery about what they were not. They were not Melanesian, they were not a Melanesian-Polynesian fusion, they were not a pre-Maori race driven from New Zealand by more sophisticated later arrivals, they did not all come directly to Rekohu from Island Polynesia — though all these claims were to be made about them.

If there is any mystery, it revolves around the identity of the *ancestors* of the Moriori — and that is not impenetrable.

The ancestors of the Moriori were the same people as the ancestors of the New Zealand Maori: East Polynesians whose own ancestors had entered the Pacific from the region now called South-east Asia and the South China Sea. Having expanded throughout the Malaysian, Indonesian and Philippine archipelagoes, one group settled the coasts of the Melanesian islands, and had arrived in Fiji, Tonga and Samoa before 1000 B.C. From there, descendants moved into East Polynesia — especially the Cook, Society and Marquesas Islands — where many of the enduring features of their hierarchical and sea-based culture were further developed and refined. From East Polynesia, some of their descendants migrated north to Hawaii, others east to Easter Island, and still others south-west to New Zealand; and from New Zealand, sometime between the twelfth and the sixteenth centuries A.D., to the Chathams.

Evidence that the final migration was from New Zealand is explicit. Artifacts have been found on both Pitt and Chatham Islands — but more especially on Pitt — made from New Zealand materials (obsidian and argillite).** Other Chathams artifacts — necklace units, bird spear points, quadrangular adzes — are shaped in styles known to archaeologists as New Zealand Archaic; and some of them have been found *only* in New Zealand and on the Chathams. Sections of Moriori vocabulary reveal inextricable links with New Zealand (kawhai [Moriori] and kahawai [Maori] for the fish caught off the Chathams and New Zealand, for example; and kopi, the Moriori name for the karaka tree is a Maori

---

* Chapter 9 explores some of these theories.

** Some prehistorians have argued that because some of this 'New Zealand' material has been fossicked or found on the surface of habitation areas, it should not qualify as evidence. I cannot agree; nor can I accept that Taranaki Maori moving to the Chathams in the 1830s would have brought Archaic tools (though this migration has been advanced as a possible explanation for the presence of such tools).

Chatham Island basalt, with its fine grain, provided a valued source of stone for adzes and chisels. Heaped up around the island in dykes and columns, some deposits have the appearance of neolithic ruins. These ones are on the north-west coast.

Guest Collection,
Alexander Turnbull Library

name for the tree and its fruit, and the tree is found nowhere else in Polynesia other than the Kermadecs). The Moriori language as a whole shows a far closer affinity to Maori than to any other Polynesian dialect, with shared innovations that set them apart from other Polynesian languages and reveal their common origin.

Precisely which part of New Zealand the first people to settle the Chathams derived from, and when, is not known, and will not be until techniques of genetic analysis and radio carbon dating are further refined. There are signposts to answers, however.

Most early canoe voyages, particularly long ones for the trading of obsidian, greenstone or food, occurred down the east coast of New Zealand, the 'sheltered' side of the country. Like the winds, the convergence of currents from this coast tends to gather up and push flotsam eastwards towards the Chathams. Axed totara and kauri logs appeared there regularly during the height of mainland logging, and objects such as boxes and bottles from New Zealand still fetch up on Chathams beaches. This suggests that any canoe voyage to the Chathams — planned or accidental — is likely to have come from that part of the country.

The chances are probably highest in favour of an accidental journey: a double-hulled sailing canoe holding fewer than fifty people being forced eastwards by a storm. The fact that the founding group included men *and* women, and that they brought sufficient tools or tool-making expertise to reproduce their artifacts in local bone and stone, suggests a substantial trading party; or evidence of a planned migration, though not necessarily to the Chathams. Some writers have claimed that a study of the migratory paths of petrels and albatross would have signalled the existence of the islands to people who had never seen them. On the slender and hypothetical nature of evidence available, the verdict on deliberate or accidental colonisation has to remain open.

Linguistic and skeletal analysis show a closer affinity between Moriori and the Maori who lived in Murihiku (southern South Island) at the time of European contact than between Moriori and any other group (other than Taranaki Maori, whose invasion in 1835 had profound effects on Moriori language). This fact, combined with the probabilities of wind and current convergence, points to a likely voyage to the Chathams from some point south of Cook Strait.

Typical limestone cliffs and kopi trees on the west side of Te Whanga lagoon.

Burt Collection, Alexander Turnbull Library

As the traditions suggest, there may have been more than one colonising group. There could, indeed, have been several voyages between New Zealand and the Chathams. But this is conjecture. An analysis of Moriori bone shapes reveals such distinctively Polynesian forms — particularly the so called 'rocker jaws' and large skulls to match them — that they are likely to be the outcome of a limited gene pool; which in turn suggests the arrival of a single founding group.*

The group's time of arrival is even more susceptible to speculation. The absence of greenstone from Chathams archaeological sites appears to point to a landfall prior to the fourteenth century, by which time that stone was being traded around New Zealand. But the earliest undisputed carbon dates for Chathams habitation sites go back no further than the fifteenth and sixteenth centuries. The most cautious estimate would be that the ancestors of the Moriori arrived between the ninth and the sixteenth century. The balance of probabilities is that it was around the thirteenth or fourteenth century.**

Nor is it likely that the location of the first landing will ever be known. Two early sites on the east coast of Pitt have revealed a proliferation of material in the New Zealand Archaic style; it is possible (as at least one of the Moriori traditions claims) that the initial settlers colonised Pitt before they attempted a landing on Chatham. But there is also at least one clearly Archaic site on the north coast of Chatham Island; and many former beach sites — particularly those on Hanson Bay on the east coast of the main island — have washed into the sea, distorting the surviving archaeological record. However and whenever they arrived, the ancestors of the Moriori would have found themselves sharing the Chathams for much the same purposes as the marine and pelagic creatures drawn there from the entire southern ocean for breeding and feeding, nesting and resting. Indeed, it was the presence of these animal predecessors — fur seals, petrels, albatross — that determined the population distribution and seasonal activities of the people who were to become Moriori.

All the islands — Chatham, Pitt, South-East and Mangere — are volcanic in origin and total just under a thousand square kilometres in area. Chatham rises steeply from a turbulent sea in a great curtain of basalt cliffs along its southern coast. It slopes upwards into a tableland, which was covered in tarahinau forest, with a variety of broadleaf trees, tree ferns and nikau palms running down the gullies to the coast. Further north, the land falls away in a series of small hills and valleys, intersected by rivers and streams and formerly covered in mixed forest. The centre of the island is flat, made up of limestone and old sand bars, much of which is overlaid with peat. Trees such as kopi, coprosma and akeake grew in profusion in the better-drained areas. But the centre is dominated by Te Whanga lagoon, which covers about one-fifth of the island's area. The northern coast is mainly low-lying schist, topped with dunes and peat and dotted with a dozen volcanic cones on the western side.

Pitt Island was less varied in appearance. It slopes from a volcanic upland down to a sandstone northern coast. It too had extensive areas of broadleaf and nikau forest, whose trees, plants and forest birds, like those on Chatham, derived from New Zealand. Mangere and South-East Islands had some low trees but were

---

* Some scholars, including Duff and Sutton, have suggested that more settled weather conditions could have permitted two-way voyaging prior to the onset of a 'little ice age' in and after the fourteenth century. Subsequent research has thrown doubt on this theory and Sutton among others has moved away from it.

** This conclusion could, of course, change dramatically if earlier dates are verified. At the time of writing some of the most likely early sites, on Pitt Island, had not been systematically excavated or carbon dated.

too small to support permanent human occupation. The outlying rocks were populated seasonally by ocean birds and seals; the most densely occupied — which became the target of hunting expeditions — being the Sisters to the north, the Forty Fours and Star Keys to the east and the Pyramid to the south.

Migrants from the sea were the most conspicuous inhabitants of the islands and sources of food for their human colonists. At least sixteen species of flying oceanic birds and penguins went ashore to breed or moult. Petrels, prions and (on the outlying rocks) albatross were taken for eating at the young or 'mutton bird' stage. Whales, especially blackfish, stranded frequently on the main island's northern, eastern and western beaches. Leopard seals, sea lions and elephant seals were available periodically on the coast. And the fur seal had extensive breeding colonies on Chatham and Pitt (one estimate of the pre-European seal population

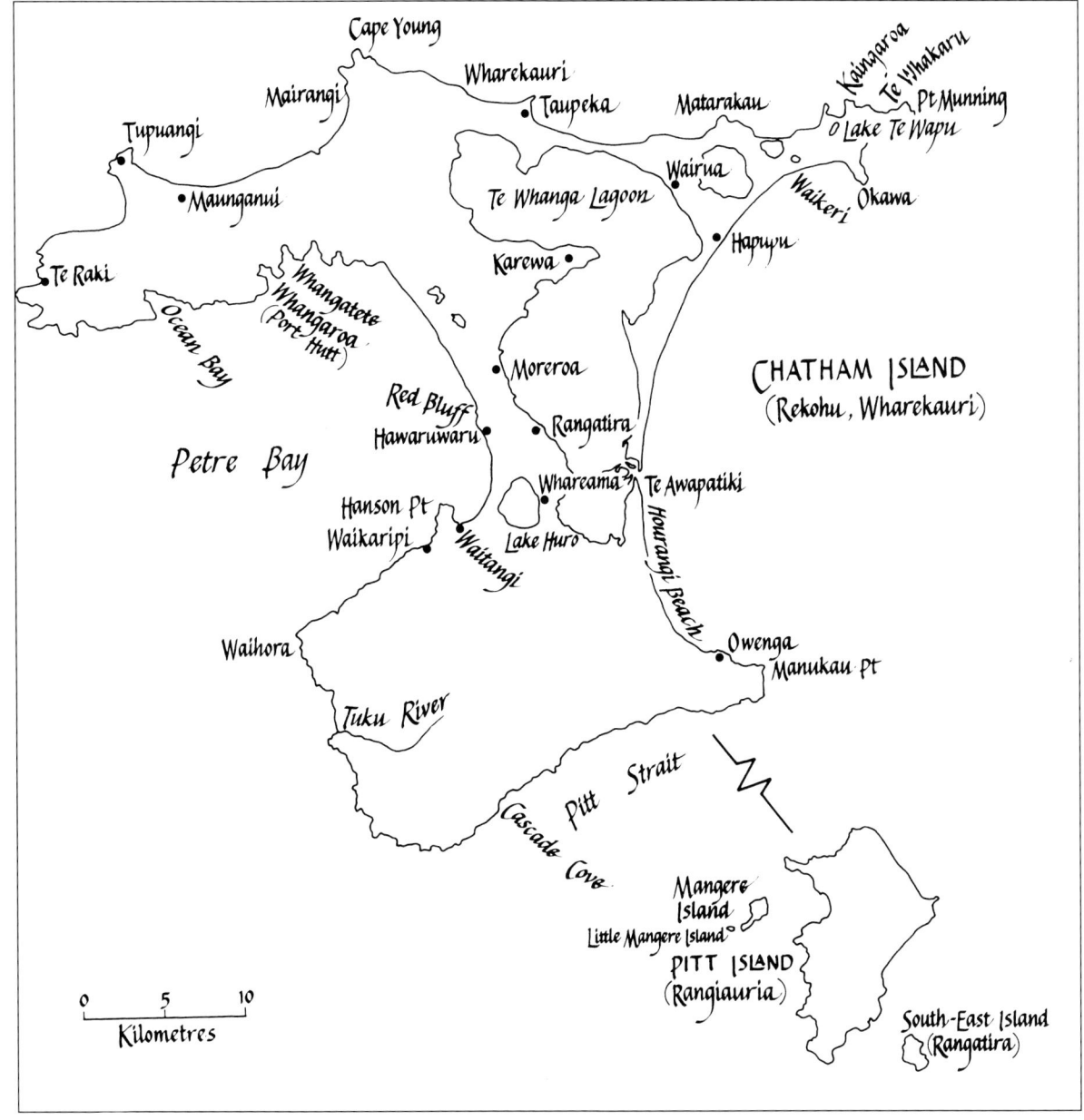

there is 20,000 animals, though not all writers agree that they were so prolific).

Fish too were also plentiful — not large in species types but certainly so in numbers: cod, groper, greenbone, moki, tarakihi. Crayfish and crab made up another food source, as did shellfish and seaweed. For the Moriori, marine food resources on the Chathams were to prove far more abundant, diverse, reliable and resilient than land foods.

The latter included forest birds (especially the parea or wood pigeon), rails in the bog scrublands, vast numbers of duck around the lagoons — easily caught during the moulting season — and fish and eels in the inland waters. Thirty plants were potentially edible, and heavy use was made of pounded bracken; though none other than the kopi kernels and nikau and cabbage tree hearts were readily collected or especially palatable.

There were no naturally occurring land mammals. The Polynesian rat was introduced — deliberately or accidentally — by the Moriori ancestors and provided an additional source of protein. Dogs may have been brought with the first colonists and died out — or were deliberately exterminated because of the effect of their presence on seals, which are believed to have been a major hunting target and food source. If the founding group brought cultivated vegetables, as some traditions claimed, these plants failed to grow because of insufficient sunshine and other climatic disadvantages.

This, then, was the environment into which the ancestors of the Moriori moved, in or before the fourteenth century. The process by which they matched

The density of the broadleaf forest which characterised Pitt Island (shown here) and most of the coast on Chatham is clear in this nineteenth-century photograph. Such bush was home for pigeon, tui and bellbird, and several other species that originated on the New Zealand mainland but developed local features in isolation.

National Museum

their cultural resources and skills to the new conditions and materials they encountered is the process by which an Archaic New Zealand Polynesian people became Moriori, distinguishable from the Maori who emerged in New Zealand from the same stock over much the same period.

Insufficient archaeological work has been carried out on the Chathams to determine precisely how and over what period the transformation took place. What can be said is that by the sixteenth century, Moriori culture had developed most of the features that European observers were to record in the eighteenth and nineteenth centuries.

There had been a considerable reduction in the range of artifacts compared with what has been found on the islands' probable earliest sites. Personal ornaments, highly polished adzes, and bird spears had become uncommon. Moriori material culture was characterised by flake tools, adzes, several forms of unpolished patu and wooden implements.

Whereas in the Archaic phase settlements were found only on a few sheltered east coast sites, Moriori ones are scattered around the most exposed locations and appear to have been occupied periodically according to the resources found there and seasonal variations in their availability. Hence, while mainland Maori were moving towards a permanent village system, Moriori were not.

Most important (and this is deduced from a combination of archaeological evidence and records from the historical period), Moriori culture was moving away from the traditional hierarchical Polynesian model of chiefs and commoners and developing an egalitarian structure. Moriori came to live in kin-based groups of around thirty to a hundred people. Each occupied settlements seasonally within an area to which they probably had prior but not exclusive rights. Community decisions were made collectively, and elders were senior members of the group whose powers were persuasive rather than arbitrary and hereditary.

Leaders worked on subsistence tasks alongside their followers; they were not tattooed, nor did they typically wear distinctive clothing and ornaments. This level

Blackfish, or pilot whales, are known to have stranded themselves on Chatham Island beaches for as long as the island has been settled. They were regarded by Moriori as gifts of the seagods Tangaroa and Pou, and their appearance was often associated with human death. They would have sustained large numbers of Moriori over a long period, but were an unreliable food source.

Burt Collection,
Alexander Turnbull Library

social order is reflected in the diminution of burials with elaborate grave goods — artifacts and ornaments; and in an eventual preponderance of less complex interments, which often involved simply leaving the crouched corpse half buried in the sand, 'looking' out to sea; or tied to a tree with some symbol of the deceased's occupation, such as a fish hook or carving tool. This suggests mana arose increasingly from accomplishment rather than from hereditary status.

According to tradition (and the archaeological record does not contradict it), Moriori had also abolished lethal combat between and within kin groups, a feature of their culture that was unusual in Polynesia. The stories tell of an ancestor, Nunuku-whenua, who became sickened by bloodshed and cannibalism while two tribes, Rauru and Wheteina, were fighting at Karewa on the western side of Te Whanga lagoon. Nunuku pushed between the warring ranks and ordered each side to retire.

> Stricken with stupefaction at this apparition, without striking another blow, they so retired. 'Follow me!' Palsied with a fear of the unknown, they followed. When they reached the shore he cried: 'You, Rauru, sit there; you, Wheteina, here!' They sat accordingly. 'Onlookers, gather all arms and stack them there!' Obediently the arms were stacked. 'Build a fire and cast the arms on top!' The fire was built, the spears and claymores of wood were burnt, yet no word was spoken in protest. 'Rauru! Wheteina! arise and meet!' They arose and met. 'Touch nose to nose!' Nose to nose was touched. 'Listen all! From now and forever, never again let there be war as this day has been! From today on forget the taste of human flesh! Are you fish that eat their young?'
>
> So it was there agreed that because men get angry and during such anger feel the will to strike, that so they may, but only with a rod the thickness of a thumb, and one stretch of the arms in length, and thrash away, but that on an abrasion of the hide, or first sign of blood, all should consider honour satisfied. 'And,' said the teller, 'all obeyed! Why? Because of the Nunuku curse: "May your bowels rot the day you disobey!"'

Traditional and historical evidence suggests that Nunuku's injunction was largely honoured (though oral tradition did preserve war chants, and assertive Moriori behaviour was to frighten the first Europeans to set foot on the islands in the eighteenth century). Certainly those who broke it were ostracised; and most Moriori seem to have been familiar with the tradition in the nineteenth century and cited it as the reason why they had not taken up arms against the Taranaki Maori invaders.

Whether or not the *story* of Nunuku is literally true, the ritualising of aggression (which is what enforced single-combat represented) was a sensible way of ensuring the survival of a viable population on two small islands. Each clan occupied largely exclusive territories where it knew every rock and tree, had ample food resources, and was no threat to any other. When a dispute did break out — over sex, firewood, food or a boundary violation — they had a method of dealing with it that did not threaten annihilation. In this respect, as in others, the Moriori had found a way of living in a state of equilibrium with their own species as they had with available resources.

Their distance from other islands and the consequent absence of outside aggressors also helped keep the Nunuku tradition alive; as did the control of birth numbers by the castration of some male infants. Population growth was not allowed to put pressure on either boundaries or food resources. And hunting expeditions, sometimes involving up to sixty people travelling in wash-through rafts to outlying islands as far as forty-five kilometres from the coast, were carried out cooperatively rather than competitively.

Because masculinity was not expressed — as it was in other Polynesian

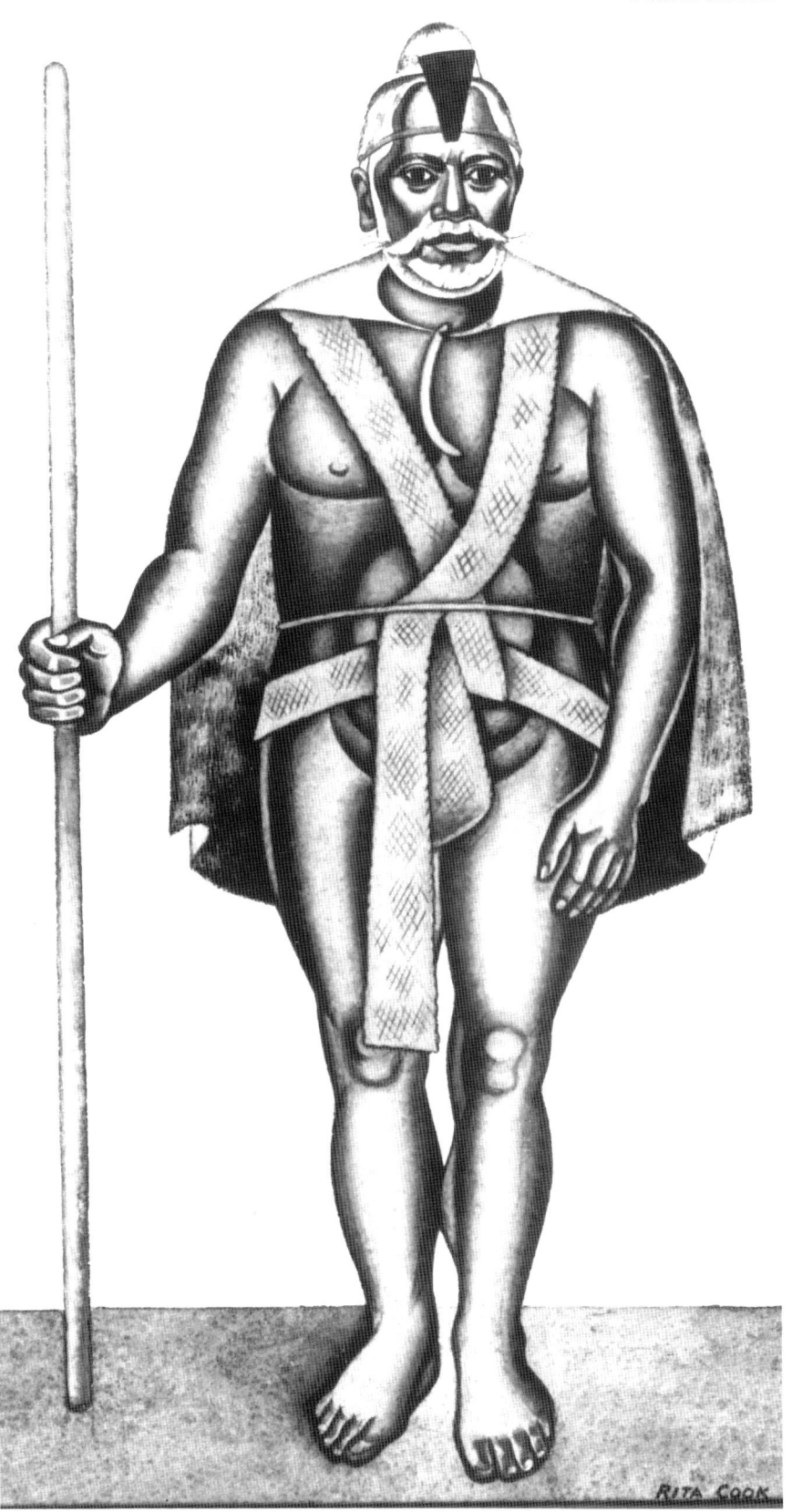

Moriori wore few clothes, usually a rain-proof flax mat or sealskin around the hips or shoulders. This drawing by Rita Angus, commissioned by Canterbury Museum, is a kind of Moriori fashion show that displays authentic items of costume, but ones that would only rarely have been worn simultaneously. The hair is in a topknot, a kura (red parakeet feather) ornament adorns the forehead, a sealskin cloak fixed with a bone pendant covers the shoulders, and a marowhara (flax girdle) is wound about the body. The tupuari (staff) could be used in one-to-one combat.

Canterbury Museum

cultures — through warfare or enduring the pain of tattooing, the Moriori substituted other activities as proving grounds for manhood. One was the demonstration of bravery on birding expeditions, particularly when landing on sheer or even concave rock faces; another was the manufacture of a hafted adze; and a third was the capacity to dive in rough seas for crayfish and come up with one in each hand and a third in the mouth.

The most detailed archaeological study of the Chathams to date has been carried out by Douglas Sutton of the University of Auckland. He has described in detail the organisation and workings of a sixteenth-century Moriori village on the south-west of Chatham Island, which he excavated over two years. The site, Waihora, was a central settlement from which small parties dispersed to gather food or minerals. It was occupied by up to fifty people, who lived in rectangular houses which stood between burial sites (on the seaward side) and a food preparation area in the centre of the settlement. Refuse was placed in heaps on the leeward side.

> The people who occupied Waihora and the related sites lived by sealing, shellfishing, fishing, fowling and some collection of plant foods. They killed fur seals throughout the year at a rookery just 400m away and took other large seals whenever the opportunity presented itself. The seal carcasses were butchered near the rookery and meat blubber and other edible materials moved to Waihora. Sealing was easily the most important subsistence activity in the economic cycle.
>
> Shellfishing was a seasonal activity in so far as it was most often possible to collect shellfish efficiently during the calmer months from October to April. Shellfish were collected off the large areas of intertidal platform . . . and many shells were left neatly in big dumps, now identified as specialised middens. Women and children probably collected the shellfish and they were very selective. The three largest, most conspicuous and easily taken species comprise over ninety per cent of the shellfish recovered from three of the specialised middens which were excavated . . .
>
> The men caught inshore fish species by using nets set and cast off the less kelp-covered promontories, again most frequently during the calmer months from October to April. Line fishing was very uncommon. Netting was an efficient strategy given the concentration of fish inshore and the frequent and unpredictable changes of wind speed and direction which occur in the Chathams. It produced a lot of potential food with only relatively simple technology and little or no risk . . .
>
> Several species of marine birds were killed in large numbers during their short breeding seasons. For instance, Chatham Island taiko fledglings were taken from burrows during January after a six-month-long absence of the birds from the area. The taiko colonies were on the ridge-tops and along the edge of the tableland scarp. The inland middens were left by people exploiting those colonies. Considerable numbers of penguins were killed during summer and autumn. Despite their selective and in some cases intense exploitation, marine birds were not a major source of food.
>
> Forest birds were also relatively unimportant in terms of food values, but again fowling, like all other subsistence pursuits, was very selective. Pigeon, tui and bellbird, the heaviest, most conspicuous and stationary forest bird species present, make up over 85 per cent of the forest birds identified . . . Coastal birds, apart from the diving petrel and two shag species, were not hunted systematically, evidently because they were more dispersed, smaller and harder to catch than the selected species. There was some systematic hunting of rails, with spears and snares. Their absence and a specialisation in the capture of other more economic species may account for the late survival of the large and vulnerable endemic rail, *Diaphorapteryx hawkinsi*.
>
> Plant foods were collected but very little evidence of them survives in the archaeological record. Fern-root was collected and chewed. It is possible that the burning of the tarahinau evident in pollen spectra from the Durham area and a location 8km to

the north-west, was deliberate and designed to cultivate bracken. Karaka kernels were collected, probably with some of the large berries and nikau, when available in the area. It seems likely that wild plant foods were valuable as a carbohydrate source in a very high fat diet.

Trade and exchange of durable materials from areas beyond the south-west coast of Chatham Island was very limited. For instance, 5 per cent of the sourced stone flakes found at Waihora came from within 8km of the settlement. The very small quantity of material from further away was imported on an ad hoc basis for specific tasks when locally available materials were not suitable. For instance, 80 valves of a soft shore bivalve were found amongst the shellfish in Waihora. Some came from a location 13km away while others were brought at least 24km. They were used as scrapers, a purpose for which they are much better suited than the rocky shore shellfish found on the Durham coast.

One particularly interesting exception to the general practice of exploiting locally available resources involves the albatross bone from pre-flight individuals. Immature bone of each of the three species of *Diomedea* which breed on the Chathams was found in Waihora. This reflects exploitation in early spring of breeding colonies on the Pyramid 56km to the south-east, the Forty Fours 69km to the east, and the Sisters which are 53km to the north-west, either by the Waihora people or some others from whom they obtained these very highly valued birds.

By the time European witnesses were able to observe and record some Moriori customs in the eighteenth and nineteenth centuries, other features of their culture less evident in the archaeological record were noted.

Moriori 'houses' for example, seemed to vary according to the location and purpose of settlements. Some were mere arbours made by bending growing trees, some single-screen windbreaks, some double-sided windbreaks set up in an inverted-V structure. Others may have been circular huts, or roofed and porched rectangular houses. Moriori carving (one set of low house gables from the late

Moriori group dressed partly in traditional costume. From left: Te Ropiha, wearing a flax mat under a European shawl; Uauroa, Ropiha's wife, in a European blanket; Te Teira, maternal grandfather of Tommy Solomon, wearing a kura (parakeet-feather head ornament), albatross down in his beard, a flax rain cape and holding a tupuari; Pumipi has a woven flax mat and also wears albatross tufts in his beard.

Canterbury Museum

1840s and an upright funereal figure have survived) shows an extremely limited range of motifs compared with that from other Polynesian cultures. Rock carvings (petroglyphs) appear to have celebrated the importance of seals and albatross in the tribes' economic and spiritual life. Tree carvings (dendroglyphs) on the bark of living kopi were similarly unembellished but effective in their graphic simplicity.*

Although they did not cultivate traditional Polynesian vegetables (kumara, taro, yam) on the islands, the Moriori became sophisticated in the manipulation

---

* The 'dancing' posture of many dendroglyphs closely resembles some early South Island rock drawings; but the form was probably one common to early Polynesia.

Carved planks from the front of a low Moriori house, believed to have been standing at Owenga in the 1840s. Some motifs are curvilinear, not unlike the Maori koru pattern, and others bird-like. These are the sole surviving examples.

National Museum

of wild plants, to make them grow more prolifically and more fruitfully (especially kopi — for its berry kernels — and fernroot, which they grew in clearings and around the edges of the kopi groves, where the richer soil gave it a pleasantly nutty taste).

Large dugout canoes had long since disappeared, because of an absence of suitable trees. But their place had been taken by the korari or so-called wash-through rafts, which had a base of inflated kelp for buoyancy and a floor and sides of bound reeds. Although they looked cumbersome and were difficult to carry, they were well suited to the strong winds and rough seas around the Chathams. They lay low, partially waterlogged, and were far more stable than conventional canoes in such conditions. In these crafts — some measuring up to fifteen metres in length (including bow and stern projections) — Moriori made safe journeys between Chatham and Pitt Islands, out to the cod-fishing grounds, where they tied the craft to long arms of kelp, and forty to fifty kilometres out to the offshore rocks for seal and albatross hunting.

Moriori language remained closely related to Maori — so closely that analysis reveals the common origin of both. The major differences were in pronunciation of certain consonants and vowels ('tch' in Moriori for the Maori 't', 'h', for 'wh', 'hoko' for the Maori causative prefix 'whaka'); final vowels were often clipped so short in speech that they appeared to have been dropped. The eventual transcription of the language in a form that emphasised pronunciation had the effect of making Moriori seem more removed from Maori than it was. In fact only about ten per cent of Moriori words preserved roots lost to Maori (ririma for 'hand', for example, is closer to the early Polynesian 'lima' than the Maori 'ringaringa'). The Maori who settled the Chathams in 1835 had little difficulty understanding Moriori, and vice versa.*

The number of tribal districts, identified by Moriori themselves, was seven: one in the north-west of Chatham Island, which held about 200 people in 1791; two on the western side containing 330 and 230 respectively; one in the south-west with 170 people; another in the north-east with 430; one in the south-east made up of 360 members; and one more on Pitt of around 300 people. This gave a high population density: about 2000 on a total of 108,000 hectares of land — sufficient to make animal and bird resources and seals potentially vulnerable unless they were carefully conserved.

The actual settlements in which these people lived in 1791 probably ranged from ten to fifty people, in closely related family groups. The rights to resources within the territories belonged primarily but not necessarily exclusively to the tribes, and precedent and discussion would have determined which extended family groups had access to them and at what times of the year. The Moriori Koche noted that his people had 'enjoyed a democracy and conducted their simple affairs by a council of notable men'. Most of the organised food gathering took place in autumn and to a somewhat lesser extent in the summer, and at those times adults would have had to work very hard indeed. For the remainder of the year a good deal of time would have been spent trying to harvest scarce resources, but living mainly off dried or preserved foods.

Life for the Moriori may not have been nasty and brutish, but it was busy and harsh at times; and it was made more harsh by a combination of excessively damp weather in winter and sparse Moriori clothing (sealskins were available, of

---

* There is of course the problem that the Moriori language was not written down systematically until its speakers had been heavily influenced by Taranaki Maori dialect over three decades. This fact may have disguised or obliterated earlier distinctions between Moriori and Maori.

Stylised representations of seals emphasise the importance of these mammals in the Moriori diet and spiritual world. These examples are carved into a limestone cave known as Te Ana a Nunuku, near Moreroa on the western side of Te Whanga lagoon.

Lovell-Smith Album,
Alexander Turnbull Library

A characteristic kopi grove, of the kind planted and nurtured by Moriori for berries. Some mature trunks were carved with dendroglyphs.

Alexander Turnbull Library

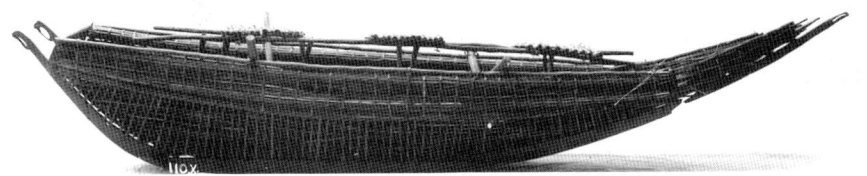

Replica of waka korari, or
wash-through raft.

National Museum

course, and widely in use with fur side inward; but flax fibre was shorter than in New Zealand and the leaf more difficult to work into adequate garments).

Life was also short. Analysis of human remains indicates that the average span for adults (those who survived beyond fifteen years of age) was about thirty-two.* The life expectancy of the population as a whole would have been about twenty-two. This seems low, particularly given that skeletal remains show adult males to have been tall by standards of the time (1.71 to 1.74 metres) and robust, possibly the result of a diet in which seal meat and other forms of seafood were a large component.

Apart from a high rate of infant mortality (probably up to 350 — one-third — per 1,000 births), what killed most residents of the Chathams and reduced life expectancy in general was damage to their teeth. This was the consequence of a highly abrasive diet, particularly fernroot and gritty shellfish. Most people would have developed bacterial infections through the gums by their early twenties, which in turn led to respiratory and other problems. These would be at first debilitating; and — after a few years — life-threatening and life-extinguishing.

Moriori had an elaborate system of spiritual beliefs and practices, which distanced them from the horrors of life and death and established their place in the world in relation to their environment (although they did not, of course, separate spiritual matters from temporal ones — each interpenetrated the other in a unified vision of reality). Like Polynesians everywhere, carrying a culture that had evolved on islands, they developed a strong sense of place. Ancestral and mythological names occur in several tribal districts, transported to new homes and attached to neighbouring features; known deities were localised in the elements, the trees, the rocks, the birds and the fish.

In the tribal areas in which they lived, Moriori would know every geographical landmark and tree, the gods who lived in them and protected them, and the chants that would appease those gods, particularly when a resource was about to be exploited. Hence the first fish taken would be left for the fish gods Tangaroa and Pou, in both propitiation and thanksgiving; hence paua and fernroot could be eaten outdoors, for that was part of the thanksgiving ritual; but certain birds were only allowed to be consumed inside a dwelling.

All rituals made use of the materials nature provided and viewed natural processes as a metaphor for the spiritual and physical growth of man. Here, for example, are two chants that accompanied the planting of a tree to commemorate the birth of a child. The second is based on the sky's mythical creation of Tu, the first man:

---

* Individuals lived longer — but not much longer. The few forty-year-olds would have been venerable elders; and remains have been found of one fifty-year-old man, which revealed calcification from extensive hardening of the main artery from the heart.

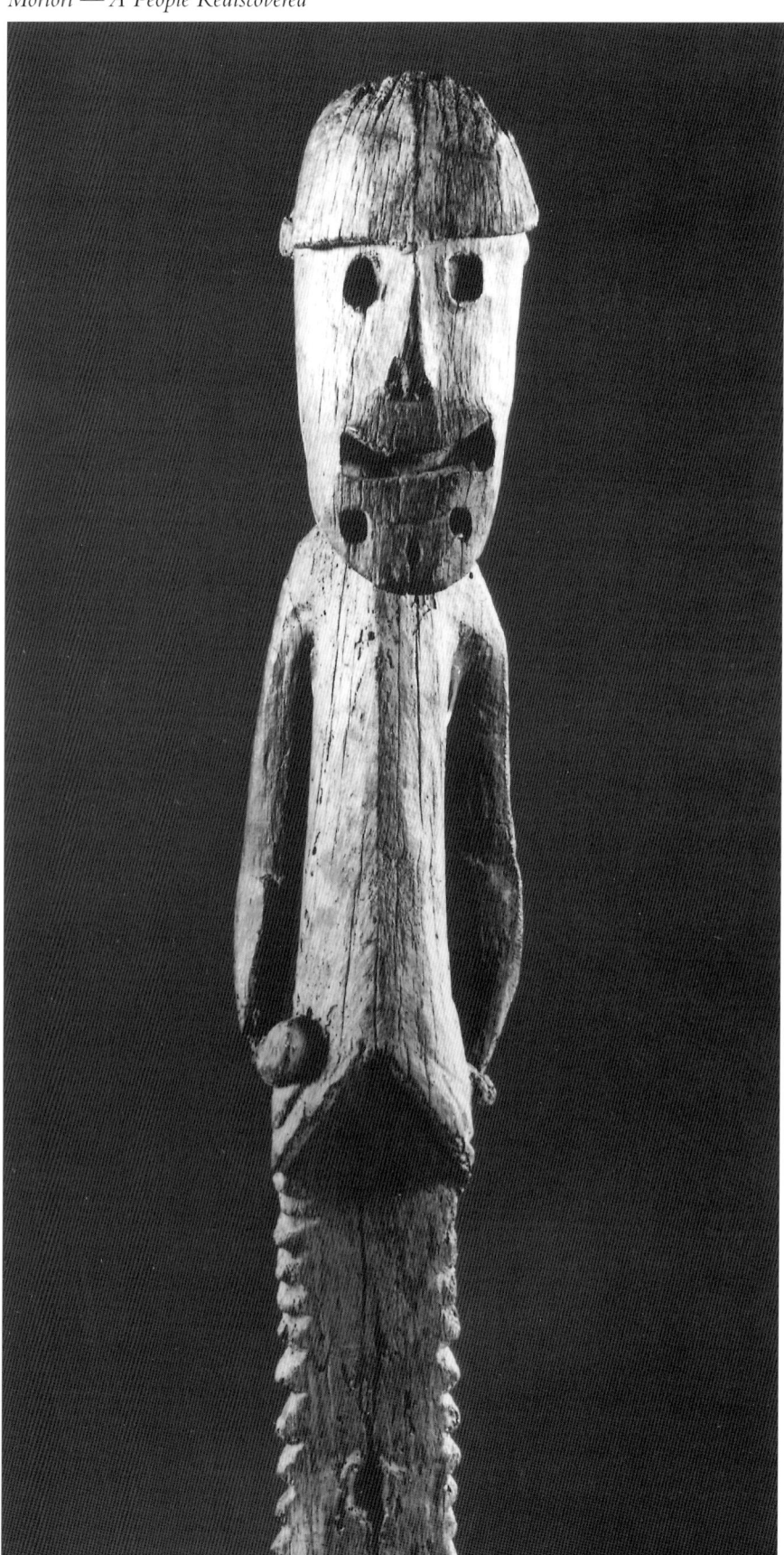

This figure of the Moriori god
Hatitimatangi was rescued from
a cave by Thomas Ritchie, a
nineteenth-century European
settler. The holes in the chin
appear to have been drilled for
the attachment of a beard. The
legs have rotted at the bottom
and an erect penis was chopped
off by a Pakeha woman when
the figure went on display in
New Zealand in the early
1900s. It is the only example of
Moriori wood sculpture known
to have survived.

Brian Brake

Stem heaped up, heaped, heaped up,
Stem gathered together, gathered, gathered together!
Heap the stem of the tree,
Heap the base of the tree,
Heap the fibrous roots of the tree,
Heap the butt of the tree,
Heap the roots of the tree!

Heap it, it grows! Heap it, it lives! The sky lives!
Stem heaped up, stem heaped up!
Let the living sky stand!

Heap the flowers of the tree,
Heap the leaves of the tree,
Heap the swaying of the tree,
Heap the waving of the tree,
Heap the pattern of the tree,
Heap the finishing of the tree!

Heap it, it grows! Heap it, it lives! The sky lives!
Stem heaped up, stem heaped up!
Let the living sky stand!

Man's soul is gathered into the world of being, the world of light,
The flying bird is placed in the body. Breathe,
Sneeze, living soul, into the world of being, the world of light!
The flying bird is placed in the body. Breathe, soul of Tu, breathe!

No one now knows the exact nature and function of the Moriori dendroglyphs on the kopi. The groves may have served a ritual purpose similar to that of marae or meeting houses (midden outside the circles of trees — but never inside — suggest a tapu/noa division). They could have been associated with the practice of each person having his or her own tree, and the human images carried on them may have represented those people after their death.* This would have been consistent with the widespread Polynesian belief that ancestors were among the atua or spiritual presences who controlled and protected the lives of living descendants. Other motifs that appeared on the kopi and on the limestone walls alongside Te Whanga — flounder, seals, albatross — are likely to have represented a deification and hence a protection of the food resources central to Moriori survival.

The spirituality of the Moriori is nowhere more apparent than in the surviving dendroglyph groves of kopi. They have a quiet cathedral-like atmosphere: their relative luxuriance silences the otherwise ever-present wind, light strikes the eye and the ground through the leaf canopy in an effect not unlike that produced by stained glass, and the eyes of the dancing Polynesian figures — many of them still vital after two hundred years — look inwards at the human observer. Of such things was the mental soil of the Moriori built up, mulched by layers of metaphorical association. They were, as even the Maori said of them, a very tapu people.

Apart from Lieutenant William Broughton and his crew and a couple of generations of sealers, Europeans did not observe the Moriori, nor begin to record their customs, until this cultural humus had been shattered and scattered

---

* See, for example, p. 90.

by trauma. The people who survived did so without the protection of their former gods and chants. And they had, consequently, lost their confidence and assertiveness. They were also judged — misjudged — by the simplicity of their art and their technology: their dendroglyphs, their petroglyphs, the wash-through rafts, the rough stone implements. Here as elsewhere, Europeans confused simplicity of technology with simplicity of mind and — by further implication — with backwardness. The Maori colonists, a martial people at that time in their own history, confused the Moriori adherence to the law of Nunuku with cowardice and — by implication — worthlessness. They also regarded the Moriori dialect as a debased form of their own language spoken by idiots, and they forbade its use.

Thus was Moriori culture revealed and reviled when taken out of its own context and juxtaposed with the nineteenth-century world of imperial expansion, Maori and European colonisation, notions of racial and cultural superiority, industrial and scientific development, and Darwinism. It was judged technologically and artistically inferior to that of other peoples, the product of slow, unsophisticated and unenterprising minds.*

In its own context, however, before the membrane of distance protecting it was broken, the pared-down simplicity of Moriori life was analogous to that of the Australian Aboriginal (and equally misunderstood): it was an appropriate and efficient response to the restricted circumstances in which the Moriori found themselves. It offered physical and spiritual security in what could otherwise have seemed a harsh environment. And it provided a programme for living in harmony with nature and with themselves.

---

* William Baucke, who grew up with Moriori in the second decade after the Maori invasion of the Chathams, spoke of 'our lowly tchakat . . . who had not yet evolved a brain to solve abstruse eclectics . . .' (Skinner and Baucke, 1928, p. 382).

Flounder dendroglyph on a
kopi between Lake Huro and
Te Whanga.
Bertha Wilson

Dendroglyph at Hapupu, east
coast, Chatham Island.
Michael King

37

TWO

The Sun People

I F THE DISCOVERY OF REKOHU WAS *PROBABLY* ACCIDENTAL, THE EUROPEAN rediscovery of the same island was certainly so. Betwen the middle of the seventeenth century and the latter part of the eighteenth, the mainland of New Zealand was encountered and explored by half a dozen Dutch, French and English mariners, the most important of whom was James Cook (who circumnavigated the country in 1769-70). On none of these voyages was the island of Rekohu and its neighbours sighted or suspected. They and their inhabitants remained unknown to the European world, literally and figuratively off the map, until a navigational mishap brought them into view in November 1791.

George Vancouver, who had sailed twice with Cook to New Zealand, was in 1791 in command of a British naval expedition to seek a north-west passage around the top of North America and to complete his mentor's mapping of that same coast. He left England early in the year in the warship *Discovery*, accompanied by Lieutenant William Robert Broughton in command of the brig *Chatham*. Broughton was one of the Royal Navy's rising stars, a twenty-eight-year-old scion of a Cheshire landed family and grandson of a baronet. He had already served as an officer in vessels off the coasts of North America and India, and had taken part in vigorous but indecisive combat with the French in Indian waters.

To reach the North Pacific, the two vessels sailed in convoy to the South Atlantic, around the Cape of Good Hope, along the southern coast of Australia, which they surveyed, and into the deep fiords, which Cook had identified as safe anchorages, of New Zealand's south-west coast. There they replenished wood and water and took on fish, birds and greens. From Dusky Sound, where Vancouver proudly drew attention to the signs of Cook's visit eighteen years before, they set sail for Tahiti.

On the first day out from New Zealand a severe storm separated the two vessels and drove them further south than their intended course. Both crews — independently — sighted small unmarked islands which could have wrecked the ships had they sailed into them at night. Vancouver named them the Snares. Still out of sight of each other, the respective captains headed north-east for Tahiti. Vancouver saw no more islands until he reached the atolls beyond the Tropic of Capricorn, 4,800 kilometres from New Zealand's southern coast. Broughton and the crew of the *Chatham*, however, pushed further east by the weather, found what the ship's journal called 'a Strange Land', where no land was indicated on Admiralty charts.

On 27 November 1791, battered by squalls, the crew reported large congregations of seabirds and patches of floating seaweed. Two days later, at 2 a.m., a lookout spotted land ahead and the brig hove to. Broughton noted that the island 'appeared of considerable extent'. Daylight confirmed this estimate. The brig lay off one of the north-western extremities, which Broughton named Point Alison after the seaman who first saw it. Cautiously, for there was a proliferation of offshore rocks, the *Chatham* negotiated and mapped the north coast, sighting the bluff Maunganui, which appeared higher than its 178 metres because of the flatness of the land on either side of it. He named it Mount Patterson. Inland from Cape Young, which Broughton also named, they saw an even higher peak, which much later came to be called Mount Chudleigh. The ship's log recorded that

> the land was low in general but some hills gradually rose up to a very moderate height, whose sides were beautifully clothed with Wood up to the Tops and the verdure on the rising grounds was exceedingly gratifying to the crew. We ran along the shore about 14 miles, but observed nothing like a Bay or Harbour. The depth of the water was moderate and gradual, and the ground good for Anchorage, being fine sand and shells. We saw smokes in several parts, particularly on the high land, but we did not see any Inhabitants till we had run a good way, when a few Indians were observed running along the Beach, who were join'd by more as we proceeded.

Broughton and his men saw 'the Indians'; the Indians saw the ship. While the Europeans were apprehensive about the encounter to follow, they were at least familiar with the scenario; it had unfolded within recent memory in other parts of the Pacific; they knew what they ought to do and ought not to do. The Moriori on the shore, however, had been separated from other peoples for at least 400 years and possibly longer. They had never seen anyone who was not Polynesian like themselves. Removed from other races and cultures, they had at this time no words for race or culture, not even for their own. They believed that they were humankind, and all of humankind. They had seen no vessels larger than wash-through rafts; now they watched one, sails filled, billowing across their familiar seascape like a mighty bird (indeed, 'Bird' was the name by which they were to identify Broughton). What they saw was as unfamiliar to them as extraterrestrials approaching in a spaceship. The membrane of distance, which had protected the Chatham Islanders from contact with peoples who thought and behaved differently from themselves, which had allowed the uninterrupted evolution of their culture and the successful observance of Nunuku's law, was about to be perforated; the Moriori were to discover that they were not alone in the world.

At 11 a.m. Broughton found the anchorage he was seeking off Kaingaroa, near the north-east tip of the island. There he observed 'people hauling up a canoe, and several others behind the rocks . . .' He decided to go ashore in the ship's cutter, which was fitted for rowing or sailing, and he took eight men with him, including his clerk, Mr Johnstone, and Mr Sheriff, one of the mates.

Kaingaroa Harbour is a broad crescent of white sand bounded at the tips by reefs and rocks. On days such as the one that Broughton and his men went ashore, it is a bright, open place, with no sense of menace or mystery. Such danger as there may have been came from the rocks that speckled the water at the entrance to the bay, and from the dense akeake trees that carpeted the low hills behind the beach, concealing unknown people harbouring unknown intentions. The Englishmen headed for the western side of the bay, site of the future European settlement of Kaingaroa, in the hope of making observations before being

interrupted by the inhabitants.

'Here we found two canoes,' Johnstone recorded, though they did not at first identify them as canoes.

> In shape they were not unlike the body of a common Wheelbarrow, their sides were made of small sticks lash'd tightly with withs upon one another about eight or nine feet long. The widest end about three feet, the other about two, and narrowing downwards, left a flat-bottom better than a foot broad. The depth was nearly two feet, and compactly filled with seaweed almost to the top. The paddles were a rough piece of wood crudely made into a flat form without the least neatness. The whole of the construction made it pretty evident that they would never be employ'd upon any distant embarkation, but were most probably used merely in the bay amongst the rocks for fishing . . .
>
> We saw some fishing Nets that were made of small two strand line evenly twisted and others that were made from the simple Fibres of the Plant, apparently without any other preparation than being made even . . . two of these were Scoop Nets, the others were made somewhat in the shape of a Bell, the width of the mouth about six feet in diameter, kept open by a large rim or Hoop made from the Supple Jack, the length from eight to ten feet, tapering gradually to the small end, which was not wider than a foot and close netted . . .
>
> The Trees we saw were but of small size, straight and free from Branches to near the tops, where they spread forth in great profusion, and whose foliage afforded a pleasant shade to the ground below, which was so free from all kinds of Bush or Underwood as might have led one to imagine that it had been clear'd by Art; this with the Trees growing so far apart render'd travelling amongst them not only easy but pleasant.

At this point the inhabitants, who had disappeared into the trees as soon as the Englishmen stepped ashore, now reappeared and advanced on Broughton's party.

> The Men were of a middling size, some stoutly made, well limbed and fleshy; their Hair, both of the Head and Beard, was black, and by some was worn long. The young Men had

The shore of Kaingaroa Harbour where in 1791 Moriori were coerced into contact with a world beyond the Chatham Islands. Lieutenant William Broughton named it Skirmish Bay, to mark the hostilities that resulted in one Moriori, Tamakaroro, being shot by British sailors.

Michael King

it tied up in a knot on the crown of their Heads, intermixed with black and white feathers. Some had their Beards plucked out; the complexion and general colour was dark brown, with plain features, and in general bad Teeth. Their skins were destitute of any marks, and they had the appearance of being cleanly in their persons. Their dress was either a seal or bear-skin, tied with sinnet, inside outwards, round their necks, which fell below their hips; or mats neatly made, which covered their backs and shoulders. Some were naked, excepting a well woven matt of fine texture, which, being fastened at either end by a string round their waists, made a sort of decent garment. We had not observed that their Ears were bored, or that they wore any ornaments about their persons, excepting a few who had a sort of necklace made of mother-of-pearl shells . . . We noticed two or three old Men, but they did not seem to have any power or authority over the others.

Broughton's men saw no women or children at close quarters, though some were visible peering from the trees before the sailors landed. Apparently they were concealed for protection.

No comparably detailed description of Broughton and his men survives first-hand from Moriori observers. But Europeans were told over seventy years later that the inhabitants of Kaingaroa were 'amazed' by the strangeness of the sailors, deduced that the God of Fire was inside them (some were smoking pipes), and believed that the rigging on the *Chatham* was fishing nets. The uniforms made the Moriori uncertain about the sex of the visitors and some were sure that they were women. What finally induced them to overcome their fear, come forward and confront the intruders, was the belief that the Englishmen were about to remove their belongings.

With forty Moriori bearing down on them, making gestures that were unmistakably threatening, Broughton ordered his men to retreat to the cutter, 'where more in safety we might endeavour to engage their friendship. With the oars we kept her just afloat. They, without making the least stop, rush'd hastily on, some of them up to their knees in water, brandishing their Spears and Clubs with much vociferation. They . . . were totally ignorant of the effect of our Fire-Arms, and only reckon'd strength on the superiority of numbers.'

Broughton and his sailors remained where they were, trying to indicate peaceful intentions by gesture and expression. They finally pacified the Moriori by placing gifts on the ends of the spears which were thrust at the cutter and its crew. 'They now became to all appearances perfectly reconcil'd, and received ev'rything which we offer'd with avidity, but amongst the Articles, which were pieces of Red Cloth, Helmets, Beads and Nails, we could not observe if they gave a preference to any one more than another . . .' Broughton tried to indicate to the Moriori, unsuccessfully, that the Englishmen wished to barter. The Polynesians, however, treated all the items offered to them as gifts and tried to snatch them away. Then the sailors conveyed by signs that they wanted something to eat and drink in exchange for their trade gifts. The Moriori simply indicated the trees beyond the beach and the point at the far end of the bay. Deciding that nothing else would be gained by unsuccessful attempts at communication, Broughton ordered the cutter to make for the opposite point, on the eastern side of the harbour. This initiative was negated, however: 'tho' we had changed our situation we had by no means changed our company, for our new friends . . . follow'd us along the Beach as we row'd down [and] arrived at the same time.' The cutter turned about and went back to the western shore of the bay, this time without company. The Moriori remained on the eastern point, apparently to protect their 'canoes' and nets.

Finding themselves alone again, the sailors disembarked and walked up the beach to the edge of the bush. There they 'found no other signs of Habitations than a small circle of clear ground, sometimes fenced in by a simple palisade. In the centre of this circle was the mark of a fire place, and a great number of Fish Shells particularly the Earshell. This had no other covering than the growing branches of the trees.'

Still unmolested by the inhabitants, Broughton now decided to perform the ceremony that was standard in such circumstances:

> . . . we displayed the Union flag, turned a turf, and took possession of the island, which I named Chatham Island [in honour of their ship, which was in turn named for the Earl of Chatham], in the name of His Majesty King George III, on the presumption of our being the first discoverers. After drinking His Majesty's health, I nailed a piece of lead to a tree near the beach, on which we inscribed, His Britannick Majesty's Brig Chatham, Lieutenant William Robert Broughton, commander, the 29th November, 1791. And in a bottle secreted near the tree, was deposited an inscription in Latin to the same effect.

After the ceremony the Moriori returned, but straggling back and showing no sign of their former agitation. 'That they might place more confidence in our friendship,' Johnstone recorded,

> our people stay'd behind whilst we advanced to meet them. At first they were rather shy, retiring back, but at last halted till I came up, and received me by saluting noses . . . Having made them some presents of Nails they were soon perfectly easy, and were join'd by more, some of our people coming in at the same time . . .
>
> Though they took whatever we offer'd, yet so little did they esteem them that we could not draw from them any thing in exchange. One spear with a small piece of Rope wrought in fashion of French Sinnet, was all that we could procure. They would at first shew an appearance of making a return until they got in their hands what was offer'd — then would run off well pleas'd. The Spear we got was about six feet long, so thick that a man could easily grasp in the middle, tapering to a sharp point at both ends. But some of their Spears and Clubs were subject to great variety. Some . . . were very long, and pointed only at one end, without much neatness. Their Clubs were rough pieces of Wood, and very few had two stones lashed on at one end, which gave them the appearance of a double-headed maul.

Broughton then decided, by firing at some birds, to demonstrate the power of the muskets which the sailors carried — to enliven the occasion, and possibly to display the capacity of firearms and make a repetition of earlier aggressive behaviour less likely:

> They seemed much alarmed at [the] report and all retreated . . . excepting one old man who held his ground; and presenting his spear sideways, beat time with his feet; and as he seemed to notice us in a very threatening manner, I went up to him, shook him by the hand, and used every method I could devise to obtain his confidence. Observing something in his hand, carefully rolled up in a net, I was desirous of looking at it, upon which he gave it to another, who walked away with it; but he did not prevent my seeing that it contained stones fashioned like the Patoo Patoes* of the New Zealanders. They seemed very anxious to get my gun and shot belt and frequently exclaimed 'Toohata'.**

Broughton's party, while alert, was now feeling more secure. An hour had passed in what Johnstone terms 'friendly intercourse'. The sailors decided to examine a source of inland water halfway around the bay, which they had

---

* Patu: stone clubs.

** There is no obvious meaning to this expression; possibly Broughton misheard it.

originally sighted from the masthead of the *Chatham*. It was a small lagoon, which turned out to be brackish and unsuitable for drinking, a fact the sailors attempted to indicate to the Moriori. The party, followed by the Moriori, then attempted to return to their boat. Broughton described what happened when they reached the water:

> [The natives] became very clamourous, talked extremely loud to each other, and divided so as to nearly surround us. A young man strutted towards me with a very menacing attitude; he distorted his person, turned up his eyes, made hideous faces, and created a wonderful fierceness in his appearance by his gestures. On pointing my double-barrelled gun towards him, he desisted. Their hostile intentions were now too evident to be mistaken, and therefore, to avoid the necessity of proceeding to extremities, the boat was immediately ordered to take us on board. During this interval, although we were strictly on guard, they began to attack, and before the boat could get in, to avoid being knocked down, I was reluctantly compelled to fire one barrel, which being loaded with small shot, I was in hopes might intimidate without materially wounding them, and that we should be suffered to embark without further molestation . . . I was disappointed in this hope. Mr Johnstone received a blow upon his musket from an unwieldy club with such force that it fell to the ground, but before his opponent could pick it up, Mr Johnstone had time to recover his position and he was obliged to fire on the blow being again attempted. A marine and seaman near him, were, under similar circumstances, forced into the water, but not before they had also, justified alone by self-preservation, fired their pieces without orders. The gentleman having charge of the boat seeing us much pressed by the natives, and being obliged to retreat, fired at this instant also, on which they fled. I ordered the firing instantly to cease, and was highly gratified to see them depart, apparently unhurt. The happiness I enjoyed in this reflection was of short duration, one man was discovered to have fallen; and I am concerned to add, was found lifeless, a ball having broken his arm and passed through his heart. We immediately repaired towards the boat, the surf not permitting her to come near enough, we were still under necessity of walking to the place where we had originally intended to embark. As we retired, we perceived one of the natives return from the woods, whither all had retreated, and placing himself by the deceased, was distinctly heard in a sort of dismal howl to utter his lamentations.

According to Moriori tradition, the man so killed was Tamakaroro, a resident of Kaingaroa.* Moriori accounts of the incident differ from Broughton's. According to Alexander Shand's informants, the attack was inspired by the belief that the sailors were women and could be taken by force to the Moriori houses behind the beach: 'To put a stop to this the sailors fired to alarm them, on which they then remarked "Hear the crack of the kelp of their god Hauoro!"** . . . [Seeing] another party coming up from the east of the harbour, the sailors fired, killing and wounding some of the Morioris, which scared them and they fled to the bush.'

Thomas Ritchie was told that Tamakaroro had tried to acquire Broughton's coat with its bright buttons, and that Broughton had shot him because he felt threatened by this behaviour. Percy Smith's version, collected at Owenga, alleged that a sailor had tried to remove a net from the beach. When the owner objected and called in friends to help him retain it, the sailors opened fire, believing they were under attack. Whatever the truth of the affair, it is apparent that there was misunderstanding occasioned by the inability of the two groups to communicate. There is no reason to doubt the veracity of Broughton's account. He made a practice of recording everything of significance in his journal, whether creditable

---

* A memorial unveiled at Kaingaroa in 1988 identifies this man as Torotoro; this is incorrect.

** Hauoro, or Heauro, was a god associated with war.

or discreditable to himself or his crew. And, significantly perhaps, the Moriori did not blame the English commander or his men for the death on the beach. Further, they apparently decided that it was *they* — and not the visitors — who had dishonoured Nunuku's law. Shand was told that the Kaingaroa Moriori 'severely thrashed those who took part in the mishap with the strangers'. The father of Koche, a Moriori who stowed away on an American whaler in the mid-nineteenth century, told his son that a council was held immediately after the *Chatham*'s departure. The fact that the body was not carried off by the sailors was considered proof that the 'Sun People' were not cannibals. It was concluded that, in the event of their return, they would be greeted with an emblem of peace.

Members of Broughton's party, after retracing their steps to their first landing place, put all their remaining trinkets and trade goods in the canoes, 'to manifest our kind intentions towards them, and as some little atonement for the injury which, contrary to our inclinations, they had sustained in [our] defending ourselves . . .' They also left potatoes, hoping that the Moriori would plant them.* The visitors then boarded the cutter, rowed to the ship, and left the small harbour, which Broughton named Skirmish Bay. He sailed the *Chatham* a further four kilometres to round the promontory that marks the end of Chatham Island's northern coast, which he named Point Munnings, then turned his vessel north-east towards Tahiti. On Kaingaroa Beach, according to Koche's father, 'the atmosphere became dark, sultry and gloomy, and thunder and lightning descended the mountain and pursued the retreating strangers . . .'

Broughton's and Johnstone's descriptions of their encounter with Moriori display several features worthy of note. One is the directness of their accounts. Like Cook, they 'saw and reported truly'. They do not attempt to conceal what they regarded as errors of judgment, such as the shooting of Tamakaroro. And — apart from obvious misunderstandings such as their identification of seal fur as 'bear-skins' — their reports have a ring of truth to them; in instances where they can be verified from subsequent evidence, they are found to be reliable.

The second comment is that these journals provide the only substantial accounts of appearance and behaviour gathered before the Moriori were affected by further contact with Europeans, the destruction of their seal colonies, the effects of epidemics, and the invasion of Maori from the mainland of New Zealand, which resulted in slaughter, enslavement and loss of morale. Descriptions of the Moriori from the 1840s (and there are many) refer to a people who are debilitated and destroyed spiritually. Infused with prejudice, they are the source of later accusations that the indigenous inhabitants of the Chathams possessed a 'low grade intellect' and 'a brute appetite for food and sex and sleep'. So they may have seemed after being wracked by disease, deprived of their land and food, and convinced that their culture was of no value. By the 1840s their view of themselves as a people and as individuals was negative; they entirely lacked self-esteem.**

In the 1790s, however, the people Broughton saw may not have been the

---

* They did not; according to Thomas Ritchie's informants, they ate them.

** Although, as subsequent chapters show, individual Moriori recovered self-esteem once they were free of the bondage of slavery.

noble savages of European imagination; but they were confident, assertive and in control of their lives and their environment. 'They seem a cheerful race,' Broughton noted in summary, 'our conversation frequently exciting bursts of laughter amongst them. On our first landing their surprise and exclamations can hardly be imagined; they pointed to the Sun, and then to us, as if to ask whether we had come from thence.' It is this image that most accurately reflects the condition of the Moriori people when they *were* Moriori: not that of a demoralised race allegedly sunk in ignorance, sullenness and lack of initiative.

Although Broughton's chart of Chatham Island's north coast was available in London and Sydney by 1793, it was to be at least another decade before further European ships reached the group. When they did, it was to plunder the island's dense colonies of fur seals* for the lucrative Chinese market. In spite of the effect that this exploitation would have on the Moriori economy and culture, these subsequent visitors were greeted warmly by the inhabitants, a deliberate result of councils held in the wake of Broughton's expedition.

Koche reported that the first sealers sailed into Petre Bay and came ashore by boat at Waitangi to a friendly welcome. The waiting Moriori laid down their protective weapons. Their spokesman stepped forward to greet the captain and placed one end of a grass plant in his hand while retaining hold of the other. While they were thus linked, the Moriori chief 'made him a speech of welcome, threw over him his own cloak, and thus established a firm and lasting peace . . .' Sealers and whalers who made subsequent landfalls at the Chathams, Koche continued, found the Moriori 'hospitable, cheerful friends and willing assistants in their labour, and love between them flourished like a palm'.

Certainly there is no European evidence to contradict this. The Chathams acquired a reputation among Sydney-based sealers as a safe and hospitable anchorage. What *is* uncertain is when the first of the post-Broughton encounters took place. No official records were kept in or of the Chathams until the 1850s. (The islands became part of New Zealand in 1842, but were not subject to any meaningful form of administration until 1855.) Secondly, the sealing industry was so competitive in these profitable early years, when skins fetched as much as fifteen shillings each on the Chinese market, that many ships and masters took pains to conceal their movements rather than advertise them.

Circumstantial evidence suggests, however, that the first sealers were in the Chathams between 1804 and 1807. Those operating out of Australia had begun to work the New Zealand rookeries from 1803. That year, Captain Joseph Oliphant returned to Sydney from the Fiordland coast with 2,200 skins. Others followed him, and American and British sealers had reached Stewart Island by 1804.

There was a further reason for the secrecy that has left massive gaps in the historical record. Conditions under which the early sealers worked had been so appalling (groups left on exposed rocky islands for months at a time, with a minimum of food and shelter) that the Government of New South Wales had gazetted retrospective labour laws to protect them. From 1805 British craft were supposed to confine their sealing activities to latitudes north of 49° 39' South. This would have excluded the entire New Zealand coast south of Banks

---

* *Arctocephalus forsteri.*

The appearance of European ships and boats became an increasingly familiar sight in the Chathams from the 1820s. This vessel is the *Ocean Mail*, which grounded off the north coast of Chatham Island.

Canterbury Museum

Moriori as they may have appeared to European visitors to the Chathams, in a mixture of traditional and European clothing: flax mats around the waist and shoulders, feathers fixed to the front of the head, albatross tufts in beards, and defensive staffs in hand. The man standing at left is Hirawanu Tapu of Owenga.

Canterbury Museum

Peninsula, and all the islands south of New Zealand, where the concentrations of seals were largest (38,000 skins were harvested from the Bounties Islands in 1807, and 250,000 from the Antipodes between 1806 and 1810). In fact sealing vessels ranged around these coasts and beyond; they simply became even more secretive. By 1807, when two recorded visits *were* made to the Chathams, one Moriori, Hororeka, had already left on an earlier British ship, spent some time in the Bay of Islands, and returned to his home.

The first of these visits was that of the Royal Navy vessel *Cornwallis*, which passed twelve miles south of Pitt Island in May 1807 and thus claimed discovery of the southern islands in the group, some of them little more than rocks: Pitt, South-East Island, Mangere, the Pyramid, the Castle, the Fort, and Passage Rock. These, along with the *Cornwallis*'s track, were to be published in a chart in 1816. Added was the significant notation: 'Many seals and whales seen.'

Six months after the *Cornwallis*, the aptly named sealing vessel *Commerce* reached the Chathams, in late November 1807. One of the crew, Jacky Marmon, wrote subsequently:

> Besides several sealing gangs stationed here, we found a considerable amount of natives . . . who seemed in dialect, colour and custom to resemble the Maoris, as I afterwards found them. One extraordinary thing . . . was that in many places the island [Chatham] was on fire. Not a mere surface conflagration, but a steady, underground combustion. There are large formations of peat . . . and these, having become ignited, have burned steadily for years . . . after the purchase of some 300 sealskins [we] ran up the East Coast of New Zealand . . . We had a Chatham Islander on board, Hororeka, who having resided some little time at the Bay of islands, was familiar with [Maori] customs and language. He, though his dialect differed from theirs, was able to act as our interpreter and conduct our trade.

Sealing gangs had reached the Chathams months and possibly years before 1807, therefore; and at least one Moriori had had the opportunity to visit New Zealand twice and to become familiar with English and Maori.

From 1810 the visits of European vessels, most of them in pursuit of seals and whales, are recorded with greater frequency. Some left sealers on the outlying islands or rocks for months and — in at least one case, on Star Keys — more than a year at a time. Almost all would have had intercourse (social rather than physical, though the latter was not excluded) with the Moriori. They, surprisingly, given the attitudes of other Polynesians, showed little interest in bartering or in acquiring European tools and vegetables to reduce their daily toil. Some Moriori must have assisted with provisioning, however, and with supplying ships with pigs, which had been introduced by sealers. It was reported in 1829, for example, that the ship *Samuel* was leaving the Chathams for Sydney loaded with pork and potatoes in addition to sealskins.

There was a price to pay for this contact. While the Moriori may have been provided with pigs and potatoes by the late 1820s, it is doubtful if these acquisitions would have outweighed the loss of other resources. The seal population of the islands was slaughtered ruthlessly, without regard to future

---

* There is insufficient data to establish how many seals were killed on the Chathams. One estimate, however, suggests that over forty years, 1804 to 1844, the renewable seal population dropped from around 20,000 to 'very few' (Douglas Sutton, letter to Bill Saunders, 14/11/79). In the final years, the 'sealers' ashore spent more time growing potatoes and raising pigs than they did hunting seals.

replenishment.* Whereas the Moriori practice had been to kill only male seals, usually older ones, and to remove the carcases, European sealers killed indiscriminately and left flensed carcases to rot around the rookeries, driving away even those animals that survived outright killing. By the 1830s the rookeries on the main island were virtually bare of animals; and those on the outliers were reduced to numbers that made further exploitation difficult and uneconomic (the more so, since fur prices in China, Russia and London had collapsed — in the case of China, the fall was from fifteen shillings per skin to five by 1829). This catastrophe deprived the Moriori of their major source of winter clothing, a major source of food, and the presence of an animal that had figured intimately in their mythology and religious ritual. The slaughter and disappearance of the seal was a prefigurement of the fate of the Moriori themselves. The rock carvings of seals at Nunuku's cave on the edge of Te Whanga lagoon would come to represent a memorial to both the hunters and hunted of pre-European days.*

There were further consequences of the European presence. The sealers' pigs and guns depleted the habitats and numbers of birds and seafowl on areas of the islands where previously they had been plentiful and easily caught, and the introduction of cats and ship's rats resulted in the deaths of many more. Worse, Europeans brought bacterial and viral diseases to which the Moriori, thousands of years isolated from the continent of Asia, had no immunity and no resistance.

Measles, influenza and venereal disease took a heavy toll of the indigenous population. Like their distant relatives on the New Zealand mainland, Moriori often took to the water when they became fevered with viruses such as influenza. This 'treatment' made them all the more likely to succumb. Traditional herbal remedies and healing karakia had no effect on these illnesses, which were unknown to their ancestors and their gods. They were all the more horrifying for the swiftness and indiscriminateness with which they took hold. The prospect of sudden death at the hand of such an unseen enemy, and the need to come to terms with the sudden and premature deaths of loved ones, made living all the more unpleasant for those who survived.

How many Moriori died through this period will never be known. No records were made or kept. Years later, Alexander Shand estimated from Moriori oral evidence that possibly half the population had been wiped out in a series of influenza and measles epidemics between 1828 and 1832. Given that the population in 1835 is known, around 1,600, this may be an exaggeration. Later authorities have suggested that, more probably, one-fifth of the original population, some 400, had died from European-introduced diseases before 1835.

Nor were the detrimental effects confined to sickness and death. Many of the sailors were misfits, habitual criminals and other riff-raff; and some may have treated the Moriori cruelly, taking women for sexual gratification and treating both sexes (and children) with contempt and physical brutality. The newcomers 'looked upon them as little more than beasts,' one writer has claimed, 'and treated them as such'.

Members of one crew that visited the Chathams in 1829 were not former but current convicts, who had pirated the ship *Cyprus*. They landed at Owenga and raided both the Moriori settlement and a party of sealers. Then two boatloads rowed up to Te Awapatiki and tried to enter the lagoon. Their boats were

---

* The Indians of Tierra del Fuego had a similar experience as a result of the activities of European sealers. This was reflected in their use as synonyms of the terms 'fur seal' and 'relatives of a murdered man'.

swamped in the surf, however, and several of the convicts drowned. The survivors returned to the *Cyprus* and sailed away, only to be arrested by a British naval vessel in Canton. Five were tried for piracy in London in 1830.

Even the behaviour of so-called 'civilised' men towards the Moriori sometimes exuded distaste. Captain John Biscoe, who visited the islands in November 1831, noted in his journal:

> . . . at 5 p.m. the boats returned bringing with them three Natives who seemed willing to remain with us, but . . . as I did not wish to encumber the vessel with these People who for some time to come could do nothing but consume the provisions, I set them on shore again. They were quite naked with the exception of a coarse mat over the shoulders which seemed to be used as a roof to them to turn the water off, as the moment they came on deck they squatted down like so many monkeys and the mats, being stiff of course, stuck out like the shell of a turtle. Added to this, a scrap of the same material passed under the crotch completely concealing what might otherwise have appear'd indelicate . . .

Whatever provocations the Moriori might have endured, there is no record of their ever again breaking the law of Nunuku (or, at least, not by killing Europeans. There is a story of one Chatham Islander who killed a relative in the early 1800s after a disagreement over a woman. He was subsequently ostracised by his people — social and spiritual death for a tribal person — and committed suicide by jumping down the blowhole at Mairangi. All of which serves to illustrate how highly the law of non-violence was valued). The Chathams

The extraordinarily mixed ethnic communities spawned by sealing and whaling on the Chathams is illustrated by this group photographed at Tennant's Lake. From left: Pumipi Te Rangaranga (Moriori), Ellen (Maori), Rihania (Maori, adopted daughter of Bill Tennant), George Kanaka (Hawaiian), Tarata (Moriori), Bill Tennant (American, known also as 'the Sail-Cloth Man' on account of his clothes), Karete (Maori, Tennant's wife), Parawa Kanaka (Hawaiian, brother of George) and Joe Flores (Azores).

Canterbury Museum

preserved its reputation as a safe place to visit and provision. Danger from other than natural causes was more likely to come from renegade Europeans than from Moriori.

It is not surprising, therefore, that by the 1830s there were several Europeans living permanently on Chatham Island. The first is thought to have been Jacob Tealing, who had been aboard the brig *Glory* when it was wrecked on the south-west coast of Pitt Island in January 1827. The crew sailed a longboat back to the New Zealand mainland, arriving in the Bay of Islands in March after a voyage of 800 miles — one of the great survival stories of the sealing era. Tealing chose to remain on the Chathams, however, where he lived at Owenga from 1827 until his death in 1855. He is believed to have been English, and possibly an escaped or former convict.

Another sealer, Shera,* was at Te Whakaru with a Moriori wife by the early 1830s 'with a view to raising produce for whaling and sealing expeditions'. Two others, John Bailey and Tommy King, lived at Ocean Bay in 1832. (One of their companions, though known as 'Charley', was a Ngati Toa Maori.) They were joined in 1832 by a former Sydney sealer named James Coffee, who took a Moriori wife; and by another European, named Baker. With a small group of Taranaki Maori men and women, they apparently co-existed harmoniously with local Moriori. In 1835, the captain of the Sydney brig *Bee* reported there were 'eight to ten runaways on Chatham Islands'. This combined presence of residents and itinerant sealing gangs ensured that Moriori would have been well acquainted with Europeans by 1835.**

New Zealand Maori, too, had visited the islands during the sealing period, having joined vessels as crew in the Bay of Islands, Cook Strait, Port Nicholson, and from the South Island. Some of these became residents. There were mixed Maori-European settlements at Whangaroa and Ocean Bay prior to 1835, and several Maori (including Paki Wara of Ngati Tama and Ropata of Ngati Toa) lived

Owenga, a sheltered bay on the south-east coast of Chatham Island, where the first permanent European resident, a sealer named Jacob Tealing, settled in 1827.

Auckland Institute & Museum

---

* Whose Moriori descendants spelt their name 'Hira' and 'Shearer'.

** Koche found wheat growing on Pitt Island in 1836, an indication of how long some of the 'itinerant' sealing gangs stayed in one place.

at Wharekauri. It is likely that it was these latter Maori who named the small kainga on the northern coast, allegedly after a house there built from salvaged kauri timber. Subsequently Maori used this name to refer to the whole of Chatham Island, because, as Alexander Shand wrote, 'they could pronounce [it] more easily than the Morioir one of Rekohu'.

Maori residents and visitors liked what they found at the Chathams around the mid-1830s: a small population (about 1,600) of contented and unassertive Moriori tangata whenua;* a handful of Europeans who were relaxed about living in association with Moriori and Maori; much unoccupied and uncultivated land; the presence of the kopi tree with its edible berries; a prolificacy of eels and waterfowl around Te Whanga lagoon and Lake Huro; ample fish and shellfish in the sea and edible birds on the outlying islands; and the growing whaling industry that was beginning to use the islands as a provisioning base. In all, it was a situation that appealed to entrepreneurial people who, for a variety of reasons, were not content in their current circumstances; and it was to lead to the most traumatic chapter in the history of the Chathams and of the Moriori.

---

* 'People of the land', indigenous inhabitants; the equivalent Moriori term was tchakat henu.

CHAPTER

THREE

The Gods Are Dead

OCEAN BAY, A WEDGE-SHAPED INLET WITHIN THE NORTHERN TIP OF THE Petre Bay crescent, offered sheltered anchorage close to deep water on the one hand and fresh water on the other. In the early 1830s, it was a port of call in the Chathams for sealers and whalers.* No detailed contemporary description of the harbour survives. But it was a quiet and pleasant enough place, particularly on calm summer days, when its waters took on the opalised blues and greens of a tropical lagoon. It was bordered by a line of rocks and, behind them, two low promontories covered in akeake. A strip of brilliantly white sand lay at the head of the bay, dissected by a stream. Behind, on a low, cleared slope, jostled the ponga huts of resident sealers, Tommy King, John Bailey and their small entourage of Maori and Moriori domestics and gardeners, mainly women. Behind this again was a Moriori community housed in lean-to shelters made from lashed vegetation from the coastal broadleaf forest.

Ship visits at this time were increasing and were encouraged. King and Bailey rejoiced in the opportunity to speak and drink with fellow Europeans, and to sell their pigs, potatoes and other vegetables and their few sealskins. Local Moriori, who had already participated in some bartering for clothing and utensils and picked up a little English from the sealers, welcomed a distraction from food gathering and a chance to test and extend their borrowed language. They were equally interested in contacts with visiting Maori crew, with whose tongue their own coincided sufficiently to allow communication. Relations between the Moriori and Maori, on the island and on board vessels, had to this point been fraternal: more so than among Maori in different parts of New Zealand, because the two peoples had no known traditions of tribal competition or animosity. That situation was to change, however, with the appearance of the sealing ship that slid into Ocean Bay in the summer of 1832-33.**

As this new crew rode ashore below the Moriori settlement, the inhabitants ran down to the beach to greet them and make them welcome — as they did on all such occasions. Among the locals was Koche, son of a chief who had taken part in the councils that followed Broughton's disastrous encounter with the Moriori forty years before. Koche was a charismatic figure, popular with his own people for his energy, initiative and sense of fun. 'Little above middle height, he

---

* It was soon supplanted by Whangaroa (Port Hutt) and, from the late 1830s, by Waitangi. Shore whaling did not commence in the Chathams until 1840; but ocean whaling vessels were visiting the islands from the early 1830s and reached a peak in the years 1839–40.

** There is a possibility that the vessel was the Sydney sealer *Bee*, the same ship that brought James Coffee to the island. If so the incident that follows occurred in January 1833.

was broad and deep-chested, with sinews of iron, and capable of immense exertion,' according to a passenger on an American whaler to whom Koche later dictated his life story. Above all, noted the American, he was 'animated'.

The excitement of the visitation turned very quickly to fear. For the ship brought a dancer, a prancer, who came ashore high stepping, rolling his eyes and flicking his tongue, a performance that stirred atavistic dread in the bowels of his fellow Polynesians. He was

> a New Zealand chief armed to the teeth. His hair, carefully combed and oiled, was tied up on the crown of his head, and surrounded by a fillet of white feathers, and from his ears protruded bunches of soft down. Evidently a man of power, accustomed to command . . . The future darkened as he walked the beach, questioning the [Moriori] people on their politics and religion, manners and customs; it was long remembered that he highly commended the veneration they entertained for sacred places, and walked off musing when in answer to his inquiry one was pointed out.

This disturbing apparition was the Ngati Mutunga chief Matioro. Born in north Taranaki some thirty years previously, he was described by Europeans as an impressive figure, over 1.8 metres tall, tattooed, weighing some 90 kilograms. More relevantly, he was a product of a vigorous warrior culture whose restlessness had been engendered by a series of forced migrations. His people, displaced from their traditional home north of the Waitara River by the Waikato tribes, had been fighting other Maori more or less continuously for a decade: down the west coast of the North Island, at Waikanae, around Cook Strait and into Port Nicholson, up into the Wairarapa, south to the Marlborough Sounds and the South Island. At first they had fought to defend, then to survive in hostile territories, and then to secure footholds in new ones. By the 1830s they sought to fight because combat among their warriors had become habitual and an antidote to their sense of dislocation. They were also nervous about what they regarded as the treachery of their Ngati Toa allies, under whose sufferance they had been allowed to drive out the Ngati Ira and occupy Port Nicholson.

The sacred place pointed out to Matioro at his request was the summit of a volcanic cone, Hokopoi, twelve kilometres to the east. Being subject to the laws of tapu, no cooking was allowed, nor the carrying of cooking utensils, within its vicinity. Shortly before dawn one morning after Matioro's arrival, a local Moriori climbed the hill to pray. He was horrified to find there an iron pot: a cooking vessel. He ran back to the village to report the violation and returned with thirteen companions, one of whom was Koche. Koche threw off his cloak, picked up a piece of rock and tried to smash the pot, which — of course — belonged to the visiting ship. Why it should have been placed there is a mystery; the idea of cooking on such an elevated, isolated location made no sense. The Moriori suspicion was that the bellicose Matioro, having been told of Moriori sensitivities towards such a place (and having had the summit itself pointed out to him) had placed the pot there to provoke a confrontation.*

And, indeed, retribution followed swiftly.

> A party of sailors, with a couple of bull-dogs, guided by Mateoro, [*sic*] pursued and overtook them. He shot dead one who turned and attempted an explanation; the

---

* A Maori writer has interpreted Matioro's behaviour, on this occasion and on his arrival, as 'testing the mettle of the local Moriori with a view to later conquest' (Mikaere 1986, p. 60).

remaining twelve [including Koche] were bound and hung by the feet from a tree, head downward until nearly dead.

Koche and his relatives believed that it was Matioro who reported back to his kinsmen at Port Nicholson about the advantages of the Chathams, and that he was consequently directly responsible for the Maori invasion of the Chathams two years later. This accusation could be a reaction to the unjust punishment Koche received at the Maori's hand. Given that Matioro stayed on at Ocean Bay with his sister Mukakai and other members of his Otaraua hapu, and that they subsequently moved to Whangaroa with Coffee and Bailey, it seems more likely that it was other Taranaki Maori who carried the news of the noncombatant stance of the Moriori back to Port Nicholson — perhaps after consultation with Matioro and his group. The missionary Engst was told that the messengers were Te Ururanga, Rihari, Arangata and Te Ira. Rihari had been one of the party who arrived at Ocean Bay with Matioro, and all four mentioned by Engst returned to New Zealand in an American whaler in 1834. Back on the mainland, they found their fellow tribesmen at Port Nicholson discontent and insecure, short of food, tired of Port Nicholson's inclement weather, quarrelling with Ngati Toa, and ready to move again.

The Chathams veterans 'related their experiences to their wondering friends, telling them of the sunshine and warmth of those islands, and the abundance of fruit so easily gathered there', Alexander Shand was told years later by those who participated in the discussions. One in particular, Paki Whara of Ngati Tama, said:

> It is a land of food — he whenua kai! It is full of birds, both land- and sea-birds of all kinds, some living in the peaty soil; with albatross in plenty on the outlying islands. There is an abundance of sea and shellfish; the lakes swarm with eels; and it is a land of the karaka berry . . . The inhabitants are very numerous, but they do not understand how to fight, and have no weapons.

It was this crucial intelligence, Shand's informants said later, 'which induced us to go to the Chathams'.

The Huro is one of the more than a dozen lakes and lagoons that perforate Chatham Island and provide a rich source of bird and fish life.

Alexander Turnbull Library

By 1835, the Moriori at Rekohu had been in intermittent contact with Europeans — mainly sealers — for some thirty years (given that they had remained unmolested in the decade following Broughton's visit). Their life had undergone some irreversible changes in that time: they were aware now of a world beyond the Chathams, and in particular of Europeans, of British people with a king; of New Zealand Maori with whom they shared some affinity and could converse; and of the islands of New Zealand only 870 kilometres to the west. Some few of their number — it is not known how many — had moved between New Zealand and the Chathams and now spoke English and Maori in addition to their mother tongue; others may have crewed on vessels further afield, throughout the Pacific.

The seals had largely disappeared from around Chatham and Pitt Islands and this had brought about alterations in the seasonal and ritual hunting life; birds had been killed or scared away from favourite hunting grounds close to settlements; numbers of some species, especially grey ducks, petrels, the large rails and snipe, had been reduced dramatically by the scavenging of rats, cats, dogs and pigs — all introduced by sealers before 1835. Some of the wild dogs had become so ferocious that they had attacked and killed Moriori. Worst of all, a large segment of the Moriori population, probably some 400 to 500 people, had died in the measles and influenza epidemics of the late 1820s. Those who survived were subject to illnesses that had previously been unknown — seasonal bouts of influenza, colds that frequently progressed to pneumonia, syphilis, dysenteric disorders; all of which had a detrimental effect on the quality of life for both sufferers and caregivers.

For all this, however, Moriori were still in control of their lives. In spite of physical and climatic hardships in winter — which had not changed — they were described as 'cheerful, full of mirth and laughter'. Their lives were based around some twenty small settlements on Chatham Island and one on Pitt, of which the most significant were those which had regular contact with ships: Ocean Beach, Whangaroa, Wharekauri, Waitangi, Owenga and Te Whakaru.* The presence of a small but growing number of European residents at some of the settlements added to their importance, because it enhanced the prospect of visiting vessels. For most Moriori, their dwellings had changed little since the appearance of Europeans. They still built thatched inverted triangular shelters, and they sometimes lived in modified arbours in the course of summer foraging. A few may have had small ponga huts, built with horizontally laid logs, in settlements with European residents. They still cooked on outside fires and in earth ovens, and used wash-through rafts as their only form of transport other than walking.

Some sealers such as Tealing and Shera now cultivated fruit and vegetables on a small scale in bush clearings sheltered from the frequent winds.** Moriori may also have had access to pigs, released by sealers, although these appear not to have been raised domestically prior to 1835. While the seal was virtually gone, Moriori still relied heavily on other traditional foods — fernroot, karaka berries, cast blackfish, eels, fish, shellfish, birds — gathered seasonally and (where necessary) sparingly, to allow replenishment. There is no record of any Moriori possessing

---

* James Coffee's description of the Te Raki-Wharekauri district in 1835 suggests that communities were made up of extended families and numbered about thirty persons each (Richards 1982, p. 352).

** Potato growing on a large scale seems not to have been carried out on the islands until after the Maori invasion.

firearms at this time,* and even metal tools and utensils seem to have been scarce and restricted to settlements with European residents. Farm animals seem to have been absent, though cats and dogs were in demand as communal pets, and dogs as hunting aids and companions. Less welcome, Norway rats had made their way to the islands on ships and, in addition to affecting the bird life, may have contributed to the spread of disease.

Some Moriori, especially those who had travelled on ships, may have worn European clothing and footwear part of the time. What evidence has survived suggests that most still wore traditional garments made from traditional materials, — especially loin coverings and capes — although sealskins had become far more difficult to procure.

Most important, the Moriori view of life had changed very little. They defined themselves by whom they were related to and descended from, and settlements were still family-based and located in one of six tribal territories. They still spoke their own language, recited their own genealogies and traditions, and practised their own religion. (No missionaries had reached the islands and Christianity had made no impact through the lives of sealers and visiting Maori, neither of whom were noted at this time for Christian observance or evangelism.) Moriori continued to worship their own ancestors and the gods of specific localities, to observe the old tapus and recite the karakia appropriate for every aspect of life to propitiate the gods. They still decorated their kopi with human and bird motifs and buried their dead in a sitting position in the sand, heads exposed and looking out to sea. Perhaps in part because this view of life had remained so coherently intact, there had been little intermarriage with Europeans — possibly only with the former sealer Shera at Te Whakaru and James Coffee at Ocean Bay; the products of such unions, or of casual connections with visiting crew members, were raised as Moriori.** No instances are known of Moriori-Maori marriages at this time, nor would such marriages become a feature of the new order that was about to be imposed on the Chathams.

The Taranaki Maori living at Port Nicholson (future site of Wellington and eventual capital of New Zealand) were known collectively at this time as Te Ati Awa, and all were intimately connected genealogically. They were grouped into two major tribes, Ngati Mutunga and Ngati Tama, and these in turn were made up of several hapu (Kekerewai, Ngati Whairama and Otaraua in the case of Ngati Mutunga; Ngati Wai and Ngati Haumia as part of Ngati Tama).

The decision to migrate was confirmed at two meetings at kainga on the shore of the harbour early in 1835.*** Ngati Mutunga gathered at Kumototo, home of their principal chief Pomare;**** and Ngati Tama at Raurimu.***** Other options were canvassed, including a massed invasion of Samoa or Norfolk

* Commentators have suggested that the absence of tribal warfare meant there was no incentive to acquire firearms.

** James Coffee covered himself politically by replacing his Moriori wife with a Maori one soon after the Taranaki invasion, and he subsequently claimed land through both spouses; only that through his Maori wife was allowed by the Native Land Court.

*** The exodus was to be far from total, however. Other Ati Awa chiefs and their hapu (Te Puni of Tawhirikura, for example) remained at Port Nicholson and were on hand to welcome the New Zealand Company settlers there in 1839 and 1840.

**** Close to the site of the current Ngati Poneke marae.

***** Between Pipitea Point and Kaiwharawhara.

Island. But the first-hand accounts of Chatham Island and its relative proximity decided the outcome. Both tribes agreed to proceed to Wharekauri — as they now called it — as soon as an opportunity presented itself.

That opportunity was the arrival of the brig *Rodney* from Sydney in October 1835. There are conflicting accounts about how the Maori procured the vessel. After the fuss that followed the Ngati Toa attack on Akaroa in 1831 using a British vessel, the captain, John Harewood, obviously wanted to protect himself from possible prosecution or condemnation for aiding and abetting a massacre on the Chathams. He claimed that the *Rodney* was occupied by 400 Maori, his crew seized, and his second mate taken hostage. He had no choice but to ferry his captors to the islands, he asserted. The Maori account suggests a greater willingness on Harewood's part to accept the commission, particularly after he had been offered a large quantity of treated flax, pigs and firearms in payment. There is also evidence that Harewood and his first mate had been negotiating an identical venture with Ngati Toa at Kapiti Island.

However he was persuaded, Captain Harewood sailed the *Rodney* out of Port Nicholson on 14 November 1835, with 500 Maori — men, women and children — and seventy-eight tonnes of seed potatoes. The passengers were 'packed so closely in the hold that they could only squat down with their heads resting on one another, and so sleep as best they could . . . they suffered much from wont of water, being unable, apparently, to carry sufficient for such a number; and on trying to pass the water to the women and children, the men seized and drunk it,' Alexander Shand recorded. In addition, most of the passengers were seasick without being able to move to relieve themselves. The squalor and stench below decks can be imagined. Had the Moriori attacked them on arrival at the Chathams, the Maori said later, the invaders could have been 'killed with ease'.

Whangaroa Harbour, where the Ngati Tama and Ngati Mutunga from Port Nicholson made their first landing on the Chathams. Ngati Mutunga initially remained there, while Ngati Tama spread rapidly to Waitangi and the north-east coast of the island.

Michael King

Harewood first took the *Rodney* into Whangatete Inlet, 'the best place I could find, not having any chart of the island'. The passengers began to disembark immediately, not wanting to spend a minute longer than necessary in their foul prison. Then a longboat appeared with Baker, Coffee, Matioro and Rihari on board, who suggested that Harewood move to adjacent Whangaroa Harbour, where the sealers were now established. This he did and the remainder of the passengers went ashore there and unloaded their potatoes.

On 23 November, after strenuous efforts to sanitise the hold, the *Rodney* departed for Port Nicholson. There Harewood found that the migrants still waiting had killed several dogs and a twelve-year-old girl 'for the purpose . . . of driving the ship back to them'. The girl had been cut into pieces and her flesh hung on posts, the captain noted with some horror. He was then paid (two and a half tonnes of pork, forty-one muskets, one cannon, two fowling pieces and about seven tonnes of potatoes) and 400 more passengers crowded into the ship, with seven canoes as deck cargo.* The *Rodney* sailed again on 30 November and arrived in the Chathams on 5 December 1835. The total number of Maori colonists was now about 900. In addition to their potatoes and canoes, they had about twenty pigs. After a few days' rest to recover from the effects of the voyage, they began to takahi — to take possession of parts of the island by a process known as 'walking the land'.

Haena Te Poki ('Old Iron'), daughter of the Ngati Mutunga chief Te Poki and sister of Toenga. When this photograph was taken in the early 1900s she was reputedly the last Maori alive who had eaten Moriori flesh at the time of the Ati Awa conquest of the Chathams.

Auckland Institute & Museum

Prior to the *Rodney*'s first voyage, Ngati Tama and Ngati Mutunga chiefs had agreed that no land claims would be made until the whole heke was assembled and the matter discussed. In fact, the first migrants, principally Ngati Tama, were unable to wait.

Although Whangaroa was promising at first sight, it ultimately disappointed the new arrivals. The harbour itself was attractive enough but not especially sheltered (there were no hills protecting it). Worse, most of the adjacent territory was peaty and damp and consequently not conducive to potato growing on a large scale. The landscape, too, was unlike anything the Maori had seen before and may have made them feel uncomfortable: peat flats stretched inland like a great carpet, with distant volcanic peaks rising from the horizon like islands.

For whatever reason (and it may have been simply greed), one section of Ngati Tama set out almost immediately for Waitangi, sheltered behind the hook of Hanson Point, and laid claim to that district and its Moriori villages; another, led by the chief Meremere, took possession of the north-east of the island, including Kaingaroa Harbour. When the rest of Ngati Mutunga arrived with their chiefs Patukawenga and Pomare in the second party, they were annoyed at what had transpired and decided initially to remain at Whangaroa, where they built a pa and planted as many potatoes as they could in bush clearings behind the harbour. Ngati Tama did the same at Waitangi and Kaingaroa.

At first the invaders simply ignored Moriori when and as they encountered them — with the exception of those around Whangaroa and Ocean Bay, who naively directed the Maori to water supplies and clearings, and who helped nurse and feed those most adversely affected by the voyage. It was far more difficult for the Moriori to ignore them. Parties of warriors armed with muskets, clubs

---

* Interestingly, two of the canoes had been made in Wellington from local totara and named *Rangiauria* (for Pitt Island) and *Ngawhenua* ('the lands'). These were tantamount to forward claims to territory on the Chathams. Another chief said the albatross on the Sisters Islands would be the grey hairs of his head: another declaration of prior rights.

and tomahawks, led by their chiefs, walked through Moriori tribal territories and settlements without warning, permission or greeting. If the districts were wanted by the invaders, they curtly informed the inhabitants that their land had been taken and the Moriori living there were now vassals. In December, when some of the Moriori men began to contest this process and to argue back, particularly around the northern coast, Waitangi and Waikanini, they were disinterestedly slain with tomahawk blows to the head. Fifty years later, the horror had not dissipated, and the Moriori remembered who those initial killers and victims were: 'Matahi Tepoki murdered Hikimanu, Ketu murdered Mahe, Kirihi murdered Kanangna . . .'

Initially, the Moriori had watched the arrival of the would-be colonists in surprise and disbelief. Around Whangaroa they had welcomed them, believing that the growth of the sealers' settlement there would attract trade and prosperity. Once the ritual walking of the land began, however, the sense of dread which had settled on those who had witnessed Matioro's war dance three years earlier became widespread. The first general action was to ignore what was happening in the hope that the problem would eventually disappear; after all, previous Maori residents in the Chathams had come and gone — there was no reason to believe these latest visitors would stay longer. Then, after this short period of paralysed inactivity, Moriori elders called a council of all Moriori men to assemble at Te Awapatiki, located near the centre of the island in an area not yet investigated by the invaders.

Te Awapatiki, 'path of the flounder', is literally that: the opening of Te Whanga, through which a large proportion of the island's kai moana — flounder, eels, mullet, kahawai, even shark — enter the lagoon from the sea. As such, it was a revered place. And the settlement to which the council was called

The Owenga chief Apitea Punga was a boy of eleven at the time of the Maori invasion. His father was one of five chiefs among whom Chatham Island was divided, and he claimed Pitt Island along with the east coast south of Te Awapatiki. Apitea succeeded to his father's interests and defended them in the Native Land Court. The luxuriant leaves of the Chatham Islands lily can be seen over his wife's shoulder.

Canterbury Museum

was on a plateau known as Hikurangi on the southern arm of the entrance. The participants — just under a thousand men, including 160 chiefs — gathered in an open space surrounded by an inner circle of huts and an outer one of akeake and kopi. Behind, the Pacific Ocean beat against an eroding coast of sand dunes; in front of them, they looked west across the lagoon, to where the invaders were encamped and waiting on the far shore. They needed no reminding that they faced the most serious threat in their known history, nor of the utter vulnerability of their position.

The younger men spoke first. They argued that the prohibitions on killing devised by Rongomaiwhenua, Pakehau and Nunuku were intended to prevent a small population of related people destroying themselves in a chain of blood feuds. Such principles did not envisage, nor were they appropriate for, an outright invasion by people who were prepared to kill on a large scale. Did not the Moriori already know the New Zealanders by reputation in their own wars as kaupeke — flesh-eaters? To do nothing in this instance would be suicidal. 'It was proposed to make a combined assault on the intruders [whom, after all, they outnumbered two to one] and even though many of the Moriori might fall, they would [ultimately] succeed.' There was little doubt the Moriori could have killed them all, Hirawanu Tapu told surveyor Percy Smith over thirty years later.

The Owenga chiefs Tapata and Torea put the contrary case: the law of Nunuku was not a strategy for survival, to be varied as conditions changed; it was a moral imperative. They reiterated the old maxims: 'For now and forever, never again let there be war . . . From today, forget the taste of human flesh . . . May your bowels rot the day you disobey this injunction.' That covenant envisaged and permitted of no exceptions; to maintain it was to maintain their mana as a people.

The argument moved both ways over three days, with all the chiefs taking part along with as many of the other men who wanted to speak. Ironically, while

The Moriori in 1835 would have looked much as they do in this 1877 photograph by Alfred Martin. Among members of this group were remnants who survived the conquest. Hirawanu Tapu (second left, standing), Rohana (second left, sitting) and Tatua (second right, standing) were all adolescents when the killing and enslavement of Moriori occurred. Each endured over two decades of slavery. Others, descendants of survivors, include Wari Tutaki (left), Teretiu Rehe (third left, standing), Rangitapua Horomona Rehe (fourth left, standing), Piripi (far right), Ngakikingi (middle, sitting) and Te Tene Rehe (next right).

Canterbury Museum

discussions were in progress, two solitary Maori arrived, the Ngati Tama chiefs Meremere and Nga Pe, travelling about five miles ahead of a party that was formally taking possession of the east coast. Again, the younger men advocated killing — more vehemently now, because the Maori had become aware of the nature of Moriori deliberations. Again Torea and Tapata argued that that was not the Moriori way. Finally, because it was the wish of all the elders, the view of Torea prevailed. There would be no killing from the Moriori side. They would return to their villages from Te Awapatiki and offer the New Zealanders peace and friendship and an opportunity to share the resources of Rekohu in partnership, without rancour or resentment. That was the manner in which they had greeted manuwiri since Broughton's visit; they would do so again, although the number was greater than any they had encountered previously. If their offer was not accepted, then they would take whatever consequences followed. What mattered above all else, Torea stressed, was that they did not compromise their mana.

While it is not recorded, it seems likely that Ngati Mutunga and Ngati Tama held a council of their own while the Moriori were meeting, and that this council decided to settle the question of ownership in a traditional Maori manner, by slaying sufficient Moriori to establish the Maori claim and to remove the annoyance of overt opposition. It is possible that they expected the Moriori to return from Te Awapatiki prepared to fight, and that consequently they considered a pre-emptive strike essential (a common martial strategy adopted by Maori who were outnumbered). Further, the remainder of the Moriori population would now be dealt with in a manner that made the new order explicit, and which utilised its labour to provide sustenance for the large Maori population that had few food sources of its own.

The change in Maori tactics was evident as soon as the Moriori men returned from the council meeting. Before they were able to deliver their proposals for peace and partnership, Maori attackers fell upon them in their homes. As Moriori spokesmen noted afterwards '. . . the enemy were found in possession, and the Morioris were taken prisoners, the women and children were bound, and many of these, together with the men, were killed and eaten, so that the corpses lay scattered in the woods and over the plains. Those who were spared from death were herded like swine, and killed even from year to year . . .'

Hirawanu Tapu added: '[They] commenced to kill us like sheep . . . wherever we were found. In the bush, on the oka ohere,* some of our people were eaten, and others were thrown to the birds of heaven.' And the Kaingaroa Moriori Minarapa and Kirapu told a government agent: 'We were terrified, fled to the bush, concealed ourselves in holes underground, and in any place to escape our enemies. It was of no avail; we were discovered and killed, men, women and children indiscriminately.'

Shand recorded that Te Wharekura and his hapu at Te Raki 'killed and roasted 50 Morioris in one oven'.

> Tikaokao and others [attacked] the Waitangi Morioris within their radius, killing men, women and children; and laid them all out on the sandy beach of Waitangi, in length over a quarter of a mile. One Moriori [survivor] — Heremaia Tau — said, 'they were laid out touching one another, the parent and the child . . .' Some of the women with stakes thrust

---

* The meaning of this expression is not known.

Shand's Maori informants reached a similar verdict. 'It was the infringement of their own tapu that killed them. They were a very tapu people.' And hundreds of those 'tapu people' simply turned their faces to the wall and died rather than persist in an existence that no longer had any meaning, and that was pierced continually with the shards of physical and emotional pain.

Others who clung to life, but stunned and stunted by their experience, were among those reviled by Maori and Pakeha as being degenerate, of low intelligence, and deficient in energy and initiative. For that was how many of them seemed. And when in later years some attempted to anaesthetise their suffering in cheap alcohol, that only added weight to the accusations that the Paraiwhara, these 'black fellas', were low in the scale of God's creation.

Some few Moriori continued to resist slavery and its overbearing physical and psychological weight. One such was Koche. He was the only one of his people able to leave a direct account of his experience, thanks to his contact with the American lawyer Ewing, who wrote it down about 1850. Koche told his story as the whaling vessel on which he crewed crossed the Pacific, and he spoke chiefly at night, when his duties were at an end. Ewing noted that

> In calm weather his broken narrative ran tersely, and was marked by humour and a lack of strong feeling; but when the storm-spirit arose, and washed the lower deck and enveloped the upper in spray, his voice grew hoarse, his eye flashed, and his white teeth from time to time came together with a clash that made the blood tingle.

Koche described the demoralising effect of having to labour for the Maori conquerors, often in sight of the battered skulls of his kinsmen. The result for the Moriori was physical deformity and a high death rate. 'Once cheerful, full of mirth and laughter, they became morose and taciturn.' Koche, with a few others, persistently refused to work.

> Some died under, others yielded to, the lash; and he, who had been dragged by a rope to the field, and beaten in vain, and would neither yield nor give up the ghost, was taken by [Matioro] to his house to break in. He continued moody, and maintained his independence so far as to execute only such commissions as pleased him, frequently courting death by mutely and stubbornly refusing to obey orders. Mate-oro [*sic*] seemed to respect his attitude to some extent, and employed him to supply his table with sea-fish, giving him a canoe furnished with nets and lines for the purpose.
>
> The struggle between them now ceased, for this occupation gave Koche solitude and freedom when afloat, and opportunity to muse over the condition of himself and [his] people. He soon came to the conclusion that it was useless to attempt an insurrection, the population being unarmed, dispirited, and under an iron subjugation. But for his single self, he was resolved on resistance to the last, and, as his boat tossed on the wave, he brooded over many schemes . . . A personal conflict was most in accordance with his disposition, and many a time he was tempted, unarmed as he was, to close in a death-struggle, out of which, doubtless, he would have come victorious, if uninterrupted; for though but little above the middle height, he was broad and deep-chested, with sinews of iron, and capable of immense exertion; and, above all, was animated by a spirit that would have revelled in the fight. But followed as the chief was, fair play was not to be looked for, and he reluctantly abandoned his favoured purpose. Whilst in the midst of such reflections one afternoon, he drew up from the ocean a fish seldom taken — the mo-eeka, pleasant to the taste, but a virulent poison, a small portion of which when eaten producing a deathly sickness, and a full meal, death . . . On landing he placed his dangerous prize in a small salt-water pool near the beach, into which, as he caught them, he placed others, until a large mess was collected. This he brought home one night when the wind blew from the north-west, and persuaded the cook to serve up for the morning meal. Directing her

to throw the offal to the wood-hogs, he disappeared, and soon after midnight reached the east coast, seized a canoe, and put to sea . . .

The cook, who had her more immediate grudge to gratify, regaled the favourite dogs with the heads and entrails . . . The howls of his four-footed companions in the night, followed by their death in the morning, told the suspicious [Matioro] a tale of poison, which a visit to the kitchen confirmed. A portion of the breakfast thrown to a stray dog promptly finished him.

Koche was sought for high and low, the island ransacked in vain; no trace of him was found, and the conclusion was arrived at that he had thrown himself into the sea. The chief had taken up a hatchet to kill his cook, but she sullenly asserted that she had never seen a mo-eeka before, and was believed and spared . . .

Koche, meanwhile, had made his way by canoe to Rangiauria — Pitt Island — and proceeded to establish himself there:

Near an old seal camp, he found growing some wild wheat, which he cultivated after a manner, and which, with wild celery, water-cresses, fern-root and karaka, left him nothing to desire in the way of vegetable food. On the shore, he found crabs and lobsters, and echini [sea-eggs] in the hollows of the rock . . . The blue petrel had their habitations in the woods, in the ground under the roots of trees, and in crevices of rocks, and were speared at night as they flew about in numbers with a noise like the croaking of frogs. But the subject that gave its sovereign least trouble was the dark-brown water-hen, of the size of a barnyard fowl, which inhabited the skirts of the woods, and fed on the beach. It was unable to fly, and made no attempt to escape when approached . . .

At the base of the mountain, near a strong spring, he formed a summer-house — an arbor of the trees and shrubs or aromatic myrtle — and, besides supplying his wants, did little else but wander over the isle during the summer season; but when winter came, he retired to a cave in the mountain . . . and devoted his leisure to making the utensils of the chase, toilet, and kitchen. He manufactured baskets, nets, and lines of twisted fibre, fish-hooks of mother-of-pearl [paua], knives of sharp quartz, razors of shell, and mats for bedding and cloaks.

He covered his fish alive in red-hot ashes, and, when cooked, peeled off the skin, and ate the flesh from the ribs. He cooked his meat in an oven, of which he had one at each residence, and several at points on the shore. It consisted of a hole in the ground lined with stone, in which he built a fire, and placed pebbles and stones. His game, after the ordinary cleaning, was scrubbed with sand on the outside, and well washed inside and out. Hot pebbles were placed in the belly and shaken in under the breast, and green aromatic leaves stuffed in upon them. The oven was then cleared of fire and pebbles, and lined with green leaves, and the game placed in the bottom. The fat was washed, and placed with hot pebbles in a vessel of bark, and beside it the blood, tied in a leaf, and propped with hot stones. Then came a layer of such vegetables as were in season or at hand, and the whole was spread over with leaves, on which the remaining hot stones were placed, covered in turn with leaves, and filled in with sod and earth. After an interval according to the size of the mess, it was taken out, spread upon a cloth of the glossy leaves of the karaka, and eaten hot.

Koche survived in this manner for several years. In 1840 his presence was discovered. Members of the New Zealand Company expedition to the Chathams reported back to the main island that Pitt was inhabited.* Matioro guessed that one of the refugees might be his escaped slave and sent an expedition to the island, which eventually captured Koche. Twice more the determined slave escaped, the second time aboard an American whaler. 'In the afternoon she stood out to sea,' Koche's biographer recorded, 'and at nightfall her hull was down and the island had disappeared, all save one volcanic peak that rose like a pyramid

---

* Dieffenbach reported that there were twelve Moriori on Pitt in 1840.

above the waves. Then Koche came out from the fore-chains, in which he had in some mysterious way buried himself, and caught a last glance of his native mountain as it sank for ever from his view.'

Koche never returned to the Chathams, and it is not known what became of him. He is presumed to have died at sea or in the United States.

The experience of Koche the survivor was, however, untypical. In spite of the Chathams becoming part of New Zealand in 1842, and the appointment of a resident magistrate in 1855, most Moriori remained enslaved until a general manumission was declared in 1863.* By then a terrible toll was evident. In addition to the 300 people killed around 1835, 1,336 more Moriori had died of disease and despair in the intervening two decades. Most of the 101 who survived in 1862 were either infertile, too old to reproduce, or too closely related to other survivors to consider marriage. There were few children. The tchakat henu of the Chathams were not totally exterminated, but the process that could lead to their physical demise was in motion.

For those Moriori who did survive the late 1830s and early 1840s, the one prospect that brought them consolation in the short term was that the very bellicosity of their conquerors might prove self-destructive.

Ngati Mutunga remained envious of Ngati Tama, who had claimed what were regarded as the prime locations — Waitangi and Kaingaroa — before the completion of the *Rodney*'s second voyage. Not only were more whaling vessels calling more frequently at Waitangi,** but the Maori there were able to grow huge acreages of potatoes for barter in the loamy soil close to the port. At Whangaroa, by contrast, the followers of Pomare and Te Poki had a considerable distance to carry their vegetables from cultivations to the bay. Worse, Ngati Tama refused to let Ngati Mutunga bring their potatoes to Waitangi by canoe to trade with whalers there. Pomare sent letters to Ngati Tama, apparently complaining about this state of affairs. They were torn up. This response added to a powder-keg of tension that required a spark to ignite.

Meanwhile, other Maori groups and individuals found that, with the Chathams conquered, their old restlessness returned. Matioro's elder brother Te Tupeotu returned to Waikanae to live in 1836. And Meremere, Ngati Tama chief of Kaingaroa, tried to persuade the captain of an American whaler to take his followers to Samoa to fight and settle there. The captain told Meremere to bring his people around to Waitangi, where he would take them aboard after he had finished whaling off the coast. Accordingly, the Kaingaroa community made the trek halfway around the island. Ngati Mutunga, in the meantime, had revived plans to capture Norfolk Island.

While the additional Ngati Tama and an allied group of Kekerewai were waiting at Waitangi, a French whaler, the *Jean Bart*, entered the bay. About forty Maori went aboard to try and initiate bartering (potatoes and pigs for cloth and tobacco; and perhaps for 'luxury' goods such as alcohol and ornaments). Ngati Tama were there, of course, from Waitangi; and a canoeload of Ngati Mutunga,

---

* In the 1840s and 1850s, long after the supposed abolition of slavery in New Zealand, Te Ati Awa gave pairs of Moriori slaves as gifts to Ngapuhi, Ngati Ruanui and Ngai Tahu (David Simmons, personal communication, 1/6/88). A Moriori man alive in Dargaville in the early 1920s had been taken to Taranaki as the child of a slave in the 1850s.

** Fifty in 1840, for example.

brought down from Whangaroa by Matioro. Once on the ship the Maori began to argue: Matioro wanted to persuade the captain to move to Whangaroa; the Waitangi residents wanted the vessel to remain where it was.

Accounts of what followed are confused and in some instances contradictory. But it appears that the French captain misinterpreted the Maori argument and threatening gestures and believed that his ship and crew were in danger. He enticed one section of his visitors, including Matioro, into a cabin below decks with wine and biscuits. Then, when he believed they were safely locked away, he had his crew clear the remaining Maori from the deck with harpoons, lances and blubber spades, killing a number of them. Meanwhile he had raised anchor and set sail.

The visitors in the cabin were confused as to what was happening. But less so once the decks were cleared; for the Frenchmen removed the skylight and began to thrust their whaling lances into the Maori milling about below. When this failed to kill anybody (though some were severely injured), the Frenchmen called for a truce. But by then some of the Maori had found the ship's guns and Matioro had brought cartridges with him. They began to fire from the cabin and managed to kill the ship's mate. The crew, deprived of firearms, tried to secure the skylight with chains, but the Maori kept forcing it open and managed to shoot the cooper. By then it was dark and both sides waited for the morning: the Maori — so they claimed subsequently — eagerly; they were enjoying the contest. The Frenchmen were terrified.

Daybreak revealed the crew taking to the boats and apparently heading for Pitt Island or the mainland.* The Maori burst on deck and fired at the disappearing boats, but were unable to chase them because of the need to see to the ship. Four of them, including Matioro, had been to sea previously and they managed to take control of the steering and sails, by which time the Frenchmen had allegedly disappeared. The argument as to whether the vessel should be taken to Whangaroa or Waitangi apparently resumed, but the prevailing winds made both destinations impossible. The *Jean Bart* was eventually run on to rocks at Ocean Bay, where Ngati Mutunga looted and burned it.

Shortly afterwards the whaler who had been dealing with Ngati Tama at Kaingaroa returned to Waitangi. He heard what had happened to the *Jean Bart* and judged that the Maori had been the aggressors. He left again without taking Meremere and his people aboard and sailed to the Bay of Islands, where he reported the incident to a French Navy vessel, *Heroine*. He then returned to Waitangi with the man-o'-war and sent a message ashore that he had tobacco to trade.

Most of the Maori were extremely wary. Former sealer James Coffee, who now lived at Waitangi with his Maori wife, advised no one to leave the shore until he had investigated the new arrivals. But a chief named Ngatuna, who knew the American captain, ignored this advice and set out for the ships by canoe, accompanied by his wife. They were seized by French sailors. When the wife jumped off the *Heroine* she was shot dead in the water. The French then bombarded the Waitangi pa with grape and twenty-five-pound shot, and subsequently sent an armed party ashore to burn all the houses. The residents, meanwhile, had retreated inland promptly, knowing they were outmatched in firepower. The *Heroine* sailed north and destroyed three more Maori

---

* This is the version of the Maori survivors. French authorities came to believe that the crew had been massacred, because neither boats nor crew were ever seen again.

settlements, at Ouira at the northern end of Kekerione Beach, at Ocean Bay and Whangaroa. The sailors took two further Maori prisoners and sailed with them for France.*

This double catastrophe — especially the loss of some of Ngati Tama's most able men, including Ngatuna — changed the balance of power on the island. Within a year Ngati Mutunga had decided to attack Ngati Tama and Kekerewai at Waitangi and drive them off their coveted location. The tearing up of Pomare's letters to Ngati Tama accompanied by an alleged uttering of insults was cited as the *take* or immediate cause of dispute.

Some 200 Ngati Mutunga warriors assembled from their settlements around Whangaroa and marched on Waitangi, led by Matioro. There they built a fortified pa alongside Ngati Tama's Kaimataotao Pa, near the mouth of the Nairn River. The Ngati Mutunga construction included a high tower, from which they commenced to shoot down on some 180 Ngati Tama. Returning the fire, Ngati Tama killed Te Ahipaura, eldest son of one of the attackers' leading kaumatua; and this made Ngati Mutunga all the more determined to defeat the defenders.

Eventually Ngati Tama began to run short of food and realised they could not survive a protracted siege. They decided to abandon the pa and make a run for the Ngati Tama settlement at Waikeri on the north-east corner of the island. From there they would persuade their kinsman Meremere to come south to Te Awapatiki to prevent Ngati Mutunga pursuit. While this plan was being discussed in May 1840, the New Zealand Company's survey ship *Cuba* arrived in the bay. Having been prevented by the Treaty of Waitangi and subsequent proclamations from buying further land for British settlement in New Zealand (they had already purchased Port Nicholson, Ngati Mutunga's and Ngati Tama's immediate former home), the company had decided to buy the Chatham Islands, then excluded from New Zealand's territorial limits. The company's officers came ashore, spoke with both Maori factions, and decided they had to intervene — 'not only to satisfy the claims of both parties, but to save, if possible, the weaker from destruction'. Not only would the war delay their mission, it might result in their having no Maori 'owners' with whom to deal. It never occurred to them that the Moriori might be considered owners.

Ernst Dieffenbach, naturalist to the company,** observed that the Moriori 'were serving their respective masters on each side; but, as slaves, took no part in the contest'. He noted 'the wretched change' in their circumstances since Broughton's visit, and estimated that 'not 90 of the original natives now survived in the whole group; a few years of slavery and degradation had reduced their numbers, and in a short time every trace of them will be lost'.

Dieffenbach attributed the darker hue of some Moriori (alleged source of the nickname 'black fella') to their 'greater exposure and still greater uncleanliness'.

> They are neither so tall, muscular, nor well-proportioned as their [Maori] neighbours, especially the women and the younger men. They have often short necks, thick heads, and, when young, prominent paunches;*** the forehead is often low and sloping, and cheek bones prominent, the eyes narrower, the nose flat and clumsy . . . An excess of toes, so as to have six or more on each foot is not very uncommon . . . Sometimes it is difficult to

---

* These two managed to return to New Zealand subsequently (though not to the Chathams); Ngatuna is believed to have committed suicide in France.

** And first scientist to visit the Chatham Islands.

*** A symptom of malnutrition.

distinguish their sex; and a sealer who had formerly lived among them [Coffee?] told me that they often emasculate their male children by compressing their testicles between stones . . . they have a generally downcast look.

The German doctor found most Moriori living close to but separate from their masters' settlements, 'in miserable huts in the open field; their disposition is morose and taciturn, and it was with difficulty that I could gain their confidence;* but, after I had succeeded in doing so, I found them not at all deficient in intellect . . .' He also noted that, at least in his presence, they spoke neither Moriori nor Maori, but 'an intermediate dialect, differing less in words and construction than in pronunciation'.

Looking down the Nairn Valley to Waitangi Harbour. Charles Heaphy painted this landscape in 1840 when Ngati Mutunga were attacking Ngati Tama. Only the intervention of Heaphy's employers, the New Zealand Company, prevented heavy Ngati Tama casualties.

Alexander Turnbull Library

To preserve their prospects for land purchase, the New Zealand Company's agent, the Reverend R. D. Hanson, moved the beleaguered Ngati Tama in the *Cuba* to Kaingaroa and Waikeri, and purchased the Whangaroa and Waitangi districts from

---

* Dieffenbach gained a reputation for good relations with native peoples. When news of his death in Germany was reported in Wellington in 1847, local Ati Awa were sufficiently moved to compose an apakura (elegy) in his honour. The deceased turned out to be Dieffenbach's cousin. The prematurity of the lament, however, in no way diminished its touching sincerity, noted the scientist's biographer (Bell 1976, p. 153).

Fighting Stages
Waitangi, Chatham Is.
1840

C. Heaphy

Pomare and the north-eastern coast from Ngati Tama.* This was not quite the end of fighting, however. Ngati Mutunga sent a war party around the coast late in 1840. This killed a Moriori whom they came upon by chance; then Meremere's younger brother, whom they found shooting tui. The latter death was regarded by Ngati Mutunga as satisfaction for the shooting of Te Ahipaura earlier in the year. A further taua was despatched, which lost two dead and one wounded to Ngati Tama. At this point peace was declared, the leaders of the respective fighting parties, Tatua and Meremere, being closely related.

Peace was sealed late in 1842 when a party of Church of England Maori missionaries arrived in the Chathams and converted most of Ngati Tama and Ngati Mutunga en masse.** Many of those who were not persuaded were mopped up the following year by the Reverend John Aldred, a Wesleyan, who established loyal followings of Maori and Moriori at Hawaruwaru and Tupuangi. Only the Ngati Kuri hapu of Ngati Mutunga remained aloof from both denominations.

Although there was inevitably some doubt about the depth, understanding and sincerity of such rapid conversions, the adoption of Christianity did have one immediate and long-term benefit for the Moriori: while most remained enslaved, it brought to an end the callous and spontaneous killings with which their owners had, up to this time, been able to terrorise them. From 1842 Moriori lives were still nasty and brutish; but they were not as short as they had been previously.

In spite of a gradual improvement in their circumstances, and of their apparent docility in the eyes of European observers, the Moriori remnants were never

Charles Heaphy's drawing of the pa and fighting stages on the riverbank at Waitangi in May 1840. That on the left was built by the Ngati Mutunga attackers, to fire down into the Ngati Tama pa in the centre. Ngati Tama have responded with a stage of their own but it is smaller because, being besieged, they were short of building materials. The trenches down to the river provided a covered way for the collection of water by both sides at night.

Auckland Institute & Museum

---

* On the basis of these purchases, the New Zealand Governor issued a charter to the New Zealand Company to administer the Chathams; it was cancelled by the proclamation which made the islands part of New Zealand in April 1842.

** Most of these adherents deserted Christianity in the late 1860s in favour of the teachings of Taranaki prophet Te Whiti O Rongomai.

reconciled to the events of 1835 and their aftermath. Their view of what had taken place was simple and unequivocal. Their mana whenua (which arose from at least half a millennium of occupation of Rekohu) had been ignored by the Maori, but had never been extinguished. They had not been defeated in fair contest, as they had not engaged in a contest. They had been dealt with neither as owners of the islands, nor as the partners they had been prepared to be. Their offer to share the resources of Rekohu with those who were, after all, distant Polynesian kin, had been hurled back in their faces. They had been ignored, insulted, slaughtered and enslaved — brought to their knees physically, culturally and spiritually. But because they had neither broken Nunuku's injunction nor vacated their island, their own mana was intact.

Their collective view was expressed a generation later in the plea from thirty surviving elders to Governor George Grey in New Zealand:

> Friend, let no other peoples of the world ask why this people did not hold to their lands. It was because we were a people who did not know anger or how to fight. The custom of this land was that when one bled and another bled, that was it. We were a people who dwelt in peace, who did not believe in killing and eating their own kind. Our word for that kind of person is kaupeke: a flesh-eating demon. The manner of this people was like that of a flock of lost sheep . . . when the shepherd went away, the wild dog came to eat them . . . The sheep were many, but what was that to the wild dog . . . It simply went on eating until its teeth were blunted and the sheep's numbers dwindled . . . Friend, we must have the rights to our own lands, because we are the rightful owners of our ancestors' home — of that land planted here by God at the time our forefathers arrived at this place . . .

Population of the Chatham Islands, showing the dramatic decline in Moriori numbers in the 1830s and 1840s.

After Richards (1972)

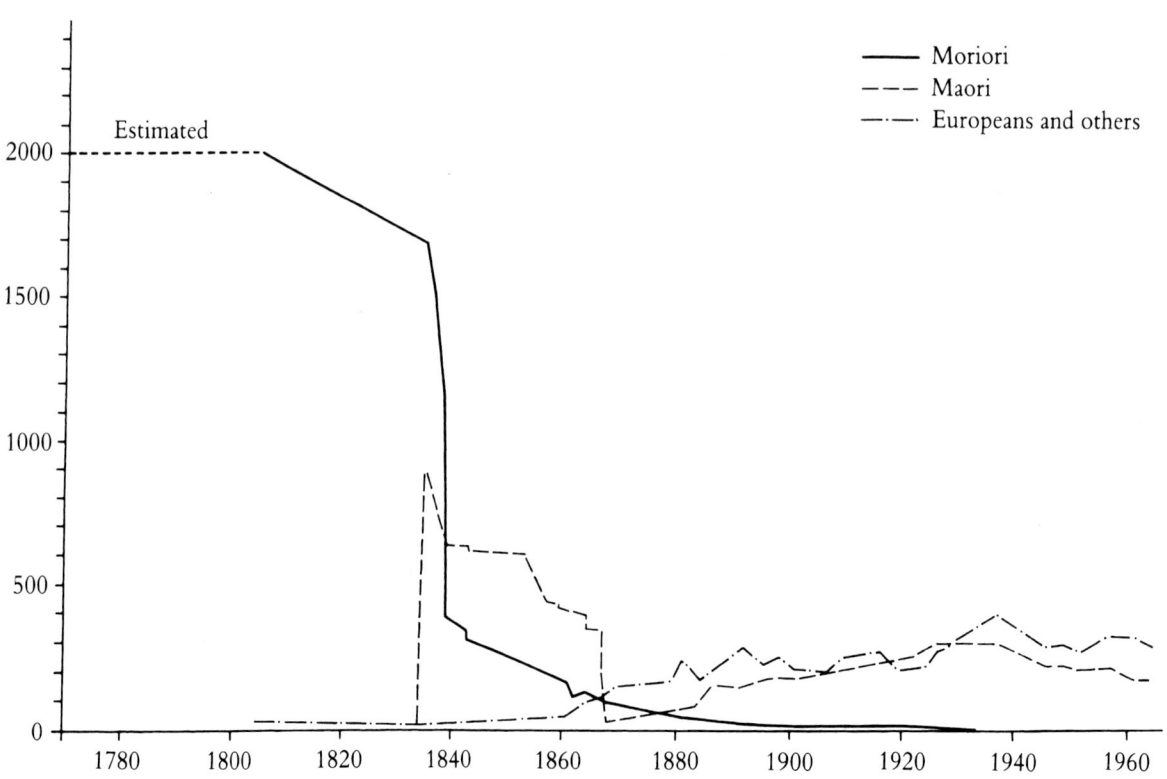

Had they possessed an intimate knowledge of Maori tribal culture in 1835, however, Moriori would have known that the outcome of the Ati Awa invasion was inevitable, given that they declined to defend themselves. This was particularly so in the light of the previous decade of Ngati Mutunga and Ngati Tama history. For these Maori at this time, displaced from their own ancestral home and insecure in their previous one, mana was to be derived almost solely from fighting, and even more so from successful conquest. There was the additional fact that the Moriori were dealing with what Rhys Richards has called 'a post-European Maori culture . . . strong tribal organisation was kept, as was communal living in well-built fortified villages; but, with the aid of European guns, gods and potatoes [the latter permitting more mobile campaigns and longer sieges], warfare was elevated to an even more important role in their lives'.

In these circumstances, even a vanquished foe could be respected — and possibly well treated — if he had acquitted himself well in combat (hence Matioro's admiration for Koche, one of the few Moriori who kept defying him). An adversary who simply gave up — as the Maori interpreted the Moriori offer of partnership and their subsequent behaviour after enslavement — was carrion on the beach. And this was how most Ngati Mutunga and Ngati Tama on the Chathams in the 1830s and 1840s viewed the Moriori, with contempt, from the time they heard that the Chatham Islanders did not know how to fight, through to the inevitable outcome of the invasion and the Land Court sittings of the 1870s.

The Moriori had learned a tactical and philosophical truth that was to be articulated by other people from other cultures in the twentieth century: non-violence is an effective weapon only against an adversary who shares your conscience.

CHAPTER

FOUR

The Maungahuka Experiment

MORIORI WHO SURVIVED THE SEVERE EPIDEMICS OF THE 1820S AND 1830s, the Taranaki invasion, the killings, enslavement and death by despair that followed the invasion, might have felt — not unreasonably — that life could hold no further horrors for them beyond mere survival. They were wrong. Late in 1842 Matioro, still belligerent, an even more imposing figure than before with his weight increased to some 160 kilograms, led a colonising expedition of more than sixty people to the sub-Antarctic Auckland Islands, 500 kilometres to the south-west. He and his fellow Ngati Mutunga compelled just under thirty Moriori to accompany them as slaves to a region whose bleakness was exceeded only by that of Tierra del Fuego and the Arctic outposts of the Inuit — and occupants of those territories had at least had thousands of years to adjust to their harsh environment.

A cluster of reasons have been cited for the Auckland Islands experiment, all of which probably had some bearing on Matioro's decision to abandon the Chathams.

First, there is every indication that the Ngati Mutunga chief and his faction were restless, confined to Chatham Island without the martial excitement that had characterised the previous two decades. Some of his people had returned disappointed to the mainland, to Waikanae, in 1836; a diverting plan to invade Samoa in 1838 had had to be abandoned because Ngati Mutunga could not find a ship prepared to transport them to a confrontation with an equally warlike people; there was still fear of further French retaliation for the loss of the *Jean Bart*, in which Matioro had been the prime mover; and the advent of Christianity to the Chathams in 1842 — brought by first Anglican Catechists and then Wesleyan — meant the likely end of local skirmishes and outright warfare. Matioro and his followers had reason to be bored and to seek the invigoration of new challenges.

Further cause to leave the Chathams at this time might have been found in the fact that Christianity was spreading at a surprising and (possibly to Matioro) alarming rate among Ngati Tama and sections of Ngati Mutunga. One of its implications was that converts should give up their Moriori slaves. Matioro appeared to have had no intention of altering his lifestyle so drastically for what he viewed as a foreign creed; and, indeed, he was still insisting on the unquestioning compliance of his Moriori slaves nearly two decades later.*

Finally, Matioro had visited Auckland Island, which was known to the

* See p. 87.

Murihiku Maori as Maungahuka*. He had landed on the group in the course of a mixed whaling-sealing expedition some years before he reached the Chathams. He must have been misled by what he had seen. The island appeared to have ample food resources (pigs, birds and fish, and the prospect of growing vegetables). If the weather was fine, it seemed a moderately appealing place. It was not owned by any colonial power and was uninhabited and ungoverned. But — whether Matioro knew it or not — the weather was scarcely ever fine; the climate was, in fact, abominable — almost impossible for the growing of vegetables and with an infinite capacity to lower human morale.

The islands had been discovered by a Captain Abraham Bristow, sailing one of the first whalers in the Pacific, the *Ocean*, in 1806. He named them 'Lord Auckland's

---

* This has been incorrectly translated as Sugar Mountain, an apparent reference to the snow which falls on the island's upper slopes. In fact, huka was the southern name for albatross down, and it was to that inhabitant of the island that the name referred. Southern Maori sealers had been visiting the group for at least a decade prior to Matioro's move there. I am indebted to Mr Syd Cormack of Tuatapere for this information (personal communication, 1/9/88).

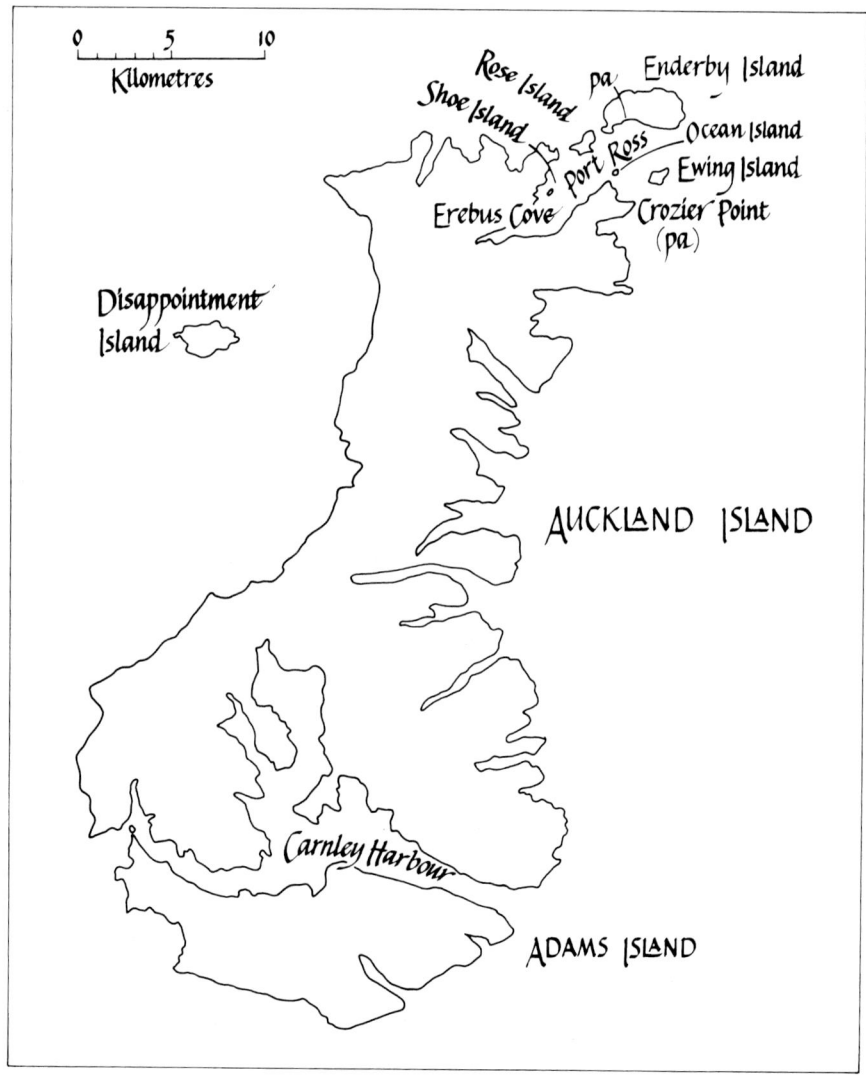

Groupe' in honour of an aristocratic friend of his father. Bristow returned in 1807 in an Enderby Company vessel, took possession of the group for Britain, and released pigs there for the benefit of future wayfarers or shipwrecked sailors.

They consist of two large islands, Auckland and Adams, and several smaller ones, of which Enderby, Disappointment, Ewing, Rose and Shoe were to be the most important historically. Collectively, they are fifty-three kilometres long and twenty-five wide. And they are, by any standards, extraordinarily bleak. Only Port Ross in the north and Carnley Harbour in the south offer safe anchorages adjacent to habitable locations. Much of the shoreline is characterised by steep cliffs and pounding sea. Low, wind-flattened forest runs around the coast on the larger islands, and the uplands on Auckland, Adams, Disappointment and Enderby are tussock-covered. Where there is soil, it is peaty. As in the Chathams, the wind blows almost continuously; but it and the rain which falls, often torrentially, are colder — much colder in winter especially, when sleet and rain alternate with snow.

Like the other sub-Antarctic islands, the Aucklands are a breeding ground for ocean birds and marine mammals — especially petrels, albatross and seals. And it

Typical Auckland Island coast: high cliffs, pounding sea and little shelter from the wind.

Auckland Institute & Museum

Rohana, longest surviving
member of the party of
Moriori slaves who made
survival possible at the Ngati
Mutunga settlements on the
Auckland Islands. She died in
1902.

Alexander Turnbull Library

was these that were expected to provide a large part of the Maori-Moriori food resource — with the bulk of the foraging done, of course, by Ngati Mutunga's Moriori slaves.

The Moriori commandeered for the expedition were Takaroa, Tarere, Tamaehanga, Tapepeke, Tamaaroaro, Pakautu, Marakapia, Tarakihi, Meke, Pita-rangi-te-muia, Matai, Ngatiawa, Ta-moko-tu-a-he, Hanga, Tiemi (men); and Kahoki, Hakina, Tongarei, Hine-kutu, Te Kore, Hine-makoko, Porou, Rohana, and Taha Patu (women).*

That is virtually all that is known about them, other than that most of them were 'young'. On the Auckland Islands, they fall into silence as far as the historical record is concerned. Whereas Maori are identified by name in accounts of subsequent events, Moriori are referred to — if at all — as 'Moriori'; they are not seen as important players in the drama that followed by either their Maori masters or the European records of those dramas. Again, an historical judgment is being made about these people; they are nobody, their doings are scarcely worth remarking upon.

And yet the Auckland Island migration was another significant event for Moriori. It removed about eight per cent of the surviving population from their homeland, reducing that population significantly at a time when it was already falling sharply. It removed them from contact with their relatives and friends for fourteen years — and some forever (at least two were murdered on Auckland Island, others died of natural causes and still others remained in New Zealand when the settlement broke up). They did the major part of the hard work — gardening, carrying water, foraging for seafood in conditions that were dangerous and cold — and it was their labour more than any other factor that allowed the colony to survive in the period before Europeans established a settlement there. Yet the historical record remains blank about who these Moriori were, how they lived, and what they thought about the experiment that involved them intimately but involuntarily. Only one of the Moriori party, Rohana,** survived into the twentieth century to tell her story about the episode. And she always referred to it as the second most harsh experience of her life (the harshest being the Ati Awa invasion and massacre of her people).

By contrast, far more is known about the major Ngati Mutunga protagonists. They were Matioro and his wife Ngakure (nicknamed Kuini or Queen), his father-in-law Te Patukumikumi and wife Tapirirua, his brother-in-law Tapae and wife Ngapera and children, Toenga Te Poki and wife Patae, Toenga's cousins Tangari Te Umu and Tupara, Manature, Motu-karaka, Ngatere, and Ngakare and his wife Piro. The total Maori party was around forty.***

For transport for the 500-kilometre voyage Matioro managed to hire the Sydney brig *Hannah* for 150 pigs. This vessel had been seized on its way from Wellington to the Chathams by a passenger named Ellis, who killed the mate. Ellis

---

* Other Moriori whose descendants reported that they had been on Auckland Island included Whiri, Titapu, Urukapu and Kurupa; another was remembered as Teone Paraire. These were either additional slaves whose names were no longer recalled when Alexander Shand collected information, because they had not returned to the Chathams; or they were alternative names for some of those on Shand's list, above.

** Later wife of Hirawanu Tapu.

*** There are conflicting estimates. Shand named twenty-six but adds 'with some children'. Other Maori names crop up later in the story which are not on Shand's list and other estimates of the Maori numbers at this time are consistently around forty.

carried the Maori-Moriori party to the Auckland Islands then returned to New Zealand. He was arrested at Mercury Bay, tried for piracy and sentenced to transportation to Norfolk Island.

There is disagreement about when the *Hannah* reached Port Ross at the northern end of Auckland Island. Some say early 1843, others late 1843; there is more persuasive evidence that it was, in fact, October or November 1842.* As soon as the migrants had landed and unloaded their own boats, potatoes and other supplies, a party of chiefs set out to takahi (take possession of the island by 'walking the land'). This brought some shocks. The chiefs Tangari Te Umu and Motu-karaka in particular were aghast at how poor the prospect was and in particular how bad the climate and the peat soil would be for growing vegetables and flax. They went straight back on board the *Hannah* and asked to be returned to the Chathams. Ellis, fearing that the remainder of the party would do the same, weighed anchor and left. When Matioro returned to the beach the vessel was gone and — whether he liked it or not — he was forced to look for the most likely site for a settlement.

Meanwhile a party of sealers was working at Carnley Harbour at the other end of the island. During the previous month they too had sailed into Port Ross and had stored some 200 baskets of potatoes in a cave on Enderby Island. At Carnley, they were astonished to see three whale boats heading up the harbour towards their camp. They presumed it was another party of sealers. It turned out to be Matioro and an advance party, scouting for a village site. The Maori stayed several days and then returned to Port Ross. When the sealers followed some time later, they were angered to find that the cache of potatoes was rapidly being consumed by Ngati Mutunga, who seemed well provided for with flour, tea, sugar, biscuits, bacon and a 'large quantity' of spirits, mostly rum. In addition to their whaleboats, they carried guns and ammunition from the *Jean Bart*. The sealer who recorded this also noted that the Moriori slaves consisted largely of 'young men and women'.

Matioro established his pa on top of Crozier Point, a headland overlooking Port Ross and opposite Ewing Island. Here his party built huts from local wood and planted flax and potatoes. They also expected to live from shooting pigs, ducks, tui, snipe, seals, sea–lions and sea elephants; from gathering albatross and petrels in the mutton bird season; from shellfish and from fishing. But it was not long before the disappointments began to pile up.

The pigs were tough and tasted strongly of fish as a result of feeding on dead seals and seabirds. They caught large numbers of cod, but they were inedible because the flesh was infested with worms. And, while potatoes did seed and grow, the tubers were the size of marbles. Apart from turnips and cabbages, other vegetable crops failed. Seals were available, but the settlers (or at least the Maori ones) grew tired of seal meat. Once the provisions ran out, life was far from pleasant. And the devastating climate — the wind, the rain, the cold, the constant dampness even inside their dwellings and clothes — sapped their physical and emotional reserves.

For six years the Auckland Island Polynesian settlement disappears from historical view. Ships must have called into Port Ross and provisions would occasionally have been replaced. But there is no contemporary record of what occurred in this period. Some children were born; some members of the group became ill and died. And there was considerable internal stress. By 1849, Matioro

---

* Testimony of Mr George Printz, who was with a sealing party on Auckland Island when the Chathams party arrived. Shand 1893, pp. 83–84.

had abandoned the Crozier Point pa to the care of Manature and moved across the harbour with his immediate supporters to build another village overlooking a bay on Enderby Island, facing Port Ross. Several family groups left both pa and settled separately on Enderby Island and the main island — but all remained within sight of Port Ross.

On 4 December 1849, two parties of Auckland Island colonists received a surprise. The Maori saw a substantial vessel, the *Samuel Enderby*, appear off Crozier Point, about to enter Port Ross. It was the first of three ships bringing British settlers to set up a base for whaling operations in the sub-Antarctic ocean; it also carried a pompous, muddle-headed scion of the commercial House of Enderby, one Charles Enderby, who had a commission from Queen Victoria as Lieutenant-Governor of the Auckland Islands.

Lieutenant-Governor Enderby and his charges were in turn shocked to see 'savages' living on an island that they had been assured was uninhabited. One settler recalled:

> When we got close into the island, to our surprise we saw a boat coming off from the point opposite . . . and with more astonishment found it to be manned by three or four Maoris completely naked, with the exception of a bit of sealskin wound round their loins. They were painted and had feathers in their hair, and had one woman amongst them. One of them came on board whilst we were still outside, we had a Maori sailor on board, who asked him to pilot us in, and from that day he was called Pilot Jack — a savage looking Maori . . .

Ngati Mutunga and the Moriori would have been more pleased to see the Enderby Company colonists than vice versa. A European settlement could mean relative prosperity after a time of excruciating hardship: work, money, provisions, medical care, and — perhaps most important — the prospect of variety and excitement in a day-to-day life that had been alternately tedious and harsh for most of the previous six years.

The two following ships arrived the same month and, although the Enderby colonists found that they had been grossly misled about conditions on the island, they set to and erected their settlement, named Hardwicke in honour of the company's governor. Lieutenant-Governor Enderby, meanwhile, had called the Maori and Moriori together and informed them: 'I am the Lord of the Island. I claim all the land which you are using and all the pigs you possess.'

Ngati Mutunga did not dispute this claim. The chiefs had probably been forewarned. And the Lieutenant-Governor swore in Matioro and Ngatere as constables with responsibilities over Polynesian *and* European settlers (they were also paid for their services). Compensation was paid for title to their land and for loss of ownership of the pigs. Some Maori obtained jobs on the company's ships, others grew vegetables for Hardwicke, and still others worked on roads. There is no record that the Lieutenant-Governor paid any heed to the existence of slaves in his colony; and Moriori continued to see to the domestic needs of their 'owners' as before.

No serious difficulties arose from the sudden juxtaposition of Maori and European, other than a single occasion when, after drinking alcohol, thirty or forty Maori came into Hardwicke one night and appeared threatening. But they had not brought guns. Minor problems such as drunkenness, European men

The slopes of Disappointment Island, characteristic of the tussock-covered uplands of the Auckland group. The improvised shelters were made by shipwrecked sailors.

Alexander Turnbull Library

chasing Maori women and Ngati Mutunga dogs attacking sheep were dealt with by Matioro (he had the Maori dogs shot).

Matioro had more trouble keeping the peace within his own family. One settler, Thomas Younger, reported:

> On one occasion an extraordinary thing happened. I found the Maoris hunting about the bush for something, but I could not understand from their imperfect English what it was they were searching for. Suddenly I came across Kuini [Matioro's wife], in a tree; she had just swung off, hanging herself by her scarf. A Maori sprung up the tree and let her down. I saw her later with her sister, she said: 'See that' — showing me a bag of money — 'me mate, moni mate' [if I go, the money goes too]. She added that next time she would drown herself . . . the fact was that the sailors had taken liquor and gone amongst the Maori girls, and Matioro had accused his wife of [adultery] . . .

More serious was a disturbance started by Matioro's cousin, Toenga Te Poki, who had become jealous of Matioro's power. He and his wife Potae killed and ate one of Matioro's pigs — a pet named after Matioro's son Pepe. Naturally, when Kuini and Matioro were told, they were upset. In fact the whole incident was contrived by Toenga to make Matioro attack him, so that he, Toenga, could fight back. Matioro did not go on the offensive, however, so Toenga armed Ngakare and two Moriori slaves and moved to attack Matioro in his house. Matioro saw them coming and fired in self-defence, killing Ngakare.

To avenge Ngakare's death, Toenga then attacked Patukumikumi, Matioro's father-in-law, who was living with his other daughter on a small island in Port Ross. Patukumikumi also saw Toenga coming and fired as his boat grounded. The bullet smashed through the craft and — again — Toenga retreated. He finally took his revenge by killing two of Matioro's Moriori slaves (names not recorded). His own position was by this time so insecure, however, that he and his wife Potae took the next available vessel out of Port Ross and returned to the Chathams. He had better luck there. Unaware of his background, the island's first resident magistrate appointed him a constable and tidewaiter — a position Toenga held when Matioro returned to Waitangi in 1856.*

Meanwhile, even though some of the disillusioned Hardwicke colonists had begun to leave as early as May 1850, the settlement continued to grow. The eighteen houses soon had their own gardens; community buildings went up, including a zinc-covered storehouse; roads became passable by foot, horseback and carriage; a Government House was built, along with barracks for the single men, a battery of four guns and, on nearby Shoe Island, a jail (known as Rodd's Castle, since the only occupant had been one of the surgeons, J. S. Rodd, imprisoned for drunkenness). The Lieutenant-Governor bought a cutter, the *Auckland*, and then a schooner, the *Black Dog*, for communication with New Zealand.

On 29 November 1850, the New Zealand Governor, Sir George Grey, arrived at Port Ross in HMS *Fly* for an official visit. The weather was continuously bad for the duration of his stay (a week) and he left feeling pessimistic about the settlement's future. Before his departure, however, Grey spent a considerable time in convocation with the Maori chiefs, who were impressed by his erudition in Maori language and thought. There is no surviving evidence that he spoke to the Moriori contingent (this would have been his only opportunity to do so, since he never visited the Chathams); nor to indicate what he thought about the continuation of slavery, which had supposedly been abolished in New Zealand a decade earlier. The only hint that the Moriori may have seen the Governor in action derives from the fact that ten years later, on the Chathams, they were convinced that Grey was the man to solve their difficulties with the Maori and they petitioned him accordingly.

The Governor's final gestures at Hardwicke were to celebrate the settlement's first anniversary by proclaiming a public holiday and to watch a regatta and sports day in driving rain.

Hardwicke in Erebus Cove as it looked when Sir George Grey visited in 1850.

Alexander Turnbull Library

* See p. 87.

Maori and Moriori births, deaths and marriages were not recorded by the Lieutenant-Governor. The exception was the marriage of one of Enderby's own seamen, Robert Reuben Bishop, to Hanna Tawerangi, daughter of the Ngati Mutunga chief Koko. This ceremony was performed by the Lieutenant-Governor himself (the settlement had five surgeons but no clergy) on 3 November 1851.

By 1852 the Auckland Islands experiment was over. Enderby's extravagant spending on the establishment of Hardwicke and the settlement's poor record in failing either to catch or buy a sufficient number of whales or to raise sufficient farm produce to be self-supporting resulted in the company sending out commissioners to investigate. Their highly unfavourable reports led to Enderby's dismissal, and to the breaking up of the community in August 1852. At its height, it had boasted 300 people — though this total included Maori, Moriori and visiting seamen. It had never come close to paying its way, let alone making a profit, and by 1852 it had become obvious that it never would. Ironically, just before the settlers dispersed, a whale was caught in the harbour — the first time this had happened in three years.

Another curious incident occurred before the Europeans left. R. E. Malone, from the naval vessel *Fantome* — which had been ordered to Port Ross to ensure that Hardwicke was dismantled in an orderly fashion — reported that an unnamed Maori woman had hanged herself on 8 July. Her husband had taken her younger sister as his second wife and she understandably felt herself neglected. Unlike Matioro's Kuini, she succeeded in killing herself on a low branch, close to the hut in which the unhappy triangle had lived.

> She was afterwards placed in a sitting position on a chair, with only her face appearing, dressed in grand clothes, with a new cap and artificial flowers, and blankets and shawls round her, some green boughs being placed to form an arched covering for her, and her husband and sister were sitting by a fire close to her. They welcomed us, and the husband showed me the tree: the branch was so slender, I wonder it did not break with her weight. The sister appeared to feel the occurrence very much, the husband not at all: he asked me if Pakeha . . . ever did the same? I was obliged to tell him yes.

The abandonment of Hardwicke seems to have been viewed as a disaster by most Ngati Mutunga on Auckland Island. It presaged a return to the hardship and stress of the years that had preceded the whaling base. According to Malone, some Maori applied for passage to New Zealand on the *Fantome* in August 1852, but were refused.

Matioro's position is confusing. In one letter to Sir George Grey, dated 23 April 1852, he says the company commissioners had offered to remove to New Zealand 'the New Zealanders of whom I am chief', but that he had declined. A month later, on 24 May, he writes again to say that he has changed his mind and has now decided to go to Parewa [Bluff] or Rakiura [Stewart Island].* Grey, apparently in response to Matioro's first letter, attempted to make provision for the Maori and Moriori settlers by ordering the company commissioners to give them a small flock of sheep and a cutter. This they did; they also left two Europeans, Whitelock and Dickens, who had 'allied themselves' to Ngati Mutunga women.

Matioro was still on the island in 1853. But by 1854 he had managed to get

---

* Interestingly enough, Matioro and two other Maori correspondents dateline their letters 'Akarana Airane', a transliteration of Auckland Islands, in preference to Maungahuka.

himself, nine other Maori men, ten Maori women and some children, five Moriori men, six Moriori women and one child transported to Port Adventure on Stewart Island. There the local Ngai Tahu chief, Maika Neera, gave them permission to remain. This left the chiefs Tapae and Tupara and their wives and families still at Port Ross.

Back in Waitangi, relatives of the stranded colonists got word that they wanted to return to their former homes on the Chathams. And so in January 1856, the chiefs Tangari Te Umu (who had escaped from Auckland Island fourteen years before) and Petere Roiri chartered the brig *Lalla Rookh* for 170 tonnes of potatoes. They sailed with the vessel first to Port Adventure, where they took on board Matioro and those Maori and Moriori who wished to return to the Chathams. Then they turned for Port Ross. Here they met unexpected difficulties.

> After landing, a very great *tangi* commenced on both sides, a mixture of love for the living and sorrow for the dead. The old lady in question — Ngapera — with her husband and others felt aggrieved at having been left alone . . . when Tangari Te Umu (her husband's younger brother) and others left them to shift for themselves, and went back with the vessel which brought them to the Auckland Islands. Although secretly rejoiced at the arrival of the vessel, it was not deemed proper to show it. In the first place she armed herself with a good stick [and] thus armed she sallied out, and addressing her nearest connections more especially (knowing they could not retaliate), poured forth a torrent of invective. 'Yes,' she said, 'you have come now after all these long years to fetch us away. You left us here to die. I will not go back with you. I will die on the land where you deserted me.' Whereupon, to give point to her scolding, she came down with her stick on the head of her unfortunate brother-in-law, causing the blood to flow, and following it up by assailing others in like manner, all of whom meekly submitted . . . She was really senior in descent to them. After she had vented her displeasure, her husband Tapae declared that he also would die in the island, to the great consternation of the rescue party, who for some time did not know what to do.
>
> At last Tangari could stand his brother's obstinacy no longer, and with a shout of pretended fury rushed at Tapae, seized and carried him out of his house bodily. Seeing that active measures were being taken, and doubtless glad of a decent excuse to yield, he said, 'Let me alone and I will leave with you,' to the great joy of all. Accordingly all proceeded on board, but the termagant old lady declared that they made her tipsy with liquor, and so by that means got her on board . . . Before returning they exhumed, and afterwards brought away with them to the Chatham Islands, the bones of their [Maori only] dead.

Archibald Shand, the newly appointed resident magistrate on the Chathams, reported that the *Lalla Rookh* reached Waitangi with the Stewart and Auckland Islands parties, '47 mostly maories', in February 1856. The Maungahuka experiment was over and never again was an attempt made to colonise the Auckland group. Unfortunately, neither Shand nor his son Alex, who subsequently wrote about the event, recorded who returned and who did not.

It is thought that most of the Ngati Mutunga migrants and probably most of the surviving Moriori came back. Some, of course, had died, on Auckland Island and on Stewart Island. For other Moriori, the break up of their sub-Antarctic colony brought an opportunity to escape what they believed would be a life of unremitting enslavement in their homeland. (The Moriori were not formally released from slavery until 1863 — and the Auckland Island Moriori would not have been able to anticipate that.)

It is known that some Moriori remained on Stewart Island. One of these, Arapatere Karaka, also known as 'Chatham Islands Willy', subsequently died there

and perception as they had survived to that time. He recalls, for example, an elderly Moriori named Pukerua stalking into his father's office one day asking that the missionary write a letter for him. Baucke senior asked William to write it.

> I did. When he had exhausted all laments and tokens of affection, and I asked him whom I should address it to, he answered: 'Ki tche' wairu o tchak' tchein', Kie Rakiu Kie whe' ranei' [To whom it may concern]. He had heard the name of Rakiura [Stewart Island] as of some distant place, and as it fell in line with the ideas of his race that the spirits of the dead roam in distant space, and that name occurred to him, why might his brother's spirit not hover there? [This instance typifies the Moriori concept of an afterlife.]

Baucke was taken on hunting expeditions because he knew Moriori rituals and could be relied upon to observe them. He remembered going fishing at night as a small boy with Kirapu, one of the Moriori chiefs from Kaingaroa. They headed for the coast with a pole net and a killing club.

> We arrive. He lights a fire of dry wood above the high water mark and performs certain rites by drawing green flax blades through the blaze, and listening to the light explosions scorching flax blades make, intermittently repeating certain charms. When the rite was ended, I asked him what the words and ritual meant. Then he told me the words of the complex jargon — he knew not what they meant — were ancient and of a language he did not understand. The whole was an offering of placation to Maru and Tangaroa (fish and sea deities) not to be angered that his food necessities compelled him to destroy their children.

On another occasion, when Baucke was ten, his father sent him home from

William, Johann Baucke's precocious oldest son, grew up speaking German, English, Maori and Moriori as first languages. He wrote graphically if long-windedly about Maori and Moriori in his later years (his best-known book was *Where the White Man Treads*). His family reported that these works were not always truthful.

Elisabeth Jenkins

The house which Johann Engst and Johann Baucke built at Maunganui in 1866 from stone off the mountain behind. The enterprise was typical of Engst's resourcefulness and the house was standing more than 130 years later.

Alexander Turnbull Library

Taupeka on the north coast to Te Whakaru, in company with a local Maori named Horomona. They were walking.

> When we arrived at Manauea . . . a large crowd on the sand dunes induced us to go up and see what might be seen. There to a stake, a Moriori corpse was lashed, upright, face seaward. We found it had been there a week or more. The Maori section of that district and their small slave colony sat hunched around some distance from the corpse, scanning the sea for the whales that the spirit of the staked cadaver would, according to Moriori faith, strand on their shore. Some of the Maoris began to credit the belief, but the bulk to treat with jeer and scorn it. Alone, stood a Moriori 'priest' delivering an oration seaward in a language he upon enquiry could not translate, but which he claimed to be an invocation to the dead man's spirit not to forget his kin now weeping here.
>
> After it was ended, the local Maori chief, perhaps tired of the farce, ordered the Morioris there to take away the corpse and bury it. This they refused to do and gave as reason that they looked on that treatment of their dead kinsman as a soil, a defilement, but said that they would burn it as it stood: so they collected a stack of dry wood, and scooping out around it a shallow pit, stood wood around it like a cone and fired it. When it was reduced they scooped back the excavated sand, leveled the spot, and the seance was over.

Blackfish subsequently did come ashore, Baucke noted, some kilometres away from where the ceremony had taken place, but sufficiently close to convince the participants of its efficacy.

Baucke recorded a further example of apparent Moriori powers when he described one of his father's farm hands being rescued at the mouth of Te Whanga lagoon by the chanting of Maikoua (also known as Makora) who lived at Te Awapatiki. Ironically, Maikoua himself drowned in the lagoon when his canoe capsized there in 1874.

In later life, when he wrote these stories, Baucke had become intensely pro-Maori (he had a Maori wife and family) and anti-Moriori. He had witnessed Moriori life at its lowest ebb, after enslavement and before the manumission and gradual recovery of spirit that followed. He made no allowances for the psychic wounds of the tchakat henu at that time, but used the gaps in their knowledge and evidence of their loss of self-esteem as a stick with which to beat them, particularly as a basis for allegations about their 'stone-dull Moriori intellect' and for unfavourable comparisons with Maori. His choice of carefully derogatory language shows a negative obsession with Moriori that bordered on the pathological.

Hence he was able to write thus about Minarapa, leader of the Kaingaroa Moriori and highly spoken of by Henry Halse, Alexander Shand and Hirawanu Tapu:

> [He] was an epileptic, a paralytic on one side, a stammerer, he was also the headman of his clan, which conditions, combined with a sinister forethrust of the simian eye pents when words eluded speech, or anger stirred his passions, had gained for him the fame of tchohung . . . medically diagnosed, Minarapa was insane, yet he passed for a recognised tchohung . . .

This warp in Baucke's vision makes him a less than reliable witness. And, indeed, other authorities such as Shand and Henry Skinner took issue with his views (resulting in Shand's case in Baucke refusing to speak to him again). But for all this Baucke was eventually the last man alive to know the Moriori language, and much of his writing is compelling because of its vividness. He did see aspects of Moriori life that few non-Moriori saw; and he wrote about them. He can be criticised, but not ignored.

Botanical explorer Henry Travers, another visitor to the Chathams at about this time, was an equally unreliable witness to what he took to be the vices and shortcomings of the Moriori. He wrote in 1864:

> The remnant of the Morioris . . . is settled at [Owenga] on the south-eastern side of the island. They do not exceed two hundred in number, and are said to be rapidly decreasing.* I believe this to be the case, for during my six months' stay, not less than eight deaths occurred amongst them. In their habits of living they now assimilate to the Maoris, and speak a language compounded of their own original language and that of the New Zealanders . . . they are much shorter but stouter built, than the New Zealanders, and have darker skins, but the same straight coarse hair. Their faces are rounder, and more pleasing in expression. Their noses are Roman in shape, resembling those of the Jews . . . their habits of living however, were originally very rude and improvident . . . like many other savage tribes they were very indolent, seldom seeking food until pressed by hunger . . . their chronology, unlike that of the New Zealanders, is very defective, and consequently they are unable to fix, even proximately, the date of their first arrival in the islands . . . they are quite in the dark as to where they came from originally; but as they resemble the Mangaia Kanakas, who form a large proportion of the crews of the American whaling vessels, I conceive it not improbable that they came from the same origin.
>
> Although I found the remains of numerous skeletons in the woods on Pitt's island, I was unable to get one in good condition: I have, however, brought over several authentic skulls, which will probably be interesting for ethnological purposes.

Henry Travers was but the first of many travellers who spoke of searching for and removing Moriori skulls. While he claimed a scientific purpose, most visitors saw them merely as 'curios' waiting to be harvested. There were similar expeditions, on the part of settlers and visitors, in search of Moriori artifacts; it became a local pastime.

The mid-1860s brought a new class of settler to the Chathams. Although sheep had been introduced to the islands in the early 1840s, and the German missionaries had raised them with some success, no one other than Frederick Hunt on Pitt had attempted to exploit them in quantity. And it was Hunt, visiting Canterbury in search of new markets for his meat and wool, who drew the attention of pastoralists there to the sheep-running potential of the islands. Although they lacked pasture, except where it was being slowly won from bushland, they had large areas of fern on peat known locally as 'clears', and it was these that would initially provide the bulk of Chathams grazing land.

The first of this second wave of European colonists to live on Chatham Island was Thomas Ritchie, an ebullient and shrewd Northern Irishman. He had reached Lyttelton in 1863 at the age of nineteen, and came on to the Chathams in February of the following year. He took up land at Okawa, under the patronage of the local Ngati Tama chief Heremaia Katene Te Raki. He grew potatoes and raised cattle to trade with American vessels and bring in an immediate income, while at the same time he cleared and fenced land in preparation for sheep, which he eventually bought from Frederick Hunt.

Ritchie worked hard and rapidly expanded the range of his operations. By 1866 he owned 9,300 hectares from Owenga to Te Awapatiki, which his brother Robert farmed. And he was to lease a further 4,450 hectares from Kaingaroa to

---

* Travers was mistaken to suggest that all Moriori lived at Owenga, though it was by then the largest Moriori community. The census taken the year of his visit revealed 132 surviving Moriori, with ninety-two living in the Waitangi and Owenga districts; Kaingaroa had twenty-five, Wharekauri nine, Tupuangi six.

This *carte de visite* of an
unnamed Moriori child is
believed to have been taken
in Waitangi by E. A. Welch
in 1867.

Auckland Institute & Museum

Te Awapatiki. On the shore of Lake Te Wapu, he began in 1867 to build Lake
House, the most luxurious and envied residence on Chatham Island to that time.
Eventually he was running a total of 16,000 sheep on these properties and on a
third, on the Ngaio coast south of Waitangi, known as the Tobacco Country.

Ritchie's genius was that he recognised and pursued any money-making
opportunity. He quickly became a trader (with a store at Owenga) and a shipping
agent, and he operated a salvage business. He was a voracious sportsman and
organised shooting competitions and the first horse races on Chatham Island. The
jockey club, which he founded in 1874, is the oldest in New Zealand to have
functioned continuously. He also introduced game birds.

Ritchie was successful in these early years because he was also a good
employer. His relations with his Maori lessors were good. He was a down-to-earth
character with no sense of superiority, and he was happy to offer work to Maori
and Moriori farmhands and stockmen. This combination of qualities produced
one of the most astonishing collections of private papers in New Zealand: a large
group of letters in Maori from Maori and Moriori correspondents that extends

over sixty-three years (Ritchie left the Chathams in 1923 and lived until 1934).

Other sheep-farming settlers who, like Ritchie, arrived in New Zealand to find the Canterbury runs all taken up, stocked and staffed, also came on to the Chathams. They included James Hay, who went into partnership with the Ritchie brothers, Walter Hood, Howel Pattison and Edward Chudleigh.

Chudleigh, from a family of Cornish gentry, arrived in the islands in 1866 and took a long lease of land on the Wharekauri block along the northern coast. Like Ritchie, he was a strong character and became one of the best-known personalities on Chatham Island and its first justice of the peace. Unlike Ritchie, he exuded an air of sanctimonious superiority and pettiness and — although he became the island's most successful farmer — his relations with his Maori, Moriori and European neighbours and employees were almost always strained. Chudleigh at times romanticised the 'old-time, noble Maori' and even had a Maori costume in which he used to pose and posture. But he never learned to speak Maori, he never had Maori in his home, and he hated having to visit Maori and Moriori dwellings and communities.

Though very different in character and mannerisms, Ritchie and Chudleigh were to dominate settler activities on the island for the next quarter-century. And life was hard for both of them. Clearing farms and maintaining them, in weather that was often atrocious, was back-breaking; getting wool out to the mainland markets was difficult and sometimes dangerous. Bales had to be taken beyond the surf line in drays, loaded onto boats, then ferried out to waiting ships. On one occasion, in 1868, Chudleigh and his men spent all day on this exercise and were soaked and exhausted at the end of it. Shortly afterwards they heard that the ship had gone down and the entire cargo lost.

Indeed, getting to and from the Chathams was part of the hazardous business of living there. Shipwrecks were frequent (thirty-four recorded between 1840 and 1868) and employees, friends and family were as likely to be lost as cargo

Thomas Ritchie.
Ritchie Family

Thomas Ritchie and Robert Shand (at foot of tree) in front of Lake House on Lake Te Wapu. Ritchie was for a time the island's most successful farmer and entrepreneur. As a young man, he enjoyed the Chathams because of its freedom from Victorian constraint. His contemporary and *bête noire* Edward Chudleigh wrote of him: 'He has turned his sisters into the kitchen and lives rampant with prostitutes and brandy.' He did not marry until 1891, when he was forty-eight.

Canterbury Museum

103

(Frederick Hunt farewelled one of his sons onto a ship that was never seen again). Transport around Chatham Island itself, and between Chatham and Pitt, was almost equally dangerous, and there is a long list of drownings and near-drownings in the 1860s and 1870s, of broken limbs, and of horses becoming bogged or throwing their riders.

Surviving these conditions, and, indeed, prospering in them as Ritchie and Chudleigh did for a time, required special qualities of toughness and resilience. These were further forged by a series of events that occurred from 1866 to 1868.

To the surprise of all the islanders, the second resident magistrate, William Thomas, returned from a visit to the mainland in March 1866 accompanied by forty-three 'Hauhau' prisoners, twenty-five wives and children and a guard of twenty-six men, half of them European and half Maori.* The Government had accepted William Seed's suggestion to use the island as a penal colony.

Waitangi, where the prisoners were to be based, had now taken on the appearance of a well-established community, described by Henry Travers a couple of years earlier:

> The huts of the Maoris and the residence of Captain Thomas are situated on low ground on the west side of the river. The Maori huts are built of fern posts lashed together with supplejacks, and thatched with toi grass . . . Captain Thomas's residence is built in the same way with the exception of the roof, which is shingled; but it is plastered inside and out with clay, and white washed. A chapel belonging to the Church of England natives is a very handsome specimen of their style of building: the inside walls are lined with fronds of treeferns . . . the building is about fifty feet long and nearly thirty broad, and about the same height to the roof. There is a smaller building used as a church by the Roman Catholic natives, built in the same style, but more highly decorated and more neatly kept . . . [the] huts are surrounded by well-fenced paddocks, laid down to English grasses, but now almost smothered by the common daisy, mustard and dock, which are spreading rapidly over the whole island. The natives generally possess considerable numbers of horses, cattle, and pigs, which run, in common, on the open lands and in the bush. They cultivate large quantities of potatoes, maize, pumpkins and onions . . .

To these features the convicts would add a redoubt, which they built from quarried stone and surrounded with a ditch and wall; a three-celled prison made from the same material;** and a long row of ponga whares, in which the prisoners were to live with their families. They were allowed to grow their own vegetables, and to work with European settlers at one shilling per day (Chudleigh, Ritchie, Engst and the Shands all made use of them). They were also put to work upgrading tracks and roads.

By 1868, 'Hauhau' had become a generic term used by settlers in New Zealand to describe any Maori who was opposed to European colonisation or was simply a troublemaker. Those who were in fact Hauhau were followers of the Taranaki prophet Te Ua Haumene who, according to the Europeans who feared him, had been teaching since the early 1860s that God would drive the Pakeha from New Zealand at the dawn of a new era of prosperity. Many Maori who believed this

Edward Chudleigh, who loved the idea of Maori but not their presence. He farmed the Wharekauri Station with considerable success for forty years and was the most respectable Pakeha figure on Chatham Island. But not respected: the Maori and Moriori knew him as Kau (Cow).

Canterbury Museum

---

* By the end of 1866, according to the *Appendices to the Journal of the House of Representatives*, the number of Hauhau prisoners on the island was 116, and with wives and children the group totalled 203. The eventual total was 163 men, 64 women and 71 children.

** This survived at Waitangi until 1979, when it was demolished to make room for a hotel extension.

took up arms to fight the settlers, to hasten the arrival of the New Canaan.

The prisoners brought to the Chathams had been fighting government troops — or supporting those who were — on the East Coast of New Zealand. They included Te Kooti Rikirangi Te Turuki, a member of the Rongo Whakaata tribe who had had a mission education and enjoyed some success as a trader. He had actually fought on the Government's side against Hauhau, but was accused of Hauhau sympathies by another Maori. He was despatched to the Chathams without trial, and he quickly became leader of the convicts.

At Waitangi, suffering from tuberculosis, Te Kooti had visions that led him to believe that God had chosen him to lead his people — the prisoners and Maori at large — to freedom. He preached this message, drawing heavily from the Old Testament, and he composed waiata that were a combination of scriptural text and traditional Maori song forms.

Later leaders of the church that Te Kooti founded, Ringatu, have speculated about whether the prophet's association with the Moriori played any part in his spiritual conversion. It is true that he came into contact with Moriori who lived in and around Waitangi, and he is reputed to have spoken to them gently and considerately, respecting more than the island Maori the tapu that surrounded the older original inhabitants. But it is unlikely that many (if any) features of Moriori

The *Jessie Readman* ashore on Wharekauri Beach, shortly after the vessel had been loaded with wool (which is here being unloaded). This was one of forty-four known shipping mishaps on the Chathams coast in the nineteenth century.

Canterbury Museum

thought or religion were on display in the late 1860s. Most Moriori had become Christian. Further, Te Kooti's religious mission is wholly consistent with the Hauhau tradition in which he had been immersed by his fellow prisoners. If Te Kooti had not been a Hauhau before he went to the Chathams, he certainly was by the time he left.*

By 1868 Te Kooti was prophesying that he and his followers would return to New Zealand — that a government vessel would be sent to transport them; or that the sea would part and enable them to walk to the mainland. This first possibility was given credence by a government decision in April to withdraw most of the guard to Hokitika, where a Fenian uprising was feared. Only six remained to guard fifty prisoners and their families.

In July, Te Kooti acted as he had planned. He recalled the prisoners working on outlying farms. Then he insinuated a group inside the redoubt, on the excuse that it was raining. The prisoners took over the fort and tied up the small contingent of guards. With this accomplished, another group seized the vessel *Rifleman*, trussed its passengers and put them ashore and threatened the lives of the crew unless they transported the convicts to New Zealand. Another, smaller boat in the harbour, the *Florence*, was run aground to prevent pursuit.

Thus Te Kooti and his followers escaped from the Chathams in the same manner that Ngati Mutunga and Ngati Tama had arrived there: by commandeering a ship. They were not immediately able to leave Petre Bay, however, because of an unfavourable wind, so Te Kooti had an 'unbeliever' tied up and

Waitangi settlement at the time the Hauhau prisoners were held there. The buildings on the beach are, from left, Beamish's hotel; the courthouse with a flagpole in front and 'Te Kooti's Gaol' behind; two private dwellings; John Alexander's hotel; and — at the end — the boatshed belonging to Captain Thomas, resident magistrate. The redoubt built by the convicts is on the hill above Beamish's. The huts on Orea Flat at right belong to prisoners and their families; one was Te Kooti's.

Alexander Turnbull Library

---

* Many Ringatu in the twentieth century have liked to draw a distinction between Hauhau (which survived in its purist form as the religion Pai Marire) and the Hahi Ringatu. While the two traditions were close, if not inseparable, in the 1860s and 1870s, they had diverged in several important respects by the latter half of the twentieth century.

thrown into the sea. After this act of propitiation the wind dropped and the ship was able to proceed, eventually landing the escapees on the New Zealand coast near Gisborne, from where they commenced a guerrilla campaign that lasted four years. Te Kooti was never defeated by government forces, and he was formally pardoned in 1883.

In spite of the fact that only one guardsman had been killed, the view of most settlers on the island was that Te Kooti was an unprincipled savage and deserved hanging. Chudleigh, who had almost been choked to death by the escaping convicts, was, understandably, especially harsh in judgment. Thomas Ritchie was more understanding of the Maori position and had some admiration for Te Kooti. But he, too, felt for a time that the lives of all Europeans on the island had been in danger.

The view of Te Kooti's departure held by his followers is different again. It is expressed on a plaque presented to the Chatham Islands museum in 1979 with Te Kooti's greenstone mere:

> In memory of Te Kooti Arikirangi Te Turuki who, while confined here as a prisoner of Her Majesty between the years of 1865 to 1868 was inspired by the Holy Spirit which resulted in his founding of the Ringatu Faith. 'The Spirit of the Lord God is upon me because the Lord hath annointed me to preach good tidings unto the meek. He hath set me to bind up the broken hearted, to proclaim liberty to the captives and the opening of the prison to them that are bound' (Isaiah 60:1). Honour, Glory, Peace on Earth, Goodwill to all men.

The departure of the Hauhau prisoners did not represent the extent of Maori exodus from the Chathams in 1868. Ngati Mutunga and Ngati Tama were

'Te Kooti's Gaol' never incarcerated the Ringatu hero; but the three-celled block was built by Hauhau prisoners from adzed volcanic rock It was later sheathed in concrete and stood until 1979.

Canterbury Museum

profoundly restless. The prosperity of the previous two decades, based on their cropping, had dwindled. A resumed life in their old homeland, Taranaki, began to seem more attractive as notification arrived of Native Land Court sittings there (and, indeed, attendance at these sittings was almost essential to ensure that their claims for ownership were heard). There were further factors. The teachings of Te Whiti O Rongomai and Tohu Kakahi were drawing many Taranaki Maori to the spiritual centre of Parihaka, where a restoration of Maori confidence was taking place.* A prophecy had been made decades earlier that the heke which had arrived in 1835 would one day return to its place of origin. And a series of occurrences on the Chathams in 1868 — including the appearance of the Aurora Australis, a measles epidemic which killed a large number of Maori and Moriori and the erasure of the settlement of Tupuangi by a tidal wave — were viewed as omens pointing to the desirability of an immediate departure.

And so, in three groups in 1867 and 1868, a total of 356 Taranaki Maori left the islands they had conquered three decades before.** They left behind only twenty Maori too old, ill or unwilling to uproot again. For the first time in nearly thirty years the Moriori population (now just over 100) was larger than that of the Maori. But now the number of European settlers (around 120) exceeded both; and would continue to do so for another forty years. The period of Maori pre-eminence on the Chathams in the nineteenth century was ended.

Waitangi Beach nearly ten years after the Hauhau breakout. The redoubt and Maori huts have gone, and ponga breastwork protects buildings and properties from erosion.

Canterbury Museum

---

* See p. 133.

** With them went at least four Moriori: and probably more.

CHAPTER

SIX

Moriori Voices

AS A DEFEATED AND PROFOUNDLY DEMORALISED PEOPLE, MORIORI languished at their nadir in the 1840s and 1850s. They are virtually absent from the historical record as individuals because so few had opportunities to make an impression on their fellow Chatham Islanders, let alone on posterity.

By the 1860s this had begun to change, however, especially after the manumission when Moriori were again free to pursue their own lives and to have some effect on the circumstances in which they lived. In this later period, visitors to Chatham Island record conversations with and impressions of Moriori leaders such as Minarapa Tamahiwaka, Kirapu and Hirawanu Tapu. Moriori themselves began meeting more frequently in intertribal council to pool what recollection remained of their history, traditions and genealogies, and to plan strategies for retrieving what they had lost. Reviving the mana of the group, these meetings also gave confidence back to individuals. Nowhere is this confidence more apparent than in the surviving letters from Moriori correspondents in the Thomas Ritchie Papers.

The departure of most Maori in 1868 had been something of a windfall for Ritchie. He chartered a vessel, the *Collingwood*, which carried much of the reverse migration back to the mainland, and there was profit for him in that too. The vacating of land around Kaingaroa allowed him to secure his large lease there, a factor which more than anything else ensured his prosperity over the next two decades.

The Kaingaroa property included the Moriori settlement of Wairua, and Ritchie recruited many of his stockmen and farm labourers there. Indeed, one of the Wairua Moriori, Hapurona Pawa, became his head stockman. But these people were more to Ritchie than employees. They were also neighbours — good neighbours — and his relations with them were at all times courteous, close and equal. This much is revealed in the letters he kept. Those same letters show that literacy among the Moriori was high in the 1860s and 1870s: a consequence in Wairua of the educational work of Maria Baucke (who had died in 1866); and (throughout the Chathams) of the fact that distance and danger made communication difficult. Letters were the only method of transmitting messages other than walking or riding all over the island oneself. They served the function that the telephone would assume in the twentieth century: communicating information of a domestic and business character, as well as informing people about major events such as births, deaths and marriages. In the case of the Ritchie letters, they were written in Maori and their grammar and spelling is, for the most part, flawless. Here is one written in 1870 from Hone Waiti, a leading Moriori at Wairua:

Moriori farm workers
photographed outside the
Ritchies' house at Owenga in
1873. The man in front with a
staff is Hapurona Pawa, Thomas
Ritchie's head stockman.

Canterbury Museum

Friend Ritchie, greetings. Friend, this is what I have to say about the horse. I gave it to you to look at on May 24 1870 at Matarakau. You told me there that you weren't sure. The thing is, the horse was for you. However, I'll look for my horse again whether at Te Hapupu, Kaingarahu or Taia. But I say this to you: when you come here to your horses, I'll be there looking for a horse for myself. At the time you come here to see to the horses you'd better come and fetch in all your horses, since you tell me I'm stealing your horses. That's all.

Friend, this is another message to you about the cow we saw at Pakauere. It's a branded one, this is the brand: . You find out the meaning of that brand. That's all.

Would you send the rest of the bales to Moko. You'd better let him know the price too — about five shillings. That's all.

Friend, greetings. Great is my love for you in the day, in the night and all of the time.

Another is from Hapurona Pawa, the stockman, who was paralysed down one side as a result of an accident and had to tie himself onto his horse each day:

Friend, greetings. Great is my love for you. Friend, this is a message to you about some poison for me*. If you are willing to give me some, that is good; if not, that's up to you. If you let me have it, give it to Hipu to bring to me. But if you are coming this way you could bring it yourself — that's if you're willing to let me have it. If you won't be coming out here you could give it to Waiti. Will you write to me now if you have got some poison, write to me now so that I will know.

Friend Ritchie, if you want Hipu,** it's all right for him to stay out there. But Robert [Ritchie] wants some tobacco for himself. His tobacco is used up. If you don't want Hipu to stay, he can come back here on Tuesday.

I also want to ask the doctor for medicine. It was actually Robert who told me to speak to Cooper about some poison. But I did not speak to Doctor Cooper.

That is all,

From your affectionate friend
Hapurona

Hapurona was also a local hero. Over the years he saved five people from drowning, three of them from Lake Te Wapu in front of Ritchie's home. Ritchie asked him to make a statement about the earlier rescues, so that he could

---

* Probably sheep dip.

** Hipu Harawira, a Moriori boy Ritchie had been looking after.

recommend him for the medal of the Royal Humane Society. That statement, taken in English, read:

> When I was a boy and before I was partly paralised I saved Mrs Heta that is now [Paranihia Heta] and then a child, with another boy, Kereopa, they fell into deep water at the Awapatiki and I fetched them both on shore. I saved Joe Mapu who was bathing in the Wapu Lake . . . he got into deep water and would have drowned had I not swim in and brought him out. He sunk twice and when I brought him on shore he was a long time before he came too, and also in the aforesaid Lake I saved Brother Te Rangihiroa while bathing. He was swimming and in the middle of the lake about he call out to me he was sinking, and to save him I swim to his assistance and brought him to shore.

Hapurona was writing another businesslike letter to Thomas Ritchie in February 1870:

> Friend, we did not finish the jobs you told us to do — drafting the rams off to Kaingaroa and the ewes to Owenga. Those two jobs were not finished. But the sheep for Te Kopa, we will have done those on Monday the 15th of February. As for Tepene's job at Kaingaroa, it's not finished yet. Most of his jobs are the same as they were when you were here. What we've done since you left is — Tio, Hipu, Robert and I are mustering sheep on the hill. That's all. Kereopa is covering all the ground as far as Waitangi. If you gave me instructions to Kereopa I did not hear them properly. Hipu is really a bit of a lazy one, but Hohepa, he's a hard worker, and when Robert and I speak to him, he really listens.
>
> But the sheep cannot be drafted because there aren't any men. There are only the two youngsters and myself to get the sheep to Patiki. Kereopa is too close to Waitangi to draft them today. As for Te Karaka, he did not want to stay at Patiki — he was asking five shillings a day. The work on those sheep has stopped, and there isn't anyone to look after them, to do the work. I wanted the sheep done in spite of the lack of men. As for Robert, he did not want them done. He is sick, and overcome by the poison.
>
> This is to let you know the things I asked you for:
>
> Coat Trousers
> 3 Waist-coats
> 1 Hat
> 1 Monkey jacket
> 1 Necktie
> 1 Crimea [balaclava]
> 4 pocket handkerchiefs, red ones and green ones — four altogether.
>
> Well, that's the end,
> From Hapurona

A letter has also survived *to* Hapurona, from the mother of Hipu, whom Hapurona and Ritchie were bringing up.*

> Son Hapurona,
>
> Greetings to you and your little brother. Great is my love for you, yes, for you and your younger brother, in the night and the day, always.
>
> I've got a message for you: give Hipu a good beating if he won't take any notice of you. Don't let him go about with Riwai, in case bad reports should reach our elder brother and me. If you go wandering about on the clears, you two go together, and not too far from home. If he won't listen to you, you should tell Ritchie to beat him. The thing is, he was sent out to you to see if it was a good thing or not. However if it is a bad thing for him to keep on staying, bring him back. If any of you go to Waitangi, you two go together.

* And who died a few years after this letter was written.

Riwai Te Ropiha, who worked for Thomas Ritchie from his adolescence. Ritchie described him as 'a powerfully strong, healthy, active young man . . .' Like Hapurona Pawa, Riwai was awarded a medal from the Royal Humane Society for saving a person drowning in Te Whanga lagoon. He was the subject of a contentious marriage, arranged by Hirawanu Tapu in an effort to perpetuate Moriori bloodlines.

National Museum

> Another message of mine to you: if you want to come to Waiteki [Waitangi], don't leave your brother behind. There's a home for you at Orea.

> Well, that is all.
> From your granny, Marara Harawira.

Life at this time was by no means composed entirely of serious matters, however. Rau Wetini, who worked for Ritchie as a general hand, wrote: 'Here comes a story for you — it's about [Hone] Waiti's wedding. When the wedding was over we all got drunk at the feast.'

Robert, Thomas Ritchie's brother at Owenga, also supplied information about Moriori activities. In one undated note he reported that Riwai Te Ropiha, a flamboyant and solidly built man from Wairua who worked on both Ritchie properties, had returned a set of stirrups he had stolen; in another he announced that Doctor Cooper from Waitangi had successfully circumcised Riwai and that the patient was progressing well.

Inevitably, some of the letters contain grim tidings. In March 1871 Robert Ritchie tells his brother that Mrs Heta (Paranihia Heta of Manukau) has had a baby son, but stillborn. Timoti Tara writes to Thomas Ritchie five years later about his brother, Rau Wetini, who had been one of Ritchie's general hands: 'We have got your letter about Rau. Rau has died . . . I have seen the accounts for Rau's long-timer [long-term debt] and the accounts for the sheep. I will find payment for the long-timers after his funeral. I send you my love. I am greatly distressed about my brother.'

While Ritchie's Moriori friends and workers were writing to him about life's mundanities and pains, an equally fluent but weightier correspondence had been going on for a decade between Moriori leaders and representatives of the Government in New Zealand. Few of these letters have survived, making those that have all the more precious; their content and manner of expression have allowed the Moriori to send significant and enduring messages to their descendants and to a wider posterity.*

Sir George Grey was Governor of New Zealand from 1845 to 1853, and again from 1861 to 1868. Although he waged war against a variety of Maori tribes during both terms, he won the respect of the Maori — adversaries and friends — for the fact that he learnt their language and recorded their history and traditions at length. Even when making submissions to the 'Kawana' that turned out to be hopeless and pointless, Maori with grievances at least felt that they were being heard and understood. No other Governor had been able to give that impression.

There is no evidence that Grey met Moriori petitioners although it is *likely* that he did so on the Auckland Islands in 1850.** At the very least the Moriori

---

* A fire destroyed most Native Affairs archives in December 1907. Documents that survive are largely those in private papers, and those that were reprinted in the *Appendices to the Journal of the House of Representatives*. The Moriori letters referred to here are to be found largely in the Sir George Grey Collection of Maori Manuscripts in the Auckland Public Library. These were returned to New Zealand in the 1920s; previously they had lain in South Africa, where Grey had been High Commissioner and Governor of Cape Colony from 1854 to 1861. Most of the relevant documents are in two sets of manuscripts, GNZMS 16 (24 pages) and GNZMS 144 (131 pages). They and individual letters elsewhere refer to correspondence from Grey, which has been lost. Further, Archibald Shand's letters make it clear that the surviving correspondence is only a small portion of the letters actually written by Moriori to the Governor and the New Zealand Government.

** See p. 84.

Moriori culture that survived passed through Hirawanu Tapu's hands. Baucke's own ethnological and linguistic contribution is miniscule by comparison. From the 1860s until his death in 1900, anybody who visited the Chathams to learn about Moriori matters — from the Governor down to amateur ethnologists — was always sent to Tapu as the most knowledgeable and communicative source of information.

With this background, it is unsurprising that Tapu was nominated as major witness for the Moriori claim in the 1870 Native Land Court sittings. He was handicapped, however, by the fact that he had never before participated in judicial proceedings and he was ignorant of court procedure and the need for a planned strategy to further the Moriori case. He placed all his faith in a rosy concept of 'British Justice', which had been explained to him by a ship's captain at Kaingaroa. By contrast, many of the Maori who gave evidence in the Chathams in 1870 had already done so in Taranaki in the preceding two years. Tapu was also unwell for most of the first session and this cannot have helped his wits or his memory. Most of the Maori witnesses in the 1870s sittings had returned from Taranaki specifically to secure their Chathams claims and thus ensure that they continued to be paid for the leases they had negotiated earlier with runholders such as the Ritchies and Chudleigh. Given that the Government was still worried about the continuing instability of settler-Maori relations in Taranaki, and in particular the growth in the following of the uncooperative Ati Awa leader Te Whiti O Rongomai, there is a strong possibility that the presiding judge, John Rogan, had been encouraged, by the Native Secretary and others, to settle Maori claims in a manner that encouraged former Chathams residents to return there permanently.* Whatever objectives lay behind the judge's decisions, in total they represented a rout for the Moriori.

The sittings opened on 14 June 1870 in the tiny courthouse on Waitangi Beach. The building stood between Beamish's hotel and two private houses. The court area measured only four by six metres, with a table down one side for the judge and court officials. The remainder of the room was taken up with long wooden forms, on which sat witnesses giving or waiting to give evidence and other interested parties. The back part of the building was a closed-in post office. Judge Rogan had a temporary shelter of native materials, shaped somewhat like a meeting house, erected to one side of the front of the building to accommodate part of the crowd expected to attend the sittings. But, even with the courtroom door and windows open, it was difficult to hear what was being said unless one was actually inside the tiny building.

Chatham Island had been surveyed into five large blocks, representing both the territories taken by the five major chiefs in 1835 and the old Moriori tribal districts. The first Maori claim and Moriori counterclaim was to be for Kekerione, which made up the shore of Petre Bay and included Waitangi. This was to be followed by hearings on Te Matarae on the south-west side of Te Whanga lagoon; Te Awapatiki, most of the east side of the island, including Owenga; Otonga in the south-west; Wharekauri along the northern coast; Pitt Island; and Rangatira (South-East Island).

---

* And, indeed, the Maori population on the Chathams was to build up again steadily again in the wake of the 1870 hearings.

The opening session was an anticlimax, owing to an unexpectedly low attendance. The court's native assessor, Charles Wirikaku, applied for an adjournment of two or three days 'to let the Natives in different parts of the Island have notice of the sitting'.

On 16 June 1870 the court resumed, with Wi Naera Pomare rising to speak as principal claimant for Kekerione. Naera was the adopted son of Wiremu Piti Pomare, who had led the Ngati Mutunga migration to the Chathams. Pomare senior had died in 1851 after an enthusiastic conversion to Christianity and building a magnificent church at Waitangi. His adopted son had become principal chief of Ngati Mutunga ki Wharekauri (Ngati Mutunga in the Chathams) by 1870. He placed before the court a list of Maori claimants to Kekerione, all of them descendants of the original Ngati Mutunga colonists. There were no Moriori names on the list. Then, speaking as if for his father, he told the court:

> I claim this land on account of my long residence on it, and having taken possession of the Island.
> *Court*: How was it you took possession of the Island?
> *Pomare*: By the power of my arm I took possession. I believe it was in the year 1836 . . .
> *Court*: Did you find any inhabitants on the Island?
> *Pomare*: I came and found this place inhabited and took possession. When we took it we took their mana from them and from that time to this I have occupied the land.
> *Court*: Did you attack or make war on them on your arrival?
> *Pomare*: We caught them and made them submit to our will.

The second Maori to speak was Toenga Te Poki, who told the court he was the oldest of the claimants.

Waitangi around the time of the early Native Land Court sittings. The courthouse is in the centre of the photograph. The temporary shelter built at the judge's request to accommodate waiting Maori and Moriori witnesses is to the right.

Canterbury Museum

> I came from Taranaki to Kapiti. I took possession of Kapiti and then Wellington. Part of my tribe went across the Straits to Queen Charlotte Sound and that land was taken, and we came to [the] Chatham Islands and we took possession of the Chatham Islands. I took possession of these places according to ancient custom, and I retained possession of this land for myself . . . and also the people. Some of those we had taken ran away. Some of those who ran away into the forest we killed according to the ancient customs. From this I knew the land was ours. We kept the people for ourselves. The original inhabitants did not dispute or in any way oppose our having sole possession of the land. It is now for the first time that they dispute our title . . .

Rakatau Katihe was the third witness.

> ... having arrived in Wangaroa we took possession of the lands in accordance with our customs and we caught the people. We caught all the people, not one escaped. Some ran away from us. These we killed and others were killed but what of that? It was in accordance with our custom. Many of those people were killed by us but I am not aware of any of our people being killed by them.
>
> *Court*: What became of the Moriori: did they live on this same piece of land?
> *Rakatau*: The Morioris lived with us in our settlements.
> *Court*: Have the Morioris separate cultivations from yours?
> *Rakatau*: Some times our cultivations were separate and at others we allowed them to cultivate with us.
> *Court*: What number of Morioris had you cultivating for you?
> *Rakatau*: I had in my settlement 40 Morioris.
> *Court*: According to Native custom, does it or not, if the people taken are afterwards allowed to cultivate and settle amongst them, give them some claim to the lands so taken from them?
> *Rakatau*: No, it does not.
> *Assessor*: Are any of the Morioris who were in your settlement alive?
> *Rakatau*: Yes, there are some here.
> *Wirikaku*: Did you hold them in any respect or hold them as slaves?
> *Rakatau*: We made slaves of them from the first.
> *Wirikaku*: Did any of their chiefs attack you in revenge for having conducted yourselves to them in this way?
> *Rakatau*: No.
> *Wirikaku*: What do you say with respect to this wish on their part to have some of this land?
> *Rakatau*: No.

The following morning the court began to hear the Moriori counterclaim. The first witness was Timoti Tara:

> I live and belong to Waitangi. I belong to tribes called Ngatihamata and Te Whetei. I belong to the Moriori people. I claim the whole block of land shown on the plan [Kekerione] and now under investigation by the Court.

Timoti then placed the names of ninety-three claimants before the judge. This appears to be a list of every Moriori then living on Chatham Island. He continued:

> I claim these lands through my ancestors ... [the Maori] landed at Wangaroa and took possession of all the land from thence to Waitangi ... at this time they commenced to kill the Morioris. They ran away and those who went to a settlement were killed. This is the way we were treated. The Maoris followed us as far as Rangiauria [Pitt Island] and killed us ... from the time the New Zealanders arrived in this Island to the time when the prisoners were taken at Rangiauria some 300 of us had been killed.
>
> My family lived with the Ngatitama Tribe. The names of those I have just given are the only survivors of the Moriori People. We were kept in servile bondage until the gospel was preached here. Even then the wood and water were held to be sacred from us. Although we made requests to have some small portions of land given to us by our masters, our request was not granted. We were told by our masters that we were to cultivate in conjunction with them. They said it would not be right for us to have separate cultivations.
>
> ... when the New Zealanders leased some of the lands, we desired that we might participate in the advantages derived from the leases. They agreed to this. When they received rents we went to receive our portion but did not get any. From this we made up our minds to take up a different line of action with regard to our masters because of their innumerable acts of deceit towards us. Hence at the present day we will not obey their orders. I still hold the right to my land to this day.

Timoti Tara, also known as Karaka and as Pawa Ngamunga Kahuki, was another authority on Moriori lore who signed petitions and letters to the Governor in the 1870s and was a major claimant for the Moriori at the Native Land Court in 1870. He lived largely at Hawaruwaru. Naturalist T. H. Potts wrote of him: 'The brows were prominent, the eyes of an almond or elliptical shape, whilst the somewhat fleshy nose curved with a fullness of form that is characteristic of the Jewish people ... the eyes ... showed a contemplative watchfulness.' Timoti had been tattooed in slavery by his Taranaki masters, but this was not a Moriori custom.

E. Dosseter

Timoti then called Hirawanu Tapu, Hori Kerei Rangimariu, Te Wetini Tara (Timoti's brother) and Heremaia Tau to give further evidence in support of the Moriori claim.

Tapu was the first witness after the luncheon adjournment and began by noting that he had heard Timoti Tara's evidence and that it was correct.

> I claim through my father. I claim a block of land as shown in this plan from a point in Whanga Lake across to the long sandy beach in . . . Waitangi called the Kekeri [Kekerione]. I also claim a block of land at the Wangatete and Ouira included in this plan.
> *Court*: Have you or any of your party ever sent in any claims to this Court for land in this Island?
> *Tapu*: We have communicated with the Native Land Court but we claim the whole Island.
> *Court*: Have you or your party sent in any claim for any land included in this survey?
> *Tapu*: Ours was a general claim.

Tapu then traced his ancestry, and outlined the sequence of the Maori invasion in 1835.

> [Soon] after . . . they commenced to kill us, our chiefs of the Moriori held a meeting at a place called the Awapatiki. At this meeting it was suggested that we should attack the New Zealanders and fight them because it was said in history that they were cannibals. This proposition was rejected because our ancestor Pakehu had put an end to war and cannibalism. There was also subsequently a chief called Nunuku who had confirmed the law and put an end to war and cannibalism. About 140 chiefs assembled at this meeting. Altogether there were about 1000 men . . . the decision of the meeting was that they should be friendly with the New Zealanders.
>
> Soon after this the New Zealanders commenced to kill us like sheep. They killed us wherever we were found, in the bush, on the oka ohare, some of our own people were eaten and others were thrown to the birds of heaven . . .
>
> As a child I learned the history of our rights to this land and having compared our rights to land with those of the laws of England, I was induced to write to Governor Browne* respecting our lands. I communicated with him and Sir George Grey . . . on account of my wishing to have our lands investigated according to English law. Captain Drake of the barque *Harriet* was our first informant as to English law with respect to land . . .
>
> I claim the whole of the land contained in this survey. Although we agreed with the Maoris to lease these lands, when the rents were received we did not get any of the money and this is the reason why I oppose the [Maori] claim . . . they have no grounds for claiming the Chathams as against us, the Morioris. I repudiate their right altogether because the blood of the Moriori as shed by them has never been revenged and therefore they have no right to the Islands . . . that is all I have to say.

Cross-examined by the assessor, Tapu was asked whether or not there had been a proposal among some of the Moriori to fight the Maori when they first arrived.

> *Tapu*: Yes.
> *Wirikaku*: Was that not the reason that they did kill you?
> *Tapu*: No, it was not.
> *Wirikaku*: When you were attacked and beaten by the New Zealanders, did they not take you and the land also?
> *Tapu*: Yes they did.
> *Wirikaku*: Have you never proposed to yourself some plan by which you could regain your land and was not that thought of before the sitting of this Court?

---

* Sir Thomas Gore Browne, Governor of New Zealand 1854–61: a high-minded but unsuccessful administrator.

Tapu: I do not understand you.

Wirikaku: Have you never wished to drive the New Zealanders out of the land?

Tapu: No. I have not.

Wirikaku: Have you ever cultivated on this block of land?

Tapu: Yes. I have cultivated at Waitangi when residing with the New Zealanders there.

Wirikaku: What was the agreement made between you [and the Maori] about leasing?

Tapu: That we shall become as one with them and forget all past wars and quarrels. We also went to Riwai* and Pamariki and made the same agreement with them . . . and that we should forget the past.

Wirikaku: Was there ever any agreement entered into between you and the Maori as to the division of the land in these Islands?

Tapu: I made a proposition to the New Zealanders that we should divide the lands. They did not agree to it.

At the close of Tapu's evidence, one further witness, Hori Kerei Rangimariu was sworn. He supported Tapu and Timoti's evidence and added: 'Our having been killed by the New Zealanders without provocation is our reason for saying we are entitled to have our lands. Our people were killed and eaten . . .'

The following morning Timoti Tara's brother, Te Wetini, gave evidence. He, too, confirmed previous testimony. He concluded:

. . . at this day the land must all come to us, the Moriois. It is correct that [the Maori] wished us to become one with them . . . and that we should have half the proceeds from the leases of the lands. But when they obtained the money for the rent they kept it all and would not give us any. Hence we have not joined and become as one with them. In 1859 and 1866. These were the years when the lands were leased. Now my land must be for me only. The New Zealanders have left the Chatham Islands and have gone with the King . . . as they are there they are with the King.** That is all I have to say.

Te Wetini was cross-examined by Wirikaku: 'Have you ever informed the Europeans that hold leases from the New Zealanders that the lands were yours?'

Wetini: Some of us have informed the Europeans.

Wirikaku: Which of the Europeans did you tell that they must cease leasing from the Natives of New Zealand?

Wetini: To Mr Ritchie, who is now in Court.

Wirikaku: Was it on account of the conduct of the New Zealanders that you wanted all your lands back?

Wetini: Yes.

Wirikaku: You are aware that you can take food out of a man's mouth?

Wetini: I am aware.

Heremaia Tau emphasised the now-familiar themes: 'I belong to the Moriori. I claim the land . . . through my father and ancestors. The land is mine . . . let the land which is mine be given back to me. We the Moriori have been treated like a flock of sheep, caught, killed and eaten . . .'

Court: Have you ever lived on any portion of this block of land?

Heremaia: I have cultivated on this block at a place called Hawaruwaru.

Court: How long is it since you left off cultivating?

Heremaia: I cultivate there to this day.

Court: What number of the Morioris are cultivating with you on this land?

Heremaia: Between 10 and 20 of us.

---

* Riwai Taupata, a Maori chief at Kaingaroa.

** The Maori King, Tawhiao, whom the Taranaki tribes supported at this time.

Court: Who is the principal man of these 10 or 20?

Heremaia: Te Wetini is.

Court: Have you homes built at this place?

Heremaia: Yes, we have houses there.

Court: Is this the only place where you cultivate?

Heremaia: No, we also cultivate at a place called Rangatira on the Whanga Lake.

Heremaia's testimony ended the Moriori claim for Kekerione, although the court minutes note: 'Hirawanu Tapu, one of the opposing claimants, addressed the Court in support of his claim. His Honor did not wish the statement taken down.'

Before Judge Rogan ruled on Kekerione, he moved on to and through the other claims. Much of the evidence repeated what had been said previously. Rakatau Katihe, however, supporting the Maori claim for Te Matarae (the smallest block), gave interesting new details about Maori attitudes in 1835:

> . . . we went and took possession of a place called Karewa. Four of us went on that expedition and caught some of the Morioris. We called them black fellows. We took the men back to Wangaroa. The women and children we left . . . each of our party took possession of different portions of the land. I took possession of . . . Matarai [sic], Awainanga, Paru. The Ngatitama resided on and took possession of [Waitangi]. Awapatiki and Ouenga* were taken by Hami and Apitea and party. At that time we each had our respective blocks of land at which time we caught the Morioris.

Surprisingly, Rakatau's claim was supported by two Moriori, Timoti Tara and Heta Namu, who claimed jointly with him. Timoti told the court: 'Rakatau and I are the owners of [Te Matarae]. When Rakatau left this place in 1867, he told Mr A. Shand to give me a portion of this block.' Heta Namu, who explained that he was half-Moriori and half-Ngati Mutunga, but lived as a Moriori, said that the block belonged to Rakatau, Hamuera and himself.

Heta Namu also emerged as a claimant for the Awapatiki block which, cleverly, he claimed both as his Moriori birthright through his mother and by right of conquest through his father. He said there were by then about ten Moriori living on the block.

The principal Moriori claimant and witness, however, was Hirawanu Tapu. He told the court that Timoti Tara claimed the land from Awatapu to Waiorua, Rehe and Teira claimed from Waiorua round the Manukau Point to Awapatiki and he, Tapu, claimed through his younger brother from Awapatiki to Kaingarahu.

> I live at Ouenga [and] have houses, horses, pigs and cultivations. I have also the same at the Awapatiki. I have the same at Kaingarahu but Naera Toenga and others turned me off
> . . .
> *Court*: Who are the leading Moriori chiefs living at Ouenga?
> *Tapu*: I am the leader of the Moriori people at that place.
> *Court*: Are you the only one?
> *Tapu*: Torea is the head chief there but I am their leader with respect to giving their opinions and advice.

One of the Maori claimants asked Tapu if it were not true that he, Hamuera, had taken the Awapatiki block by force of arms.

---

* An earlier, Moriori spelling of Owenga.

Tapu: True, but I was not cast out.
Hamuera: Did I not hold your parents [lives] in my hands?
Tapu: You did not.

In the case of the Otonga block, the Maori claimants sought to avoid a counterclaim by deposing that they had already made provision for the ten or so Moriori who lived there. Judge Rogan summoned one of these Moriori, Hori Rangi, and questioned him.

Court: Had Toenga ever spoken about locating you on the south end of this block?
Rangi: We have been informed and my only objection to it is there are 15 lakes . . .
Court: Have you arranged among yourselves to accept this block of land?
Rangi: I have not fully consented because it is wet land.

The final claims heard were for the Wharekauri block, running the length of the northern coast. Here, too, the Maori claimants had attempted to avoid a counterclaim by allocating two reserves to the Moriori residents in advance of the court sitting. Pamariki for Ngati Tama said that twenty hectares had been made available to Minarapa Tamahiwaka and his wife at Te Whakaru; and 240 hectares around Wairua to (among others) the Riwai family and Hone Waiti. Hone Waiti said that he and the other Moriori on the block knew of these arrangements and accepted them.

The claims hearings had taken ten days. As soon as they were over Judge Rogan announced his findings. In the case of Kekerione, he awarded 15,520 hectares to the Maori claimants and 240 hectares to the Moriori, which included the settlements of Hawaruwaru (Red Bluff) and Rangatira on Te Whanga lagoon.

The Court . . . is of the opinion that Wi Naera Pomare and his co-claimants have clearly shown that the original inhabitants of these Islands were conquered by them and the lands were taken possession of by force of arms and the Moriori people were made subject to their rule and also that they maintained their conquest by actual occupation without having subsequently given up any part of the estate to the original owners, they (the New Zealanders) only having given sufficient land to the Morioris to cultivate for their support . . . Wi Naera Pomare and the Ngatimutunga Tribe are the rightful owners of this block according to Native custom. But . . . as the original inhabitants have had a permissive right hitherto of cultivating certain portions of land for their maintenance, an order will be made in favour of Te Wetini and others of the Moriori people . . . without any restrictions being placed thereon.

If their statements in evidence and letters represented their expectations of what the Land Court would deliver to them, then the Kekerione decision (and its precedent-setting implication for those that followed) must have stunned the waiting Moriori. It revealed to them that their faith in British law to rectify what they saw as the gross injustice of their situation was misplaced; not only was the Maori not to be punished for their treatment of the Moriori, they were to be rewarded for it. The judgment also revealed that the Moriori had handled the hearings badly, their recitation of woes serving only to strengthen the Maori case of ownership by right of conquest and subjugation. They had not argued — as they had on other occasions — that conquest was impossible where one side declined to fight because its customary law forbade killing. The decision also revealed that Judge Rogan considered native customary usage on the Chathams to be *Maori* custom, not that of Moriori; this was another point of law that the

Moriori were not aware that they should have addressed until the judgment was made. Some Moriori witnesses, too, had left an unhelpful impression that they had opposed the Maori claim only because the Maori had neglected to pay them a share of rentals. And, finally, the Moriori had neglected to argue that their case based on original occupation and adherence to their own customary law was strengthened by continuous occupation — even in slavery — whereas the Maori sojourn had been broken by the return to Taranaki in 1867 and 1868 and earlier — all the Maori witnesses in court had come back to the Chathams specifically for the hearing.

Tactically, therefore, the Moriori case had been poorly presented. By the time the Moriori witnesses realised this, it was too late to rectify the outcome.

True, provision was made for Moriori to cultivate 'certain portions of land for their maintenance'; and this was repeated in judgments on other blocks. And those Moriori who had come to a prior agreement with Maori owners had done rather better than those who had not. But the decisions as a whole were a complete reversal of that which the Moriori leaders, Hirawanu Tapu and Timoti Tara in particular, had sought: a return of the islands as a whole to Moriori ownership, with minor provision for Maori occupation and cultivation.

In the case of Te Matarae, Judge Rogan awarded 2560 hectares to the Maori claimants and 80 to two Moriori, Timoti Tara (Karaka) and Roretana Rikipouri. At Te Awapatiki 13,150 hectares went to Apitea, Hamuera and the other Ngati Mutunga claimants and 800 to the Moriori (Hirawanu Tapu, Torea, Taitana, Heta Namu, Timoti Tara, Rangitapua Horomona Rehe, Teretiu Rehe, Wi Tipene, Hori Kerei Rangimariu and Apitia Kahuwai). At Otonga, the Maori were given 15,863 hectares, the Moriori 240 hectares near the Tuku and 20 hectares around their settlement at Waikaripi. And at Wharekauri, from a total of 11,282 hectares, the Moriori got only their two promised reserves of 20 hectares at Te Whakaru and 240 hectares around Wairua. In total, 60,156 hectares had been under claim on Chatham Island. The Maori had been awarded 58,516 hectares or 97.3 per cent; the Moriori 1640 hectares or 2.7 per cent. In almost every case the Maori had retained land with extensive 'clears' suitable for grazing and leasing. The bulk of the meagre Moriori share was forested or wetlands, that could not easily be mustered and thus could not be expected to earn money as a result of being leased.

Moriori claims to Pitt and South-East Islands were dismissed in minutes, their rights (according to the judge) extinguished by Maori conquest and by the fact that no Moriori had cultivated on either island for at least twenty years. The Moriori case was not helped by the fact that two of the principal claimants to the islands, Tame Tainui Tawarewa and Ngatiro Tekupuhanga, were drowned shortly before the court began sitting.

There were Maori and Moriori entitled to part ownership of the blocks defined in 1870 who missed out on shares because they lived on the New Zealand mainland and did not know of the court sittings or were unable to attend them.

Reference has been made to the descendants of Moriori who remained in New Zealand after the failure of the Auckland Islands settlement. In addition, Ati Awa people had given at least six Moriori slaves to other tribes in the 1850s, and had taken some back to Taranaki with them in 1867-68 (although they may not have been 'slaves' in the strict sense of the word, they were certainly 'mokai' or people exploited as a servant-class).

There are accounts of Moriori slaves seen in Otaki, gifted to Ngati Raukawa; and in the South Island, gifted to Ngai Tahu. Two Moriori who took part in a whare wananga at Taiporuhenui near Hawera in 1895 were apparently former slaves. Their names were Tahuaroa and Kapohau. And a female slave, Hineuru, had apparently gone to Taranaki in the 1850s with a young son, also Moriori.

A small number of descendants of some of these people made their way back to the Chathams in the late nineteenth and early twentieth centuries, and some succeeded in registering their interest in Moriori blocks whose owners were rapidly dying out. Most remained in mainland New Zealand, however, married into Maori or Pakeha families and lost their links with both the Chatham Islands and their Moriori cultural heritage. Indeed, the Moriori received such a bad 'press' in New Zealand publications and schoolbooks that even those who knew of their Chatham Island associations tended to remain silent about them. Three or four generations on, their descendants were often ignorant of their Moriori antecedents.

There were several ironies for the Moriori in the outcome of the Land Court sittings of the 1870s. One has been noted: the reverse outcome (formalising large Maori landholdings) to the one Moriori had anticipated. Another was that confirmation of Maori title was followed by a slow but steady buildup of Maori numbers in the Chathams as people returned to collect rents or to uphold their court-endorsed land claims. Before 1880, the Maori population there had again surpassed that of the Moriori. But the third irony was the most extraordinary.

In the late 1860s and early 1870s, the majority of Te Ati Awa became followers of the Parihaka prophets Te Whiti O Rongomai and Tohu Kakahi. These men preached that the time of European ascendancy in New Zealand was drawing to a close, and that the country would soon be left again to the rule and control of Maori. This was not necessarily a hopeful prospect for Moriori. But it rekindled the morale of many Taranaki Maori, and it was the message they brought back to the Chathams during and after the Land Court sittings. As they resumed residence in their former homes, the Ngati Mutunga supporters of Te Whiti began to collect huge quantities of eel and duck from the lagoons and petrel and albatross mutton birds, to ship back to Parihaka. They also held prayer meetings at which they discussed the teachings of Te Whiti and their significance for the Chathams.

According to the Moriori Hapurona Pawa and Horomona Rehe, both of whom worked for Thomas Ritchie, the chief Apitea had called one such meeting in September 1872 to discuss a massacre of all Europeans on Chatham Island. Hapurona warned Ritchie, and subsequently went with Horomona to the meeting at Maipito Pa in Waitangi. Ritchie noted in his diary:

> . . . the Maories appeared not to want them there at all and asked them to leave. The Morioris told the Maories that they . . . had heard from Herekia (or Pomare) all about Te Whiti's prophecies and they had now come to learn all about them. The Maories were very guarded in their conversation throughout, they talked of how true Te Whiti's prophecies were . . . all of which more deeply impressed the Morioris that there were [*sic*] going to be a massacre of the whites but they did not know when . . .

Shortly afterwards the resident magistrate, R. J. Lanauze, intercepted a letter from Wharepa to a Maori living in Taranaki. The contents convinced him that a massacre would occur, and he ordered all Europeans on the island to arm themselves and take refuge in Ritchie's house at Kaingaroa. Lanauze himself left the island by ship to 'get help' — but never returned (he was replaced in 1873 by

Te Ati Awa Maori at a tangi at Maipito Pa, Waitangi. Men on the right are wearing the raukura (albatross-feather emblem), which indicates that they are supporters of Te Whiti O Rongomai.

Canterbury Museum

Samuel Deighton). A court of inquiry was sent to investigate the incident in October 1872, and it concluded that there had in fact been no threat.

Certainly Te Whiti himself was opposed to physical violence, and all his anti-government and anti-settler campaigns in Taranaki involved passive resistance (pulling out survey pegs, removing fences, blocking roadways). 'What I said and wish to convey,' he told William Baucke some years later, 'was that the two races should live side by side in peace; the Maori to learn the white man's wisdom, yet be the dominant ruler. Even as our fathers thought and expected the white man to live among us — not we to be subservient to his immoderate greed.'

Subsequent campaigns to rid the Chathams of European settlers involved the followers of Te Whiti wearing their three albatross feathers (the raukura) and riding around the island on horseback in processions they called waka (canoes). Te Whiti was said to have told them that if they did this seven times the Pakeha would leave. The Pakeha did not.

The Moriori, however, were confronted by the spectacle of the people who had conquered and killed them forty years before now adopting a pacifist ideology; and choosing as their emblem the albatross feathers originally worn by the Moriori followers of Nunuku. It was an outcome redolent of paradox and irony.

CHAPTER

EIGHT

Fog Before the Sun

AT THE TIME OF THE 1870 LAND COURT SITTINGS, THE NUMBER OF Chatham Island residents who defined themselves as Moriori was just over ninety. By 1883 this had dropped to thirty-two; by 1889 to twenty-seven; and by 1900 to twelve. The flame of optimism which had seemed to flare briefly in the 1860s and 1870s as Moriori became free men and women living on land to which they held title flickered and began to die. Whatever resources they had started to accumulate by way of land, agricultural output, farm workers' wages, literacy and entrepreneurial skills, it was apparent by the end of the century that their numbers were not recovering. The resources and gradual reclamation of morale had come too late: although individuals such as Horomona Rehe and Riwai Te Ropiha were generally contented and forceful men, Moriori as a group were still plagued by widespread infertility, high infant mortality among those who managed to bear children, and susceptibility to disease. As time, nature, acculturation and the growth of immunity began to correct *these* problems, the pool of genetically Moriori people seemed too small for them to survive as a physically distinct group. The New Zealand Maori population began to grow from a low point of 42,000 in the 1890s. The Moriori lacked the broad population base necessary to take advantage of potentially favourable circumstances. They were fated to disperse, as Johann Gottfried Engst was fond of saying, like 'fog before the sun'.

At the same time, the Moriori ethos was diminishing. After 1870 there were no more than half a dozen elderly men (such as Minarapa Tamahiwaka) who remembered the Moriori language, hokopapa and traditions from the time when these had been part of a living culture. The younger generation had been brought up immersed in Maori and — although they labelled themselves Moriori — showed no strong inclination to reclaim the culture of their forefathers (except on albatross-hunting expeditions, where both Moriori and Maori observed Moriori conventions and ritual).

Only Hirawanu Tapu was active in recording Moriori traditions. And he, while motivated in part by personal interest, had to be prodded continually towards this task by Alexander Shand. Both Shand and Tapu believed that they were accumulating this information for posterity, 'to save the ancient thought from silence', rather than for use by living people. Both believed that the Moriori 'race' and culture would be extinct within one or two generations.

An indication of the speed with which traditional knowledge was evaporating came in an article from a Chathams correspondent in the *Otago Daily Times* of June 1872. It described the rocks on the western side of Te Whanga lagoon as being 'as copiously inscribed as the walls of Sennacherib's palace. The characters are of the rudest inscription, in basso relievo, not unlike the carvings on old Runic monuments and some are as sharply cut as if done but yesterday. The aboriginal natives are utterly ignorant of these characters, or for what purpose or by whom they were thus engraven on these rocks, no tradition relative thereto having been handed down.'

Thomas Ritchie, too, noted that Moriori friends had said they did not know who had carved the petroglyphs and felt no spiritual attachment to them. Ritchie concluded, wrongly, that the island must have been occupied by a pre-Moriori people. In fact, the group amnesia simply indicated that Moriori no longer remembered the scale of their previous dependence on seals, which had been forcibly brought to an end by foreign sealing in the late 1820s and early 1830s.

For all his friendship and easy working relationship with Moriori, Ritchie believed, with other Europeans of the time, that they were inferior to the Maori, 'lower in the scale,' he wrote, 'mentally and morally but not physically'. Alexander Shand took a similar view. Moriori were, he said, 'devoid of . . . energy, intelligence and ferocity,' and their expression was generally 'dull, with an absence of vivacity, though in many cases they were full of fun'.

Other observers were harsher still in their judgment, seeing in Moriori a 'race' that could be viewed as representing the base of the pyramid of human creation. Resident Magistrate Samuel Deighton, who had been appointed to the

This Manukau group travelling on the west side of Te Whanga lagoon includes Harirota Paua (left, on horseback), Tommy Solomon (boy sitting at left) and Paranihia Heta and her husband Heta Namu (sitting, right).

Lovell-Smith Album,
Alexander Turnbull Library

Chathams with a government instruction to compile a Moriori grammar and vocabulary,* wrote in 1875:

> I can't say I have much of a liking for the Moriois although I feel sorry for their miserable fate. They are a lazy race very deceitful in a small petty way, extremely dirty and very untruthful . . . they are a very inferior race to the Maoris having deteriorated very much since their arriving here [Deighton had no doubt that they had originated in New Zealand] . . . they are bodily a strong stout healthy looking people but they have few children, and the few they have seldom reach maturity. The invasion of the Maoris appears to have had a paralysing effect upon them from which they have never recovered . . .

For all the dilution of their culture occurring at this time, older Moriori were doing their best to arrange marriages among their own people and discourage attachments to Maori (most of whom still regarded Moriori as inferior and therefore unsuitable for marriage). Thomas Ritchie noted that they were 'very strict about their pedigree and if the slightest suspicion of Maori blood is amongst them they know it and will tell you . . .' Some of the men emerging as Moriori leaders — such as Heta Namu and Tamihana Heta — were of mixed Maori-Moriori ancestry, but had always identified with their Moriori side (perhaps in part because they had been rejected by their Maori relatives).

Torea and Hirawanu Tapu made a conscious effort to marry Moriori with Moriori for as long as there were sufficient partners. In the early 1870s they arranged a union between Paranihia Rehe of Manukau (full Moriori) with Heta Namu; and in about 1880, Tapu persuaded Rangitapua Horomona Rehe, Paranihia's brother (and one of the most able of the surviving young Moriori) to marry Ihimaera Te Teira, daughter of Te Teira Rangipewa, a Moriori chief of mixed Owenga-Otonga ancestry.** Both unions produced children: Mikaera Heta, born in 1873 (who died twenty-one years later); and Tame Horomona Rehe, born in 1884.

The other 'promising' Moriori whom Tapu patronised as a potential leader was Riwai Te Ropiha of Wairua, who had worked for the Ritchies at Kaingaroa and Owenga, and for Chudleigh at Wharekauri. As noted, Thomas Ritchie had described him as a 'most industrious, hardworking young man [who] has been living backwards and forwards with me since he was a boy'.

In the early 1880s, Tapu became alarmed that Riwai was keeping company with a Miss Daymond, one of Wi Naera Pomare's stepdaughters, and that Thomas Ritchie was encouraging this match. Tapu wanted a Moriori wife for Riwai and decided that, in the absence of suitable candidates on Chatham Island, he would import one. He sent Alexander Shand to Stewart Island to collect a fifteen-year-old grand-niece of his, Kiti Clark, who was half-Moriori and descended from one of the Auckland Island colonists. They returned together on the schooner *Omaha*.

As Tapu hoped, Kiti and Riwai were attracted to each other and she became pregnant. A Moriori customary marriage followed and Kiti Clark became Mrs Riwai. All was not well, however. Kiti's mother apparently disapproved of the arrangement (though she had released her daughter willingly enough into Shand's care); and Thomas Ritchie, equally disapproving, wrote to her:

---

* He completed the vocabulary with Hirawanu Tapu's assistance in 1887 (see Appendix One), but apparently not the grammar, although he was in the Chathams for eighteen years. Deighton was widely regarded as being handicapped by an alcohol problem and the promise of the grammar and vocabulary is said to have prevented him from being dismissed from his post earlier.

** Torea had died in 1876, leaving Tapu in charge of such arrangements.

The only Moriori meeting house in Maori style, this wharerunanga stood at Wairua in the 1890s. The woman at right is Kiti Riwai, holding one of her daughters.

Christchurch Public Library

Your daughter and Rewai Ropea [*sic*] has come to me and told me that you are very angry about their loving one another, and will take steps to have your daughter, Rewai and Tapu taken to New Zealand if they do not go up this trip. You are quite right as a mother to take such steps and have the right to do so in your, and for your daughter's interest . . .

Your daughter, child as she was, fell in love with Rewai from first she met him, became very fond of him . . . she is to all appearances pregnant . . .

All the blame is attached to the old scoundrel Tapu that you sent your daughter to, and he is the only one that has been the cause of all your trouble. My advice to you under the circumstances is that Tapu should be made to make over to your daughter all his property which I am told he promised . . . and after that is settled then you give your consent to and insist on their being legally married.

The marriage was a success, however, at least in the medium term. It produced nine children between 1885 and 1905, after which Kiti Riwai left the Chathams and married Joseph Ashton of Ngati Kahungunu, whom she had met in Taranaki. She had one further child, a son, by this second husband. The children she and Riwai shared were not the full number of *his* descendants, either. Rose Clark, Kiti's sister, followed her to the Chathams and gave birth to three sons of Riwai's between 1899 and 1903. It may have been this liaison which caused Kiti to abandon her first marriage; or a major setback she suffered in the Native Land Court. Whatever the cause, after Kiti's departure the Riwai children had to be shared out among and cared for by other Moriori families, especially the Rehes (Solomons), Hetas and that of Tamihana Heta.

The Riwai fecundity and that of the next two generations of Solomons* suggest that the Moriori population could have remained viably distinct had a larger number of people reached parental age by the early 1900s. As it occurred, the increase came too late and affected predominantly two families who, oddly, chose not to intermarry while their Moriori genetic inheritance was strong.

---

* Tommy Solomon had five children and thirty-two grandchildren.

Thomas Ritchie's Moriori correspondents continued to write to him through the 1880s with a variety of information, requests and complaints. Hone Waiti, for example (undated):

> Would you make some medicine for me to take, to clear up my insides. My insides are very out of sorts. You should explain the directions to the man who will be bringing it to me, since you won't be coming . . .

And another, also from Waiti, then living at Matarakau, placing an order from Ritchie's store:

> I've got no horse to fetch my food. My horse is sick, but perhaps you could let me have your cart? Parata and Riwai will deliver it here. I know the things to deliver here:
> 2 sacks flour
> 2 sacks sugar
> 1 sack rice
> 18 bales
> 2 balls twine
> 2 papers ammunition
> 3 pounds paraffin
>   As for the cart saddle, you'd better leave it lying there. Another day when the horse is better, I'll fetch it.

And Hapurona Pawa in October 1886, covering himself in case of misunderstanding:

> Friend, listen to me. I may not come, because I am still looking for your brother Robert's boat. Perhaps he doesn't want me for mustering sheep at Kaingaroa. One thing I know for sure is, he certainly wasn't speaking to me about the job. If he does want me you'd better write to me straight away to let me know what you think about me and Mika Heta [Paranihia and Heta Namu's son].
>   I wrote to you so you'd know, in case you'd be angry with me. That's why I wrote to you, in case you'd say it was I who didn't hear you properly. It's not my not hearing you properly: if Robert won't speak to me, I won't come. That is all.

In 1885 Moriori were back in the Native Land Court. Having lost the ownership of South-East Island and Pitt, and won back only a fraction of Chatham, Hirawanu Tapu decided to make a test claim for the outlying islands. These were a vital and continuing source of mutton birds and albatross for Maori and Moriori, and they had not been specifically included in the 1870 court settlements.

The island Tapu chose for the claim, Motuhara, was a rock that had come to be known as the Forty Fours (because it lay on latitude 44°). He told the court that the only recognised owner had been the Moriori ancestor Tamarawhaki; and that he and Teretiu Horomona of Owenga were now the only living descendants of Tamarawhaki. He added that, while the court had decided that the Maori had taken possession of Chatham Island, they had never been judged to have taken Motuhara; nor had they in fact. There had been no fight for nor conquest of Motuhara.

Wi Naera Pomare, now appointed a court assessor in addition to being an interested witness, counterclaimed and said that the Maori case in 1870 had been for the whole Chatham Islands group. Because that claim had been successful, all the outlying islands were now in Maori ownership, even if the individual owners had not been named. He added that, because Motuhara was important for birding, it had become a traditional food source for Moriori *and* Maori.

Resident Magistrate Samuel Deighton, who was acting as Land Court Judge on this occasion (though Chudleigh, as a Justice of the Peace, had frequently to sort out confusions caused by his ignorance of the law*), upheld Pomare's interpretation: '. . . the Chatham Islands were adjudged to the Maoris in 1870, and the Court is of the opinion that the adjacent islands were included in that judgment.'

This was the last attempt by Moriori in the nineteenth century to use the legal system to rectify grievances arising out of the Taranaki invasion. There was some grumbling that the court had allowed Pomare to act, in spite of what was obviously a conflict of interest; and some satisfaction within Moriori ranks when, six months after the hearing, he died of tuberculosis.

In 1889 another keen 'Moriori watcher' was on Chatham Island: Edward Tregear, an able civil servant and amateur ethnologist, had published *The Aryan Maori* in 1885, which sought to prove, by linguistic analysis, that Maori and European shared cultural origins. Tregear was to continue to research and publish on Maori and wider Polynesian topics and was, with Percy Smith, one of the founders of the Polynesian Society in 1892.

In the Chathams, Tregear hoped to find genealogies which linked the Moriori to New Zealand, and which would enable him to calculate when they had left the mainland and in what circumstances.

> I especially wished to commune with Hirioana [*sic*] Tapu, the last chief of the tribe, and the only reliable source of information now accessible as he is getting old [Tapu was then sixty-five], and no one conversant with the old songs, legends etc., will be in existence when he has left us. He gave me much information in the short time at my disposal, but was unable to recite the perfect genealogy of his forefathers. Fortunately, Mr A. Shand, of Waitangi, who is an ardent student of Moriori, had acquired the wished-for genealogy from Minarapa Tamahiwaka an old priest now dead . . .

Tregear then turned his attention to the expected demise of the Moriori:

> Some little time ago I saw in the Australian papers a discussion as to the date on which the last aboriginal native of Tasmania died, a question having arisen whether a certain woman recently dead had been a full-blooded native or only a half-caste** . . . thinking that, as the Moriori are rapidly dying out, scientists at the end of the next half-century might be interested in knowing what was the exact state of the native population in 1889, I made a census enquiry . . .

Tregear's 'census' is almost useless. He misspells about half the names, he omits others altogether, he claims that some are full Moriori when they are Maori-Moriori, and he describes Kiti Riwai, incorrectly, as a 'child of pakeha and half-caste woman'. His total is 'twenty-seven of pure Moriori descent, and five half-breeds.*** The Maoris on the islands number about two hundred and fifty souls, and there is roughly about the same number of a white population.'

---

* Chudleigh wrote in his diary for 24/5/83: 'Miserable day going through law and justice with Deighton. He is quite ignorant of all law and as he is a paid officer there is a want of justice to the public.'

** No one much admired 'half-caste' coloured people at this time. They were seen as neither one thing nor the other. Oddly, the same opprobrium was not attached to whites of mixed ethnic origin.

** Two of his 'pure' Moriori, Tamihana Heta and Wi Hoeta, were not pure; but then he omitted from his list at least two people who were — Heremaia Tau and Nga Whena. So his total may be correct in spite of errors.

Throughout the 1890s the Moriori population took its sharpest dive: from twenty-seven to twelve by 1900. Strange portents in the course of the decade — icebergs seen in the strait between Owenga and Pitt in 1892, earthquakes in 1893 and snow in 1898 and 1899 — convinced older Moriori and Maori that the 'end' was not far away. The absence of a doctor on Chatham Island for most of this period did not help. Previous medical practitioners had been classed by Chudleigh as 'Freaks, Failures or Faddists'. The last one to leave, Dr Samuel Johnson Cooper, was an alcoholic who disappeared subsequently in the Mackenzie Country after a drinking bout. In the early 1890s Moriori elders seemed to die at an accelerated rate: Pumipi, Te Teira, Timoti Tara, Apiata Kahuwai, Heremaia Tau, Teretiu Rehe and Teretiu's wife Pakura. Hirawanu Tapu, too, became seriously ill, with tuberculosis, and Alexander Shand feared that he was close to death. He was alarmed by this prospect: not simply because he would be losing an old companion, but because he was far from completing the translations of his voluminous transcriptions of Moriori traditions and chants.

Shand had left the family farm at Te Whakaru in 1870 and leased the Whangamarino block close to Waitangi with his brother-in-law, F. A. D. Cox. They farmed the land together, raising largely sheep, but built separate houses since Cox and his wife had a family and Shand remained a bachelor. From Whangamarino he took time off to attend most Land and Magistrate Court sittings. He was the resident magistrate's clerk and a licensed Maori interpreter, and frequently performed this latter function for magistrates and judges; at other times he acted on behalf of Maori or Moriori witnesses who were unable to present their own cases. It was at Whangamarino, too, that he carried on his work on the Moriori culture and language, for which he relied so heavily on Tapu.

Ihimaera Rehe, swollen with obesity and illness, just before her death in 1903.

Canterbury Museum

In April 1891 he was writing to Dr Thomas Hocken of Dunedin* to

ask your advice on behalf of my Moriori friend . . . Hirawanu Tapu Mai Tarawai who is my constant and I may say chief assistant in my Moriori work more especially in translating and arriving at the meaning of words and phrases of which none of the others can offer an explanation — we have worked together in collecting legends, songs and stories for very many years now and without him I do not know how I should get on in getting meanings which he himself has to puzzle over . . .

Last winter I had arranged with him to come here for a week at a time to help me, but owing to continuing ill health he was unable to do so and at the time when I met you he was continually unwell . . . I am much afraid of losing him if his ill health continues and in such case I should feel like a one armed man. It occurred to me [that] perhaps you could suggest something to assist him.

In a subsequent letter to Hocken, Shand described Tapu's symptoms:

. . . his complaint was called . . . 'kawei', of this he says there are two kinds and that it commenced first in the head giving intense pain and swelling it up; this kind was 'E kawei hit' te roro' a kawei turning to the brain; the other (a watering kawei) 'E kawei wai' (his kind) which was the same at first, but afterwards broke the skin . . . and the sufferer got relief to a certain extent . . . from the head it goes down the muscles of the back each side of the back-bone and ultimately lodges in the testicles producing . . . a running there also and in this case going down his legs to his feet . . . the pain and the watery breaking out, or eczema, spread downwards. His first attack was in 1856 . . . since that time he has had attacks at distant intervals but these last three or four years at much shorter ones . . . his face and head swells and his skin grows black, suffering pain and dizziness until the watery running sets in which eases him somewhat.**

Hocken apparently sent medicine by steamer, which relieved Tapu's symptoms. Writing to thank the doctor, Shand added that he had heard from Stephenson Percy Smith, whom he had met originally when Smith was one of the surveyors prior to the Land Court sittings:

. . . he is trying to organise a Polynesian Society and get members everywhere over the Pacific. I think the idea an excellent [one] and he suggests that I should contribute Moriori articles.*** I like the idea very well, but don't quite see at present how it will fit in. He also suggests that the [Moriori] Vocabulary should be published there in parts . . . in working at my vocabulary which I have been for the past 3 months more or less I found it easier to first hunt up words in the karakias, songs, legends and so forth taking each one as it turned up, jotting them down higgledy piggledy under each letter with examples showing their use in combination . . . I only wish I could get time to work properly at the thing and get on with it, but unfortunately to be frank with you I have to earn our bread and butter and like many of our friends am exceedingly hard pressed, having so much hard work to do prevents me making the headway I ought . . .

Serious as he was about his work with Shand and Deighton, Tapu was not above teasing some of the earnest but amateur scholars who came to interview him. The year after Shand sent his letters to Hocken, Henry Forbes was writing:

Tapu was an intelligent old fellow, with a very Jewish countenance, and highly developed frontal processes. 'The pouwa', he said, 'he a big bird; he die — oo! two hundred, three hundred year . . . long time ago. I see his bone stick up in Te Whanga, where Morioris

Opposite: Hirawanu Tapu, shortly before his death, with spectacles and pipe, showing the effects of age and illness. The photograph was taken by Archdeacon Woodthorpe, chaplain to the Maori Mission in the Christchurch Anglican Diocese and one of the many people who came to the Chathams to consult Tapu about Moriori culture.

Canterbury Museum

---

* A medical practitioner and eminent collector of books and documents relating to New Zealand history, whose collection formed the foundation for the University of Otago's Hocken Library.

** Shand has described a form of tuberculosis.

*** Shand did this for the first seven volumes of the *Journal of the Polynesian Society*, from 1892 to 1898.

camp long time back. Me young fellow . . . tell me Moriori make him hole in water, drive him pouwa in, hammer him dead and roast him. His bone I see him stick in hole in mud in lagoon water. Oo! big, all same as cow; he eat plenty grass swim [floating on] lagoon water, Moriori call koko.' It is, of course, impossible to describe in words Tapu's gestures and expressions; but no one who heard him could doubt that he had seen large bones in the lagoon, and that their origin had been explained to him by his father.

According to another account, Tapu told Chudleigh's farm labourer Abner Clough that

> the Moriori were descendants of the crews of three Portuguese ships which sailed to the Chathams from Lisbon after Abel Tasman had returned to Europe with accounts of the rich whaling and sealing waters around New Zealand. His story was that the Portuguese found the islands uninhabited and sent one ship to New Zealand to fetch Maoris to help kill and skin the seals. They only succeeded in bringing Maori women.
>
> A ship loaded with sealskins set off for China, but it was sunk by the British, who were then fighting the Dutch. Another ship went to New Zealand to get some Maoris but never returned. The third ship was blown ashore on the Chathams and wrecked, so the Portuguese and their Maori women were marooned. According to the tale, they lived and bred on the Chathams for the next 140 years until Broughton arrived, and became the people known as Moriori . . .

There was no giant bird on the Chathams (except for a large rail), nor any evidence of a Portuguese landfall there before Broughton. It is unlikely that Tapu believed either story.

Up to the 1890s, Moriori had stayed largely clear of the kinds of law-breaking which had got their Maori compatriots into so much trouble on the Chathams (fighting, looting, importing alcohol illegally, and so on). Frequently needing the shield of the law as a protection from Maori abuse, they seldom seemed inclined to break it themselves. But one Moriori, Tamihana Heta, was in almost continuous trouble from 1888 to 1891 for refusing to register his dogs and pay an annual tax of five shillings per animal that had been levied on the Chathams in 1887.

The tax was imposed throughout New Zealand — in other areas by local bodies. Its purpose, apart from raising revenue, was to enforce registration and control of Maori-owned dogs, which in some places were numerous. It was almost universally resisted. Many Moriori and Maori were not yet part of a cash economy. They had dogs — plenty of them — but not the means to pay for them; further, they did not see why they should have to pay the Government or a local body for what was theirs. Te Whiti stiffened resistance in Taranaki and on the Chathams by advising his followers not to pay the tax.

In June 1888, in the temporary absence of Resident Magistrate Samuel Deighton, Chudleigh and his fellow justice of the peace F. A. D. Cox issued warrants for the arrest of four Maori and Tamihana Heta for refusal to register their dogs. When that produced no result, Chudleigh returned from one of his visits to the mainland with a force of eight armed constabulary to arrest a total of sixteen offenders and remove them to Wellington for trial and imprisonment. They included Tamihana Heta.

Tamihana was born in 1865 of a Moriori mother and Maori father. Although he spent many of his early years among his father's people, he identified increasingly with his Moriori relations from the late 1880s. In the 1890s he began to appear increasingly as a Moriori witness in the Native Land Court and in the

Tamihana Heta (left) with his
first wife, Erina Winiata, and
Epiha Hough, a Maori whom
Tamihana had adopted.

Burt Collection,
Alexander Turnbull Library

following decade he adopted some of Riwai Te Ropiha's children after Kiti Riwai
had left the island.

After a month in jail, Tamihana and his fellow convicts returned to the
Chathams where, in January 1891, some of them (including Tamihana) had to be
arrested again for continuing to refuse to pay the tax and register their dogs. On
this occasion, Resident Magistrate Deighton crumbled when the Waitangi jail was
attacked by a crowd of women and released the prisoners. The matter does not
appear to have been enforced again, much to Chudleigh's disgust.

More seriously, Heta Namu, husband of Paranihia Rehe of Manukau, got
drunk after a tangi at the end of 1892 and attacked a Waitangi Maori named Paki
with an axe. Several people were hurt in the fight that followed, and Paki so
seriously injured that it looked as though he would die.

The new resident magistrate, Major F. J. W. Gascoyne, prevented retaliation
by banning the sale of alcohol on New Year's Day 1893. But he was uncertain
what to do about Heta. If Paki died, Heta would have to be arrested, charged
with manslaughter, and held in jail until he could be shipped to the mainland for
trial. If that happened, Gascoyne feared, 'there might be serious trouble and an
attempt to rescue him'. Even if Paki survived, Heta would have to be charged
with assault and this would be an unpopular move.

Gascoyne resorted to a characteristically Chathams solution (in which he
showed far greater sense and flexibility than his predecessor, Deighton). He told
the chief Pangopango, 'in great secret' that he intended to arrest Heta and put
him on the steamer that was to arrive in two days — if he could find him. 'I
guessed that Heta would hide on board the ship when she was at the other side

of the island [at Owenga], and try to get away to Parihaka . . . and I had no intention of searching the steamer for him. Things happened as I wished. Heta hid on board and got away . . . and as he knew that a warrant was out for his arrest I did not expect to hear anything more of him for a year or two.*

By the mid-1890s Moriori were also back in the Native Land Court — not fighting the common Maori adversary this time, but one another. With the removal of any possibility of challenging the dominant Maori position on the island, Moriori solidarity had begun to crumble;** and the immediate cause of conflict was competition for succession to the land shares of those who had died.

The first of many such cases involved claims for Timoti Tara's shares in the Kekerione block. The major claimant was Puti Timoti, Timoti's widow. She based her case not on her marriage to the deceased, but on the fact that they were both descended five generations from a common ancestor, Kikitauira. Alexander Shand told the court that Timoti's relatives had wanted to turn Puti off the land at Hawaruwaru after his death but did not in the end do so, because of her marriage to Timoti.

There were complications, however. In the first place, by accident, Timoti had not been formally registered as an owner of Kekerione (though everyone agreed that he should have been). Secondly, three other people claimed his share by virtue of their close blood relationship to him: Wi Hoeta, a half-Moriori from Hawaruwaru; Rohana, Hirawanu Tapu's wife; and Karaka Paoe. The presiding judge, Alexander MacKay, declined to adjudicate on the merits of the claims by accepting Timoti's right to ownership, then dividing the shares among the four claimants and adding Ngahena Parata, Puti's sister, to share her quarter.

A more acrimonious dispute was heard the same day at the same court sitting, which was in Wellington. Hirawanu Tapu wanted to survey off a section of the Te Awapatiki block at Manukau representing his shares, those of his wife, and those they had inherited since 1870 — a total of 266 hectares. The other owners objected because, they said, they held the land in common, cultivated it in common, and ran sheep on it in common. They also claimed to have dwellings on the area Tapu was claiming as his own; and that it was the best land in the block. Judge MacKay adjourned Tapu's application because of conflicting evidence.

When it was presented to the court again, early in 1898, it was at Waitangi and before Judge Butler. This time Alexander Shand acted for Tapu and said that the common cultivations had fallen into disuse and the dwellings were of a temporary nature, directed specifically to frustrate Tapu's subdivision. Tapu, too, gave evidence in support of his plan:

> Our sheep all ran together from 1874 to 1883, but in the latter year I found that the other owners were taking advantage of me and my sheep have decreased from 400 to 100; therefore I want my share located. I have had it surveyed . . . after the survey . . . some of

---

* And he did not. Heta apparently stayed with his Ati Awa relatives at Parihaka for several years, then slipped back to the Chathams unnoticed, when the warrant had expired. Five years later, Heta and his wife Paranihia did go to court — but it was to force payment for the slaughter of twenty of their twenty-six turkeys by dogs belonging to Joe Santos, a Negro former whaler from St Helena.

** By now the Maori population had climbed back to more than 200, while that of the Moriori had fallen below twenty; far more traumatic than the drop in numbers, however, was the eventual Moriori realisation that they would not be able to overturn the Land Court decisions of 1870 and 1885 which had left them in control of only a fraction of their former homeland.

the other owners came to work [there] as a protest against my claim. They put up temporary homes . . . the permanent homes are all outside my [proposed] boundaries.

Horomona Rehe, Heta Namu and Paranihia Heta all spoke against Tapu's plan, reiterating that they believed he had surveyed off the best land in the block for himself, land they had formerly all used in common. Judge Butler found in Tapu's favour, however. He awarded Tapu and Rohana the 266 hectares they had had surveyed, and allocated the remaining shares in the block as follows: Horomona Rehe, 178 hectares; Paranihia Heta, 89 hectares; Heta Namu 89.2 hectares; Ihimaera Rehe, 89.2 hectares; and Te Karaka, 89 hectares.

Ani Davis, daughter of a slave, half-Moriori and half-Negro. She moved to the Chathams from Port Underwood in the 1890s.

Wilford Davis

Further variations in the allocation of shares had to be made because of the return to the Chathams of Moriori who had formerly lived on the mainland; in some cases those who returned were descendants of Moriori who had been part of the Auckland Island colony, or who had been taken back to New Zealand as slaves.

The case of Kiti Riwai has been mentioned*, and she eventually acquired shares in Manukau. Others who moved to the Chathams after the 1870 court sittings included Harirota Paua, a niece of Horomona Rehe; Mihi Tame Tainui, who returned from Taranaki in the 1890s; Ani Davis, half-Negro, half-Moriori, daughter of the slave Kurupa who had been taken to the Auckland Islands; her son Bill; Rakete Tipene, who also returned from Taranaki in the 1890s; his niece Raukura Hetaraka; and an unnamed elderly Moriori woman, presumed to be a former slave, who was returned to the island in a lead coffin and buried at Manukau in 1904.

Wedding of Ani Davis's daughter Mary to Frederick William Eyles at Waitangi, 1909. Joe Santos stands at rear and Tommy Solomon, best man, at right.

Joseph Eyles

* See p. 138.

Several of these 'rediscovered' Moriori were to play important roles in the dwindling Moriori community. Harirota Paua married Joe Mapu, a highly accomplished half-Moriori farmer and musician from Otonga, who played the concertina at all the island dances.* Ani Davis married Wi Hoeta and helped him farm at Hawaruwaru and fight his battles for further land through the court. Bill Davis, a highly literate and intelligent man, was the only part-Moriori to volunteer for service in the First World War, in which he rose to the rank of second lieutenant. And Rakete Tipene joined Horomona Rehe and Riwai Te Ropiha as leaders of Moriori causes in the early years of the twentieth century.

Rakete Tipene set a useful precedent in 1900 for those who were part Moriori and part-Maori by successful claims in Maori and Moriori blocks. Prior to this time, only those of pure Maori descent had been given shares in Maori land; anyone with Moriori blood was made to claim as Moriori. In Rakete's case, however, Judge Edgar ruled:

> . . . the present Court cannot see any good reason for excluding such a half-caste from lands which belonged to his or her Maori parent. Of course such a half-caste would have no right to Moriori lands through his Maori parent, nor to Maori lands through his Moriori parent. But there is no reason why he should be debarred from inheriting through either parent such lands as that parent had a right to. The Court will therefore admit into the list of beneficial owners such half-caste Morioris as can show a right through the Maori parent.

The census of 1900 revealed that there were only twelve 'full-blooded' Moriori still living. They were: Rohana Tapu, Horomona Rangitapua Rehe, Ihimaera Rehe, Tame Rehe, Paranihia Heta, Riwai Te Ropiha, Hapurona Pawa, Puti Timoti, Te Harawira, Temuera, Merepaha and Ngahena Parata. There were also 'three-quarter-Moriori' — Riwai's twelve children — and at least half a dozen 'half-Moriori' — Heta Namu, Wi Hoeta, Tamihana Heta, Wharetutaki, Joe Mapu, Arthur Lockett, Harirota Mapu, Rakete Tipene and Mihi Tame Tainui.

The name missing from the list is Hirawanu Tapu. After years of ill-health Tapu had finally succumbed to a painful death from tuberculosis in May of the year the census was taken, aged seventy-six. In spite of differences with his neighbours, he remained a celebrity and the undisputed rakatira of Moriori until his death (the first New Zealand Governor to visit the Chathams, Lord Glasgow, was taken to Manukau to meet him in 1895); and he continued to appear in Land Court cases until only weeks before his death, giving evidence on Maori claims in addition to Moriori ones, because he had outlived and out-remembered Maori witnesses.

There was nobody of Tapu's stature waiting or able to assume his role. By 1900, Horomona Rehe and Riwai Te Ropiha were regarded as effective leaders of the Moriori, with close support from the 'half-Moriori' elders Heta Namu and Wi Hoeta, and from Rakete Tipene and Tamihana Heta. But none of this group possessed first-hand knowledge of Moriori language and traditions. They knew only what had been passed on to them by Tapu and by their parents' generation. They regarded themselves, at times fiercely, as 'Moriori'. But they spoke Maori

---

* Chudleigh also records Mapu describing to the Native Land Court how he had found and removed lice on sheep. 'He opened a book, bent over it in the attitude one would take examining sheep's wool, peered intently as if looking for something in the crack between the leaves, made a grab and pretended to hold something between his thumb and finger . . . the word [lice] was unknown to him . . .' Richards 1952.

and increasingly integrated themselves into the Chatham Island Maori community, socially and politically.

The only Moriori who now survived from before the time of the Maori invasion were Rohana, Tapu's wife at Manukau; and Temuera and Merepaha at Whareama. Temuera and Merepaha were an odd couple, known to Pakeha on the island as 'Ming' and 'Moo'. He (Temuera) had been castrated as a child as an apparent measure of population control and this had affected his hormone balance. He had always spoken in a high voice, chosen to wear dresses, and was regarded (incorrectly) as a hermaphrodite. Merepaha was normal by comparison, but suffering terribly from the effects of old age. Both were arthritic and blind from cataracts in the 1890s, and had a wire running from their hut to a well to enable them to find water. Individuals such as Tamihana Heta stayed with them for short periods, but they had no one to take care of them constantly. At a time when most other Moriori were living sparsely but comfortably, Temuera and Merepaha were *in extremis*: crippled with illness, close to starvation and trapped in squalor.

Around 1900, Horomona Rehe and Heta Namu persuaded them to move to Manukau, where they were put into a clean ponga house close to the rest of the Moriori community. There they were fed, washed and pampered, but seemed not to like their new lives. Both were dead within a year of the shift. They were followed closely by Rohana Tapu, who died in May 1902; and Ihimaera Rehe, Horomona's wife, who died in June 1903. By 1904, only six of the twelve Moriori counted in the census four years before remained.

Given that Hirawanu and Rohana between them held the largest share of the

Temuera and Merepaha, an elderly, blind Moriori couple living at Whareama in the 1890s. In this photograph, taken without their knowledge, they are crying out 'pra, pra' (flour, flour) to Carrie Foster at right, who found them starving. The wretchedness of their condition was not typical of Moriori life at this time, and they were moved to Manukau, where they could be cared for, soon after this picture was taken.

Canterbury Museum

Some of the prolific Riwais and Solomons, photographed at Manukau. From left: Riwai Te Ropiha, Riria (Lily) Riwai, Roger Riwai, Meri Riwai, Tommy Solomon and Rangitapua Horomona Rehe. Riria became Mrs Preece; Meri, Mrs Bragg.

Burt Collection,
Alexander Turnbull Library

Te Awapatiki Moriori reserve, and — others said — the best land on it, it was inevitable that there would be a scramble to succeed to it. What was more surprising was the duplicity with which two of the protagonists proceeded.

Without telling anybody else on the island, Kiti Riwai and Ani Wi Hoeta attended a sitting of the Native Land Court in Wellington in June 1904. They appeared before Judge Gilbert Mair and told him they were Tapu's only surviving relatives, and applied to succeed to both his and Rohana's shares. The judge accepted their evidence and their application (both of which were uncontested) and they returned to the Chathams as owners of 266 hectares at Manukau. Their ruse became public knowledge when they tried to evict Tamihana Heta from Tapu's house, which he had built and in which he had been living since Rohana's death.

Kiti's claim was not without foundation. When Tapu had brought her to the island to marry Riwai in 1884, he had called her his 'grand-niece' and his 'adopted daughter', and intimated that he would eventually leave his property to her. She had strengthened the claim by nursing him in his final illness and managing to extract a will naming her as his heir. There was the further fact that, in spite of their Moriori descent, neither Kiti nor Ani Wi Hoeta had until this time been allocated shares in any Moriori land. Kiti may have been on the verge of leaving Riwai and wanted resources of her own on the island (she had already inherited Maori land in the South Island from her mother's family).

The problem was that there were two wills. An earlier one had named Tamihana Heta to succeed Tapu, provided he built him a new house (he had already constructed the old man's previous one), fenced his land and looked after his stock. Tamihana had done all these things, except that he had not completed the new house by the time Tapu died. He had taken Tapu to his own house in Waitangi immediately prior to his death, and had arranged for Kiti to nurse him there.

When the effect of Kiti's and Ani's scheming became apparent, Tamihana Heta, Horomona Rehe and Paranihia Heta applied to the court to have their names struck off the succession order and replaced with their own. This case was heard at Waitangi in February 1906.

Acting for the counterclaimants, the lawyer C. B. Morrison told the court that Tamihana Heta was descended from Reoma (his Moriori grandmother) who was a half-sister of Hirawanu Tapu. Horomona Rehe and his sister Paranihia, he said, were both related to Tapu on their mother's side, from which they had derived their claims at Manukau.

> There is strong evidence that Hirawanu recognised Tamihana Heta as his proper successor to this land and the person to whom he should look for help in his old age . . . Tamihana Heta was put upon this land by Hirawanu . . . he expended very large sums of money, building, fencing, clearing . . . he maintained and provided for Hirawanu and Rohana until they both died. He also provided for their funeral obsequies. At the time when [Kiti's and Ani's] application was made to the Court in June 1904, Tamihana Heta was in actual possession of this land. His name was not mentioned [in court] . . .

Paranihia and Horomona indicated that they supported Tamihana's claim; while he told the court that he recognised their right to succeed to the land jointly with him. He then specified the ways in which he had acted for Tapu in his final years, including appearing in court on his behalf.

Kiti Riwai reiterated that it was Tapu who had brought her to the island and given her in marriage as his 'adopted daughter'. She presented a genealogy in court showing that she was third or fourth cousin to Tapu. Finally, she described looking after him in his last illness, when 'he kept going from bad to worse, vomiting blood'.

The process of overturning the original succession order was complicated. The counterclaim had been heard before Judge G. Ward. He was required to instigate an investigation by the original judge, Gilbert Mair, incorporating the

Wi Hoeta, his wife Ani (formerly Davis) and Tamihana Heta, Hawaruwaru, early 1900s.

Auckland Institute & Museum

new evidence; and then the case went before the Chief Judge of the Native Land Court to validate variations in the order. The result was ready for announcement at Waitangi in March 1907: the process had taken just over a year.

The effect of Chatham Islands geography and climate on court hearings was revealed when the claimants assembled on 15 March 1907, however. Application was made to have the case adjourned because Tamihana Heta was bringing in sheep from Wairua and had not yet appeared. Two days later there was a further postponement on the ground that 'owing to rain on Sunday, Tamihana Heta was unable to come in . . .'

The results of the case were eventually heard on 19 March. As expected, the succession order *was* varied. The names of Tamihana Heta, Horomona Rehe and Paranihia Heta were inserted as owners of Hirawanu Tapu's land in place of those of Kiti Riwai and Ani Wi Hoeta; Kiti and Ani lost this particular battle. But by 1913 Ani had inherited land at Manukau through her husband's death in 1911; and Kiti, too, had been awarded shares there. So both eventually achieved part of the result they had sought originally in 1904.

As Alexander Shand had anticipated in his letters to Percy Smith and Thomas Hocken, the loss of Hirawanu Tapu was a blow to him. He had been able to publish his accounts of Moriori history, chants and traditions, largely in the *Journals of the Polynesian Society* between 1892 and 1898 (and most of these were issued as a single volume in 1911). This task had only been possible because of Tapu's assistance and constant provision of information. Stressing as they did the Polynesian character of Moriori culture, these articles had also acted as something of a counterweight to some of the more bizarre theories about Moriori origins that were beginning to be published in New Zealand and elsewhere.* But

Alexander Shand, farmer, linguist, amateur ethnologist and cripple, shortly before his death in 1910.

Hocken Library

* See pp. 170–178.

Shand's Moriori vocabulary and grammar were nowhere near completion when Tapu died; without the Moriori scholar, this work came to a virtual halt. Shand was forced to seek meanings in contexts, existing translations or other Polynesian languages; but Percy Smith records that he wrote very little after 1900.

On the night of 28 July 1910, Shand's house at Whangamarino caught fire and he burned to death. All his papers — Moriori, Maori and others — were incinerated with him. The verdict of the coroner was that death was accidental, and Shand was presumed to have been prevented from escaping by his rheumatoid arthritis (which had been made considerably worse by his insistence on daily cold baths). He was found to be semi-dressed and had already thrown some papers out a window before being overcome by smoke or flames.

The island hummed with rumours in the wake of his death, however, and they were repeated for the next seventy years. The most persistent was that a member of a particular Maori family feared that an upcoming land claim would be upset by Shand's knowledge of history and whakapapa. This suspect is alleged to have set fire to the house to burn Shand's papers and, with them, evidence contrary to his family claim. Some accounts go further and allege that he remained at the scene of the fire and threw papers into the blaze as Shand threw them out; finally, it is claimed, he pushed Alex himself back into the house as the old man tried to climb through a window.

No charges were ever laid over the matter and the rumour may have no substance. But one member of the family under suspicion and his wife left the Chathams the same year for Taranaki and never returned.

The question that exercised scholars subsequently was what became of Shand's Moriori vocabulary. At first it was assumed to have been lost in the fire. But the Reverend Herbert Williams refers to having used such a vocabulary for an article in the *Transactions of the New Zealand Institute*, in 1919; and further reference to it is made in 1920 on index cards in the Williams Papers. No one other than Archdeacon Williams seems to have sighted it and its subsequent whereabouts is unknown.

In 1910 the relevant factor was that, with Hirawanu Tapu and Alexander Shand both dead, the Chathams had lost what Edward Tregear called the 'sole repositories of the knowledge of a lost race'. William Baucke would disagree subsequently, but, for most observers, the comment was fair and grounds for grief. Edward Chudleigh, always grudging with his praise, wrote in his diary: 'Poor Alex. He lived a hard life and a long one . . . his next birthday would be 70 . . . all his life's efforts perished with him . . . he was a good Colonist and a most useful Islander, also a good brother . . .'

Riwai Te Ropiha towards the end of his life.

Canterbury Museum

There were two other deaths on Chatham Island in 1910 — neither noted by the press but each as important to the dwindling Moriori community as that of Alexander Shand. Heta Namu died at Manukau, aged about seventy. And Riwai Te Ropiha, only in his fifties but looking decidedly older, died at Wairua. His passing left only four 'full-blooded' Moriori alive. And three of those — Rangitapua Horomona, Paranihia Heta and Tame Horomona — were members of the Rehe or Solomon family. For the next two decades, the spotlight of outside interest in the Moriori would be directed exclusively towards Manukau, their home.

NINE

And Then There Was One?

Tame Horomona Rehe, known later as Tommy Solomon, was born on 7 May 1884 at Waikaripi on the west coast of Chatham Island.* His antecedents were a combination of the Owenga Moriori tribe, who had settled the east coast of Chatham Island south of Te Awapatiki, and the Otonga people of the south-west coast. His grandmother Nakahu, originally from Owenga, had met his grandfather Purehe, from Otonga, on Pitt Island. They had been taken there by Maori captors to cultivate land.

After the release of slaves these grandparents returned to the main island to live primarily at Owenga and bring up their two children: Paranihia Ngamare, born in 1853, and Rangitapua Horomona, Tame's father, born in 1856.** They remained there until their deaths. But the Rehes always regarded Waikaripi on the Ngaio coast as their ancestral home. They lived there in a ponga hut for a few months of each year and used it as a base for birding expeditions up the Tuku Valley, which kept alive their ancient hunting rites. It was during one of these west coast sojourns that Tame Horomona was born.

Tame's parents' arranged marriage — Rangitapua Horomona Rehe to Ihimaera Te Teira — reinforced existing family associations. The Teira family, too, had links to both Owenga and Otonga; and they had also undergone a period of captivity on Pitt Island (indeed, Tame's great-grandparents on his mother's side appear to have been living on Pitt at the time of the Maori invasion).

Tame's home, however, was Manukau, where his parents lived the greater part of each year. Manukau was the reserve made over to Owenga Moriori by the Ngati Mutunga chief Apitea Punga in 1868 and confirmed in Moriori ownership by the Native Land Court two years later. It was largely bush covered at the time Tame grew up, a feature regarded as a disadvantage for mustering by most Maori, who in 1870 had kept the 'clears', carpeted in native grass and suitable for grazing sheep, largely for themselves.

In 1884 there were about half a dozen Moriori households at Manukau, living in thatched ponga huts strung between the bush and the coast. They were regarded as the most prosperous of the six surviving Moriori communities, because the small area of cleared land was proving highly fertile for grazing and cropping, and because the adjacent shoreline was rich in fish and shellfish. The chief at this time was Hirawanu Tapu; but the rising leader — the man who

---

* Some accounts refer to his being born at Porua, which is the same place (Waikaripi is close to the mouth of the Porua Creek).

** Nakahu had also had a girl, Merea, by an earlier husband, Matutuki.

This group at Manukau about 1889 includes Ngaria Riwai (second from left), Paranihia Heta (third left) and Heta Namu (fifth left).

Alexander Turnbull Library

played the same role in relation to Tapu as Tapu had previously in relation to Torea Takerehe — was Rangitapua Horomona Rehe, Tame's father.

If the community to which Tame Rehe belonged was Moriori by descent, its culture, however, was not. The Moriori language was no longer used there (even Tapu employed it only in the course of his scholarly investigations with Alexander Shand). Normally the inhabitants spoke Maori and some English. Their sources of Moriori tradition were Tapu and his wife Rohana, and these tended to be tapped only when evidence was required for claims in the Native Land Court. Rangitapua had shown some interest in becoming a repository for Tapu's knowledge in his early years; and he had published at least one article on the Moriori creation and arrival myths in the Maori language newspaper *Te Korimako* in 1883, when he was twenty-seven. But while Rangitapua viewed his Moriori identity as a feature of the present, he saw Moriori traditions as a thing of the past. His perspective was forward-looking; he was determined to pull his people out of the trough into which an obsession with the past had plunged them previously. Like Hapurona Pawa, Riwai Te Ropiha, Tamihana Heta and others of their generation, he was a practical man who reluctantly accepted the tragic history of his people and the findings of the Native Land Court. He had put these disasters behind him and sought to secure the physical and economic well-being of his family as best he could within the resources available.

The Chatham Islands 'culture' of the late nineteenth century was an amalgam of Maori and European elements shaped by the islands' isolation from mainland New Zealand. Most Maori and Moriori spoke Maori and some English; some Pakeha, such as Thomas Ritchie, spoke Maori. Fashions were casual in the extreme, except when a special occasion — a dance, a reception, the Waitangi races — called for dressing up. Funerals and tangihanga were conducted according to local custom. On ordinary days, boots and shoes were to be seen only in Waitangi — and then not frequently.

Chathams people had by this time turned in upon themselves. The prosperity that had seemed likely in the 1860s had not eventuated and the islands were hit hard by mainland economic depressions and the high cost of shipping stock and wool out and goods in. By the early 1890s Ritchie was bankrupt and had to abandon his leases and fine home at Kaingaroa (he raised his young family in a modest cottage at Okuki, north of Waitangi).* Walter Hood fared little better. Chudleigh survived only because of his caution, and because he had diversified his holdings by taking up land in the Waikato. The consequence was a general distrust among European settlers of the vicissitudes of the New Zealand economy, government, bureaucracies and institutions (especially banks and mortgage companies); Maori on the island had always mistrusted them.

Visitors noted this distrust, and a grim preference on the part of islanders to 'go their own way'. When Queen Victoria and her son Edward VII died, Chathams residents showed none of the near hysteria of imperial fervour provoked in New Zealand.** They showed no enthusiasm for filling in forms or setting up committees to satisfy public service procedures. The islanders developed a growing suspicion of strangers: because they so often brought influenza and other epidemics with them; and because many of them became instant experts and spoke and wrote about the islands and their inhabitants in highly pejorative terms when they returned home.

A succession of authority figures (resident magistrates, constables) reported their inability to persuade islanders to cooperate willingly with them. Yet, when threatened by authority, those islanders displayed a fierce loyalty to one another (and an unwillingness to inform on one another). And all activities could cease for a week if somebody died and a tangi was held, involving a blend of Maori and Pakeha practices unique to the island.

There were splits in the ranks, however. A few Europeans such as Chudleigh, the resident magistrates and their wives and the schoolteachers from 1890, lived apart from the rest of the population, like self-appointed gentry, and disparaged the coarseness of island life. All European settlers continued to recognise the Moriori as an older people, separate from the Maori. Many Pakeha residents and visitors discussed Moriori traditions and culture with them (with Tapu, until his death in 1900, with Rangitapua, with Riwai, Joe Mapu and Tamihana Heta). Maori, on the other hand, increasingly regarded the Moriori remnants and descendants as just another hapu on which intertribal marriage had already encroached. The Maori expression most often used to describe Maori-Moriori relations from this time was 'we are all one family'. Once the Land Court battles were settled in the 1870s, Ngati Mutunga on the island came to terms with the invasion and the killing of Moriori by mental and emotional absorption of their former slaves. Ngati Tama abandoned the Chathams and returned to their holdings in North Taranaki and around the Nelson district. There were no longer victors and victims on the Chathams: just one family that incorporated both and eroded the distinction between the two. This amnesia intensified throughout the twentieth century so that in time the Moriori position as tchakat henu (based on more than 500 years' occupation of the islands before the Maori arrival) was

---

* After fifty-nine years, he eventually left the island in 1923 to live in New Plymouth, where he died in 1934 aged ninety-one.

** A resident magistrate reported that when a steamer approached Pitt Island in 1910, a crew member hailed a resident ashore and said, 'Have you heard that the King is dead?' 'No,' came the reply, 'have you got my kerosene?'

overlooked entirely. By the 1980s, when most Maori first began to speak of tangata whenua rights on the islands, they were speaking of Maori rights.

Tame was not the Rehes' first or only child; but he was the first and only one to survive. In later life he told his farm manager Bob Jacobs that his brothers and sisters had all died within two weeks of birth. When Tame was born, however, Rangitapua decided that the child would be fed on condensed milk rather than at his mother's breast. This is reputed to have saved him and, according to Tame, to have been the source of his subsequent gargantuan appetite.

He grew up at Manukau with two other children: his cousin Mikaera Heta, who was eleven years older; and Ngaria Riwai, one year younger, who had been adopted by his aunt and uncle Paranihia and Heta Namu. In addition to Tame's parents, Rangitapua and Ihimaera, adults living at Manukau at this time included his father's cousin Teretiu and his wife Pakura, Hirawanu and Rohana Tapu, Apieta Tehume (another elder), and Joe Mapu and his wife Harirota (Tame's older cousin).

They grew their own fruit and vegetables, the latter in common plots. Meat was available from their own sheep. Cod and paua were taken from the rocks when the weather permitted. And there were periodic family foraging expeditions for eels, flounder, swans' eggs and ducks from Te Whanga. Further afield, the annual mutton-birding expeditions up the Tuku Gorge produced hundreds of birds for preserving.* The annual seasonal expeditions to the Sisters, the Forty Fours and the Pyramid, undertaken with Maori and other Moriori, brought back albatross and mollymawk chicks. The Manukau community worked hard for its sustenance; but it was well fed. And older members, such as Tapu, Rohana and Tehume, were always given a share of the fruits of foraging.

Six years after Tame was born the first school opened on Chatham Island, at Te One. He was enrolled and attended periodically from 1890 to 1896, sometimes from Waikaripi and at others riding the twenty kilometres to and from Manukau. He learnt to read and write and displayed a general intelligence well above average. There was no thought that he should pursue his studies, however. His father pulled him out of classes at the beginning of 1897 to help him work the land at Manukau, and to look after his mother, who was by now overweight and chronically ill.

At this age and throughout his adolescence, Tame coped easily with everything that came his way. School had taught him to read, write and count, and that was as much as he wanted from it. He grew into a fit and good-looking young man, not tall (1.74 metres) but muscular. He had no trouble with the physical side of farm work (his father was clearing land and planting additional pasture for sheep). He was a powerful back in the Owenga rugby team. And from his mid-teens he was regarded as sufficiently strong and responsible to join the older men on birding expeditions.

William Baucke has left a description of one such expedition — catching taiko petrels on the Tuku hill — which would have been little different from those in which Tame participated at the same age:

> The birds tunnel out carved burrows, which each revisits year by year. There they lay their
> egg — one — hatch it, feed their young till the pinfeathers appear, after which the parents

Opposite: At Manukau: Paranihia Heta, Ngaria Riwai and Pakura Teretiu. This photograph was copyrighted by Muir & Moodie in 1905 but was taken in 1889.

Auckland Institute & Museum

---

* In one expedition alone, led by Rangitapua and Riwai in 1903, the party returned with a thousand taiko, the bird that would be thought to be extinct before the 1970s, and which was rediscovered in small numbers in the 1980s.

Rangitapua Horomona Rehe, father of Tommy Solomon and leading Moriori elder from 1900 until his death in 1915.

Auckland Institute & Museum

return no more, and the youngster, now a mere globe of adipose, waits in its burrow till that fat has been transmuted into flesh. It is at this moment that [the hunter] comes along, and maybe sees a new burrow; in that case he gets a rod, chews the end to burr it, inserts it in the hole, jabs it about, withdraws it, if he sees fluff adhering, he inserts it in the hole, marks off the depth, lays the rod upon the surface in the direction of the hole, and at the end drills a neat round hole to admit his arm, takes out the bird, cuts the butt end of a tree fern whose curved cone, when ground into the hole, plugs it airtight, and lifting the plugs of previous seasons, continues his harvesting, chanting the while an exorcism to shoo away the demons that surround him everywhere. Each bird as he extracts it, he breaks the thigh bones of, interlocks the wings, forces the upper mandible through the V of the lower to seal the beak and prevent oil-soil of the feathers for ease of plucking, and goes home. There he hangs up his birds in bunches waiting to be plucked, the while the ambience vibrates with the wails of bird agony: for his teachers had not taught him that keeping mutilated birds alive waiting to be plucked, was more barbaric than mutilating humans for a difference of opinion, as our not too remote forefathers did. He however could reply — 'where were my cauldrons to scald them in?' — for when cold they cannot be plucked without tearing off therewith large clots of the outer tender flesh.

Far more exciting were the expeditions for albatross mutton birds. These were carried out each year by joint Maori-Moriori expeditions of several boats. The young of the para (royal albatross) were taken from the Forty Fours and the Pyramid in March and April; of the tataki (wandering albatross) from the Sisters between August and October; and of the ruru (Chatham Island mollymawk) from the Pyramid in December and January. Again, Baucke has left a characteristically vivid description:

Our trip . . . shall be to Tarakoekoea [the Pyramid] an islet southward of Pitt Island, distant seven miles, and rising from the sea in a 566 ft of, from one aspect, perfect pyramid, and, by clear moonlight, a towering majesty of frosted gold. It is the end of March. We are waiting for calm and tide at Glory Bay. Our boat's crew is a bunch of seven fearless stalwarts. No bribe will tempt admission of a white man to that crew: but I, knowing all the rites to be observed, and utterly trusted not to break them, am yearly 'counted in'. The night before we start, the roll is called and all the ancient rites handed down by the Moriori — in our case, consisting of instructions for behaviour — are delivered with stern solemnity. No useless words — no vague attention — to touch neither lizard, worm, small bird or other living thing we meet, mutton bird and albatross, and, above all, for instant obedience to every order, no matter what the hap or circumstance. Such as we feared that they may break the rules, are weeded out, no matter who they are or of what lineage.

  The adventure we are on is not a play of jests — every nerve is tense with alacrity to serve. It is 4 a.m. and the boats are afloat. The rowlocks 'chok' in unison. Just as the sun looks over the rim to see what we are at, we have arrived. A mass no longer of frosted gold with angles ruled by a master hand, but a distortion of eroded slabs, heaped in rocking libration higher up, glare down at us: no seeming landing anywhere: Yes at one spot, 30 ft above reach, a narrow shelf juts out. But how to get there? Watch us. Our Captain lays us off two boat lengths or more and tensely judges the majestic moving heaves of ocean hunch their backs and hurl their weight in ear-rending roars against the rock to half-way up, and retiring, fall in Niagaras of spume and froth, as if some stumbling titan had spilt his milk. Four times we make good our drift — those to land are forward in their place — a fifth sea-mountain approaches, we climb its camel hump; — 'Pull all'; we face the cliff, lifting with the rise; we all but touch the rock; 'Jump': The foremost and 'jump' have leapt together; 'Stern all', and the boat sinks in froth and boom and smother. Not an instant must she linger, but be clear of the long rock-slope or impaled upon its jags. So the process is repeated till those to land, with water kegs and biscuit bags, are landed. The same dexterity must be employed as we reship. The boat's nose rises to your level. Your Captain nods. You claw hold somewhere, and hanging grimly on, clamber in as best you can. All this has been rehearsed in dumb show thrash, calls commingle with the tumult, and are lost . . .

We have landed. We look well before we tread; displace one of those rocking slabs and you set free a torrent of destruction to those below. Above the highest storm line our slaughter begins, for from here to the summit, every flatlet the size of a waiter's tray contains a bird. It stares with glass-clear eyes at your approach and backs away, but your 18 inch long waddy clips it exactly where head and neck conjoin, and you pass on. New chums hit it 'on' the head, an insult it requites by squirting a stream of oil against your leg. Here and there you see a mound of blue mould with a monstrous beak attached. These are late chicks — you pass them by; for should you interfere with them, or rock larks, or lizards, destructive storms will instantly maroon you there — a Moriori code we, too, observe.

The birds we are after are full-fledged, but not yet lean enough to fly, whom, since their pin-feather appearance, the parent birds have left to be nourished by their own enormous fat. A handsome fellow, he sits there waiting for release — not the release he meditates. Our slaughter is now ended, so we collect the slain into convenient heaps to throw them down in stages; one lot we had to shift 13 times. We pile our 1280 cadavers on the lee side of the rock to cast them to the sea. Two men grasp each a wing of one bird, swing it twice and catapult it into space.

Presently, the sea below is dotted with floating blobs, which the waiting boats employed in fishing utterly disdain. At last I transgress the code anent 'useless words' and hazard 'Call the boats, the birds will scatter'. My answer is prompt and stern, 'you wait'; even so, for presently, as if by magic of an unseen broom, the birds are swept into a long queue, like a tail to our monster rock. At once the boats row to its outer end, gathering up to the last bird of the tail. Then only I am given reasons why — that the mana of the Moriori in that ritual last night was still in force, for, had I not seen? Of course, I remembered that jargon which not even the two Morioris of our party understood. After a secret ponder the mystery cleared, as thus: the wind split into two streams by our rock, followed its curve, and in seeking to rejoin, each swept up the flotsam in its path and laid it on the junction where their reunion met. On our return to shore I ventured to parade my find. 'Ha: Ha: listen to the infidel' 'Maringanui kai kore rangona te kanga i wako: (Fortunately your blasphemy was not heard at sea, or you had ruined us)'.

I have attended these adventures many times, and at each met some previously undiscovered joy of life. For there was coarse fare . . . coarse, but intimately understanding partnership of danger and mutual help . . . of various instant death and callous at the stare of it . . . of reading the meanings of customs, whose origins, ages long extinct, and crusted mayhap with the layers of aeons, are still charged with mana and essences to such as open them with faith . . . here one reads the inmost worth of the words, 'naked truth'.

As Baucke indicates, such expeditions required courage and strength of a high order. In the absence of other challenges, participation had become a proving ground for manhood on the Chathams, an initiation rite into adulthood. On his first such venture, however, at the age of sixteen, Tame Horomona almost lost his life.

In August 1900 the Maori and Moriori elders agreed that there would be no expeditions that year to the Sisters, twenty kilometres off the northern coast. The birds had been too depleted from previous harvestings; and the weather continuously rough. A group of young men, some of them, like Tame, waiting to make the journey for the first time, decided to go in secret. Twelve of them left Mairangi in three boats in the early hours of the morning of 28 August. They reached the rocks and gathered what they considered to be a good harvest of birds.

As they returned, however, the weather worsened. The wind was strong and the waves driving into the northern coast far higher than normal. In an attempt to land on Tupuangi Beach, two of the boats were swamped and all the occupants (nine men) drowned. The third boat, under the guidance of the most experienced member of the group, Robert Richmond, succeeded in racing the sea and was carried high up the beach on the crest of a wave — without overturning.

Richmond, Tame and Reta Brown — the boat's crew — were the only survivors. But they encountered no jubilation. The accident was the worst boating mishap involving islanders to that time, and the survivors were admonished and abused and forbidden to take part in further albatross expeditions for several years.

Tame's excess of high spirits — an outgrowth of his physical stamina, his gregariousness and a sense of mischief — got him into further trouble at the time. When he was in Christchurch with his father in 1901 aged seventeen, he asked for money to spend. Rangitapua, believing it would go on alcohol, turned him down. So Tame stole one of his father's cheques and forged his signature. Exasperated — this was apparently but one in a long line of instances of dishonesty — Rangitapua allowed a prosecution to proceed.

In court, Rangitapua apparently had second thoughts about the consequences of what he had set in motion and asked the judge to issue a warning, because Tame was 'a bad boy'. The judge did so and Tame left the court in a state of glee, immediately stole a bicycle, and was shortly afterwards stopped by police. Returned to court, he was sentenced to twelve months' imprisonment. Receiving news of the conviction by mail, Chudleigh commented in his diary, with characteristic lack of humanity: 'This boy is a man and could give many convicts many points in downright badness.'

Those who knew Tame well, such as Noel Cox of Whangamarino, disagreed.

Tommy Solomon, the year he survived the boating accident at Tupuangi Beach in which nine others drowned.

National Museum

Tommy, bearded, taking a boat ashore at Owenga in 1907 at the time of Lord Plunket's visit to the Chathams as Governor. The caption in the Christchurch *Weekly Press* read: 'The last of the Morioris bears a merry heart.'

Canterbury Museum

They believed the offences arose out of devilment and high spirits, and an unwise application of Chatham Islands *mores* to life in mainland New Zealand. They claimed that Tame did not have a calculating bone in his body, nor did he do or wish anybody harm. He simply did not foresee the consequences of his impulsive pranks or sleights of hand.

Tame's problems with money continued. He forged a further cheque in Christchurch and was fined for the offence. His father refused to pay and Tame was faced with the possibility of a further term in prison. This time, however, Noel Cox came to his rescue by borrowing money from his uncle, Bob Shand. Cox then took custody of fifty of Tame's sheep and kept them until the sale of wool had paid off the debt.

After his mother died in June 1903, Tame's succession to her land was delayed, 'for the son's protection against himself, as he [is] likely to be a spendthrift'. Instead, the Native Land Court gave Rangitapua lifetime ownership of Ihimaera's Manukau shares.

In an effort to help Tame accept responsibility, Rangitapua settled him on a forty-hectare farm at Whareama (where the elderly couple Temuera and Merepaha had lived before their removal to Manukau). At the same time he sought a wife for his wayward eighteen-year-old son. The obvious candidate for marriage with Tame was Ngaria Riwai, oldest child of Riwai and Kiti Te Ropiha and 'three-quarters' Moriori. It would have been a union that would ultimately have combined the resources of the Moriori reserve at Wairua with that of Manukau, and it would have united the island's two leading Moriori families. But for some reason, now unknown, the match was rejected: it is possible that Tame and Ngaria, who had been brought up together, decided that they knew each other too well and were not compatible; or that they felt their relationship was that of brother and sister; or that Riwai may have forbidden the union on some other pretext. Meri, his next youngest daughter, was only eight years old in 1903.

For whatever reason, Rangitapua looked to the South Island of New Zealand. The whole weight of Moriori experience in the nineteenth century led him to reject the possibility of marriage with a Ngati Mutunga woman (by this time there were no Ngati Tama still living on Chatham Island). South Island's Ngai Tahu, on the other hand, were the Maori with whom the Solomons felt closest affinity, and there had been a good deal of movement between the Chathams and Arowhenua Pa near Timaru and Rapaki and Port Levy on Banks Peninsula.

However it was arranged — and the details are no longer known — Tame Horomona Rehe was betrothed to Ada Fowler of Arowhenua, a seventeen-year-old half-Maori, part-Malay girl. The arrangement was made between Rangitapua and Ada's mother, Mata Kahu, a powerful matriarch at Arowhenua. Ada was her youngest and favourite daughter. The couple were married on the Chathams on 13 January 1903, and they moved at once to the farm at Whareama, where they lived for the next ten years.

Tame *did* settle down as his father had hoped. He worked conscientiously at Whareama and frequently found time to help Rangitapua at Manukau, particularly during shearing. He continued to throw himself into every sport offering on the island: athletics, rugby, shooting, boating, horse racing. In December 1905 he won the Chatham Island Jockey Club's cup for the first time on a horse named Manukau (he rode the same horse to victory again in 1910). He was energetic, successful and popular — all the things school textbooks were to claim that Moriori were not.

At times, however, he could not resist showing off. His strength was considerable and became a matter of legend. Once at Lyttelton, staying at a hotel, he uprooted a verandah post for a bet. On another occasion, also at Lyttelton, he asked a Japanese seaman to show him the full set of ju-jitsu holds. Some months later, when Constable H. Scott tried to remove him from the Mangoutu Hotel at Waitangi for disorderly conduct, Tame had a counter for every move that the policeman tried. He was eventually allowed to leave the bar of his own accord.

Tommy Solomon shortly after his marriage.

National Museum

Tommy with his first wife Ada (left) and Riria Riwai, later Mrs Preece.

B. M. Wilson

His most potentially serious offence also involved alcohol. The Chatham Islands was a 'proclaimed area', which meant that 'Natives' (a term that embraced Maori and Moriori at this time) were not allowed to drink alcohol off licensed premises.* In fact the law was broken frequently, especially at weddings and tangi. But Constable Scott's successor, G. H. Fry, heard that Tame was giving away whisky and wine and went to investigate.

The allegations were true. Tame had ordered a five-gallon keg of whisky and a case of twelve bottles of port from Forbes and Company, wine and spirit merchants of Lyttelton. Never one to drink alone, he had invited friends around to share this cache and given most of the port away. When Constable Fry arrived at his house, Tame offered him a bottle of port and — when this was refused — told him that the order had been delivered in error. He had wanted five gallons of vinegar and a case of tomato sauce, he said. Somewhere, somehow, the order had been misunderstood and whisky and port was the result.

Fry did not believe a word of the story but undertook to investigate before he prosecuted. While the constable was writing to the Lyttelton police, Tame telegrammed Forbes and Company, at sixpence per word, and asked them to back up his story. The telegram arrived well ahead of the police, and Forbes and Company obliged. As a consequence, Constable Fry was unable to press charges. Tame always claimed subsequently that the cost of the telegram had exceeded that of the likely fine.

As the years passed, it became apparent that Tame and Ada were unable to conceive children. This was a source of immense regret to them as would-be

A shearers' camp near Owenga with Ada Solomon (second from right) and Paranihia Heta, Tommy Solomon's aunt (right).
Auckland Institute & Museum

---

* This legislation remained in force until 1943.

Rangitapua Horomona and
Ada Solomon (seated), shortly
before their deaths in 1915.
Behind are the Riwai sisters
Ngaria and Riria. The boy at
left is believed to be Naria's son,
who died in 1920.

Hocken Library

parents; and to Rangitapua, who was distressed that the Rehe family (and the
Moriori line) would die out. It was possibly in response to this fear that the older
man married again in 1909. He was fifty-four; his bride, Ria Piwari, twenty-two.
She had already established her fertility by having two children, one of them,
Nuku Davis, to part-Moriori Bill Davis, Ani Davis's son. Rangitapua began
building a new homestead on the hill at Manukau to accommodate what he
hoped would be a large new family.

This move was made possible by a fortunate coincidence. A fishing company
had been formed in Wellington to catch and freeze blue cod at Owenga for transport to the mainland. It was decided to fuel the freezer's huge steam boiler with
wood, and the nearest source was the Rehe land at Manukau. Rangitapua was
offered four shillings and sixpence per cord, and the likelihood was that the company would need 400 cords per year. Thus he was able to expect (and got) an
annual income of more than £7100 from the sale of trees alone; and at the same
time he was getting the rest of his farm cleared for pasture at no cost to himself.
Tame came from Whareama to help with the cutting and carting of wood.

This enterprise, and the fishermen, houses, shop, post office and school that
followed, lifted considerably the prosperity of the district and the quality of life
at Manukau.* By 1913 Rangitapua was a comparatively wealthy man, a result of
royalties from timber and judicious farming. But his health was failing and his
second marriage was not a happy one (and there had been no children). So Ada
and Tame left Whareama and came to live and work at Manukau full time. They
were there when the First World War broke out in August 1914. The Chathams'
fifteen volunteers included one Moriori descendant, Bill Davis, and Rangitapua
made one of the largest donations (£11 16 shillings) to the islands' war fund.

The following year Tame suffered a double loss. First his father died, aged
fifty-nine. Then in November 1915, after being sent to Christchurch for the
treatment of tuberculosis, Ada died, aged thirty. Tame Horomona Rehe, now

---

* More than 200 people lived at Owenga before the freezer closed in 1937.

widely known as Tommy Solomon, was the owner of one of the best farms on Chatham Island and a widower. He still had no descendants and — as far as he knew — he and his father's sister Paranihia Heta were now the sole surviving 'full-blooded' Moriori.

Tommy Solomon's new life began very soon after Ada's death. At the tangi at Arowhenua, Tommy's powerful Ngai Tahu mother-in-law, Mata Kahu, decreed that he must marry again, and that 'what is in the family must stay in the family'. And so he was betrothed at once to Whakarawa Rene, a niece of Ada's (her mother had been Ada's sister Rora) and daughter of Pita Paipeta, one of the most influential men at Arowhenua.* She was sixteen, Tommy thirty-one. They were not strangers, as Rene had often stayed with Tommy and Ada on the Chathams, keeping the family link with Arowhenua alive. The following year they were married and Rene went to live with her new husband at Manukau.

Like his father, Tommy had ambitious plans for the farm. The property now had almost 720 hectares cleared of bush. Because it had rich forest soil that had not been overgrazed like most properties based on the peaty 'clears', it was fertile and grew luxuriant grass. Tommy was eventually able to run 7000 sheep on it, far more than the neighbouring Owenga Station, which was 11,600 hectares but able to carry only 5000 sheep. He extended and completed the homestead, filled it with high-quality furniture which he chose in Christchurch (including a pianola), obtained a diesel generator for electricity, finished fencing the property and built a new woolshed. And he was still collecting money from bush clearance. Most important, perhaps, Tommy now revealed himself to be a superb manager. He knew exactly what needed to be done on the farm to keep production levels high, and he had an exceptionally good working relationship with the men he

Owenga school pupils in 1930 including Bully Solomon (next to teacher George Gubbins at left), Bu (in front of Bully), Flora (centre at back) and Mannie (second from right, top, next to Mrs Gubbins). Other Moriori children include Charlie Preece and Stella Martin (at left below Mr Gubbins), Mattie Preece (sixth from left, back row) and Herbert and Bunty Preece in the centre rows.

Pat Prendeville

* There is a story at Arowhenua that, after Ada's tangi, Tommy and Rene were locked in a hut together for the night. When they were released by elders in the morning they were pronounced married. Tommy was always spoken of at Arowhenua as Tommy 'Chatty' — because of his Chatham Island origin, and the fact that he talked a great deal.

employed, who lived in and ate with Rene and him. For her part, Rene proved an excellent domestic organiser, able to grow vegetables, cook for large numbers of men, clean the house and outbuildings, mend clothes — and bear healthy children, all without appearing to extend herself.

Their first child, Charles Te Teira ('Mannie') was born in 1917; Thomas Tutanekai ('Bully') in 1918 ('Tutanekai' was in commemoration of the government steamer, which appeared around Manukau Point just as the child was born); Ngamare ('Bu') in 1920; Flora in 1922; and Eric Rangitapua in 1924. Mannie was named after Tommy's maternal grandfather, Thomas after his father, Bu after Tommy's aunt (Paranihia was also known as Ngamare), and Eric after Rangitapua. The Solomon clan was established, just as Rangitapua had hoped it would be. And all the children — with the exception of Flora, who died in 1935 — were to bear children of their own.

In 1918 the Rehe name was again before the court, this time because of the misfortune of Ria, Rangitapua's widow.

After Rangitapua's death in 1915, Ria had had a child, to another man, whom she named Wairata [Violet]. The baby died of bronchitis in 1917, and Ria's Piwari relatives believed this was an outcome of makutu. One year later, in June 1918, Ria was helping her family round up a mob of horses while she was heavily pregnant with another child. The animals swung towards her and bolted, and she was unable to stop them breaking away. This was regarded as further evidence that there was something wrong with her.

Within a week the baby was born, and Ria sank into what appears to have been puerperal fever. The family was now convinced that she was possessed by some evil spirit, and as she cried out in hallucination, they decided to beat the spirit out of her. They believed they had been 'told' to do this with kitchen utensils (noa objects for the removal of something tapu) and they flattened basins and enamel cups so as to use them as weapons. Then they hit Ria with them, and with a knife, an axe, and the butt of a gun. After the family had inflicted horrific injuries, they stripped her and plunged her into a cold bath. As a result of this maltreatment, Ria Rehe died on 29 June 1918.

Ria's father Hare Piwari and two other relatives were charged in Christchurch with Ria's murder. Before the trial could run its course, however, the influenza epidemic reached New Zealand and all three suspects caught it and died — an outcome which others in the Chathams were to see as spiritual retribution for Ria's death.

Other victims of the 'Great Flu' included Tamihana Heta's wife Erina; and Homai Heta, aged eight, whose tombstone identified her lovingly as 'mokopuna of Paranihia Heta'. In fact Homai was the daughter of Ngaria Riwai and Jack Martin, and she had been given to Paranihia as a baby because the old lady had brought up Ngaria, and to compensate for Heta Namu's death in 1910.

To take Paranihia's mind off this tragedy, and to give her some company in her small house on the flat at Manukau, Tommy and Rene Solomon gave her their first-born, Mannie, to bring up. This she did for four years, until her own ill-health made her unable to cope with a small child. In later years Mannie Solomon recalled little of that time, except that 'she only spoke Maori, and if I tried to speak English I'd get whacked over the head with her walking stick'. He did not remember whether or not she tried to instruct him in any of the Moriori customs she would have remembered from her own upbringing; except that she observed a rigid distinction between male and female functions and activities (if Mannie was bathed, no girl was allowed to wash in the same water, nor to use his flannels and towels; nor would she permit males and females to eat together).

In December 1919, Tommy Solomon and Paranihia had a visit from Henry Skinner, a thirty-two-year-old veteran of Gallipoli (where he had won a Distinguished Conduct Medal) and ethnologist at the Otago University and Museum. Skinner had come to the Chathams in the course of the most important study of Moriori origins and culture since Alexander Shand's investigations. Ambitiously, he summarised the background to his fieldwork:

> The view that then prevailed in New Zealand . . . was that the ancestors of the Morioris were representative of the earliest ethnic wave into New Zealand, whence they had been driven by later and more warlike immigrants from Tahiti. If this were the true account of their origin, and the Morioris did represent the earliest stratum of mankind in New Zealand, it was evident that a study of their social system, of their religion and of their art would yield results of the first importance . . .
>
> That explanation was based on traditional evidence derived from the Maoris, for Moriori tradition was vague and uncertain.* The [alleged] Maori tradition stated that the people whom the Tahitians found in New Zealand were black and that their culture was extremely primitive. But Moriori culture, though simple, was not in any way more primitive than that of the Maoris. And since a series of investigation in Moriori craniology had shown that the Morioris were in no degree less Polynesian than the Maoris, it became evident that the Maori traditional account was not in consonance with the facts and that an examination of all other lines of evidence was called for.

Skinner was being charitable. In fact, the state of knowledge about Moriori in New Zealand was more confused and contradictory than he indicated, and the so-called 'Maori traditional account' was largely fabrication.

Mention has been made of some of the theories about the origin of the Moriori that had been current in the nineteenth century. Most amateur scholars accepted that the Moriori were a 'different people' from the New Zealand Maori, and that they had been driven from New Zealand when the more enterprising and more combative Maori arrived there. The assumed differences of achievement between Maori and Moriori were thought to arise from different racial origins of the two peoples. Another question that had engaged scholars — but which remained unanswered — was where the Moriori had come from prior to their occupation of New Zealand.

In 1893, Professor J. H. Scott, Professor of Anatomy at the Otago Medical School, published a paper proposing that the Moriori and the Maori were both derived from an ancient interbreeding of Melanesian and Polynesian peoples, and that the Melanesian element was stronger in the Moriori, whose 'cranial capacity is somewhat less'.

The picture was further confused by a study by German scientists, published in 1903, which suggested that there had been a migration of peoples around the southern zone of the Pacific and made the absurd claim that the Moriori most closely resembled the Tasmanian Aboriginal.

Captain Gilbert Mair voiced the consensus current in New Zealand in 1904 when he said at a meeting of the Wellington Philosophical Society that 'originally the Morioris were quite a distinct race from the Maoris, but . . . they appeared sub-

---

* See Appendix Three. Skinner did not, of course, have access to material later available in the Sir George Grey collection of manuscripts.

sequently to have intermingled . . . and formed with them a mixed race, introducing into their own language a proportion of Maori words'. To dramatise his case, Mair then 'exhibited a skull of a Moriori slave who was killed in 1839 or 1840'.

This view received support from Professor John MacMillan Brown of Canterbury University, who, in 1910, dissociated himself from Alexander Shand's contention that the Moriori were Polynesian. This opinion was wrong, said the professor. 'I think they are merely a slight infusion of one aboriginal race, a small, dark race that occupied the Marlborough Sounds, and dwelt in . . . pit dwellings.' The dark colour was 'a sign that a large element of the ancestry of the Morioris had come from the hotter tropics . . .' Professor Macmillan Brown completed his interview by noting that 'he possessed a photo of the last chief of the Morioris, a youngish looking man, still alive, Solomon Rangipuni [sic] by name, of Manakau [sic], Chatham Islands. Unfortunately, there had been no purebred Moriori for him to marry, so he had had to content himself with a half-caste [sic].' The distinguished professor had never been to the Chathams.

The most coherent statements about the relationship between Maori and Moriori (but — as it turned out — the most misleading) were made by Stephenson Percy Smith in *The Lore of the Whare-Wananga (Part 2)*, published in 1915; and Elsdon Best in an article 'Maori and Maruiwi', published in the *Transactions of the New Zealand Institute* the same year.

Smith's book was based on Maori manuscripts that purported to record the teachings of an ancient school of learning of the Ngati Kahungunu tribe. The history of the manuscripts does not inspire confidence in their authenticity or reliability. They were rewritten and amplified on many occasions by different people. One ostensibly originated in material taken down in English in 1840 by J. M. Jury, an Englishman. These were copied into another book in 1876 and given to Whatahoro, Jury's son. The government interpreter, Thomas Young, then translated this material into Maori, and this version was copied by Whatahoro Jury. Percy Smith then copied out Whatahoro's version and translated part of it back into English for publication.

The resulting text appears to be the work of many writers, as the style changes from narrative to narrative. The provenance of the manuscript is one objection to *The Lore of the Whare-Wananga*. Another is that it contains information that could not possibly have been known to Maori until after Maori contact with the Chathams in the 1830s. It refers to the people of the Chatham Islands as Moriori — when there is no record that this term was in use before 1840; and it calls the main island Wharekauri, a usage that dates from about 1835; and all this while purporting to be the ancient lore of the pre-European Maori.

The parts of Smith's book relevant to the Chathams claim that the Polynesian navigator Toi-te-huatahi found New Zealand occupied in the middle of the twelfth century by a dark-skinned, inferior 'Mouriuri', who were partly absorbed by later Polynesian arrivals, and then attacked and driven from New Zealand, the remnant ending up in the Chathams. *The Lore of the Whare-Wananga* also purported to present evidence of a 'fleet' migration of canoes to New Zealand, this being the infusion of Maori which resulted in the inferior Mouriuri people being driven from the country. An examination of Smith's sources reveals that he concocted the fleet story by averaging out canoe traditions back 22 generations from 1900, coming up with the date 1350. In fact, prior to 1862, there were no Maori traditions of more than two canoes arriving in New Zealand at the same time, other than those of the *Arawa* and *Tainui*, whose genealogies are linked by marriage anyway.

Elsdon Best (left) and
Stephenson Percy Smith,
founders and stalwarts of the
Polynesian Society and creators
of myths about the Moriori.

Alexander Turnbull Library

Elsdon Best, an amateur ethnologist working for the Dominion Museum in
Wellington, had an even more detailed and more explicit story involving the
'Maruiwi' (which, as he admitted, was not the name of a tribe, but of one of the
chiefs of the early inhabitants of New Zealand):

The first of [the] Maori settlers are shown in tradition to have reached New Zealand
twenty-eight to thirty generations ago. At that time the Maruiwi folk were occupying
many portions of the North Island. They were the descendants of castaways who had
reached these shores in past times, and landed on the Taranaki coast. They had been driven
from their own land by a westerly storm. Their homeland, according to the accounts given
by their descendants, was a hot country — a much warmer land than this. In appearance
these folk are said to have been tall and slim-built, dark-skinned, having big or protuberant
bones, flat-faced and flat-nosed, with upturned nostrils. Their eyes were curiously restless,
and they had a habit of glancing sideways without turning the head. Their hair in some
cases stood upright, in others it was bushy.

When, during the fighting on the East Coast in the 'sixties', native prisoners were sent
down to the Chatham Isles it was noted that some of the women of No. 4 batch, who
came from Tarawera and Te Whaiti, much resembled Moriori women in physique, and
more particularly in their frizzy hair of Fijian appearance. A member of the Ngati-Awa
tribe there remarked, 'They are exactly like Moriori women.' A few of the Tuhoe hill tribe
seen by the writer at Te Reinga in 1877 had the same Fijian-like heads of hair.

The culture plane of these Maruiwi seems to have been lower than that of the Maori
of Polynesia, so far as we can gather from tradition. They are said to have been ignorant of
their own lineage, a sure mark of an inferior people in Maori eyes: 'They were an indolent
and chilly folk (*kiriahi*), fond of sitting round a fire. They slept anyhow, and in summer-
time went almost naked, wearing merely some leaves. In the winter season they wore
rough capes made of the fibrous leaves of *toi* (*Cordyline indivisa*), of *kiekie* (*Freycinetia
banksii*), and *harakeke* (*Phormium*). They were improvident in the matter of food-supplies,
and did not construct good houses, but merely rude sheds that our ancestors called
tawharau. On account of these peculiarities of those people our ancestors called them, in
contempt, *kiri whakapapa* and *pakiwhara*. It is also said that Maruiwi had overhanging or
projecting eyebrows, and were thin-shanked: an unpleasant and treacherous folk. Our
ancestors from Hawaiki and Rarotonga were given some of these women as wives when
they first arrived. Later-comers asked for them; in yet later days they took them, enslaving
women and young men. They always selected the best-looking women as wives; and those

women approved of it, for the Maori men were much better-looking than their own, and more industrious. Now, as time rolled on and generations went by, the mixed folk became numerous in the land, the result of the Maori taking Maruiwi wives. Then troubles between the two peoples became frequent, Maruiwi stealing from our folk and murdering them. At last it was resolved to exterminate them, and they were attacked in all parts. War raged all over the island — a war of extermination against all of Maruiwi not connected with the Maori. Thus were they slain at Te Wairoa, Mohaka, Taupo, Rotorua, Maketu, Tauranga, Tamaki, Hauraki, Hokianga, Mokau, Urenui, and all other places where they lived. Thus originated the famed saying "Te Heke o Maruiwi," as meaning death. But ever were spared those living with the Maori people. Some of the survivors of Maruiwi are said to have fled to forest ranges in the interior. Some fled to Arapaoa from Taranaki and Te Whanganui-a-Tara (Port Nicholson). These were attacked by the party of Tama-ahua that was going south to seek for greenstone. The survivors of Maruiwi fled to Rangitoto (D'Urville Island), where they were again attacked, and many women captured. The last seen of the remnants of these folk was the passing of six canoes through Raukawa (Cook Strait) on the way to Whare-kauri (Chatham Isles). Such is the story of the folk to whom this land belonged, and it is known that all of us are descended from Maruiwi — from those women taken by our Maori ancestors.'

Such is the account of Maruiwi, though much abbreviated, preserved by oral tradition. We here have, if reliable, a description of a people much inferior to the Maori in appearance and general culture. We are also told that the thick projecting lips, the bushy frizzy hair, dark skin, and flat nose often seen among the Maori are derived from Maruiwi. The writer has seen many natives showing these peculiarities among the Tuhoe Tribe: and we know from the traditions of that tribe that some of the Maruiwi folk at one time lived at Te Waimana, in their territory. Another tradition of much interest has been preserved by the Ngati-Awa people of the Bay of Plenty, to the effect that about five hundred or more years ago a canoe reached Whakatane with a number of black-skinned people on board. Presumably these were waifs from some island of Melanesia — possibly Fiji or the New Hebrides, or even New Caledonia, where the natives used double canoes. Forster's description of the natives of Malekula, as seen during Cook's second voyage, reminds us of the Maruiwi of Maori tradition. He remarks, 'They were all remarkably slender, and in general did not exceed 5 ft. 4 in. in height. Their limbs were often indifferently proportioned, their legs and arms long and slim, their colour a blackish-brown, and their hair black, frizzled, and woolly . . . They had the flat broad nose and projecting cheek-bones of a negro, and a very short forehead . . . All went stark naked . . . Their ugly features and their black colour often provoked us to make an ill-natured comparison between them and monkeys.'

This story drawn from the unreliable and polluted sources used by Smith, and from some additional unspecified ones, did more damage to a public understanding of the history of New Zealand than any published before or since. Its transmission through the Department of Education's *School Journal* imprinted on the minds of scholars, teachers, schoolchildren and journalists the notion that New Zealand was first inhabited by an 'inferior' Melanesian people, that they were driven from New Zealand by the more virile Maori of the Great Fleet migration, and that they fetched up on the Chathams. For Mouriuri and Maruiwi read 'Moriori', and there is an 'explanation' for the apparent backwardness and lack of resilience displayed by the Moriori in the nineteenth century. There, too, lies an implicit justification for the European conquest of New Zealand: 'Our ancestors only did to the Maori what the Maori did to the Moriori.' The pleasing, reassuring reverberations of this story in the mind of Europeans ensured the endurance of this myth for more than sixty years after Henry Skinner had set about disproving it.

For disprove it he did. In December 1919, he reported,

I was able to see the two surviving Morioris, to examine a number of old settlement sites, to study the carvings on the kopi trees and the so-called inscription above the cave on the west shore on Te Whanga, and to collect a considerable amount of hitherto unrecorded information from the settlers. Both of the inhabited islands were visited, and so it was possible to study at first hand the environment in which Moriori culture was nurtured. To me the islands will always be associated with memories of boundless hospitality, of long days in the saddle, and of nights spent before the great wood fires when talk, centering first on the ancient inhabitants of the group, passed on to every subject under the sun . . .'

Of his visit to Manukau on 19 December 1919, he wrote:

Solomon is of medium height, deep chested and stout . . . he has a brown complexion, black eyes, a well-shaped straight nose, good teeth, and straight black hair. He appears to be in every aspect a typical Polynesian, more so, in my opinion, than the average Taranaki Maori, and might easily be figured as a native of Tonga or Tahiti. He is very intelligent, speaks excellent English, and is a member of the local school committee. He lives in a well-built house of modern design, and farms his own land.

And of Paranihia Heta:

I also visited his aunt, who speaks Maori and knows no English. Her complexion is brown, with a very distinct ruddy tinge on the cheeks, much like many Maori-European half-castes. I have not seen anything approaching this ruddiness in any pure Maori, and I would have attributed it to a European strain had I not been assured to the contrary. Her teeth are extremely prominent, her nose is well formed, her hair is coarse, and black, and is curled in loose ringlets. She remained seated, with legs crossed in the usual Polynesian manner, throughout my visit. She appeared of average height and stout. She wore glasses, and was reading when I entered. I was informed by a neighbour that she was a good businesswoman, standing by her word, and very reliable, though perhaps a trifle keen.

Henry Skinner with members of the 1924 Chatham Islands expedition, about to leave Lyttelton. From left: R. S. Allen and J. Marwick (geologists), Skinner, G. Howes (entomologist), M. Young (marine biologist) and E. F. Northcroft (botanist).

Hocken Library

Combining his Chathams fieldwork with studies he had undertaken earlier of Moriori material in New Zealand and British museums, Skinner concluded that:

> The evidence derived from Moriori material culture is . . . decisively in favour of the New Zealand origin of that people . . . their relationship was closest with what I have elsewhere called the southern culture of New Zealand. We do not know from what district the Moriori ancestors migrated to the Chathams, but it must have been [one] in which this southern culture existed . . . the Moriori culture and the southern culture of the Maoris have points of relationship far and wide in the Pacific regions and . . . this relationship seems closest with eastern Polynesia and particularly with Easter Island.

Thus Skinner demolished the basis for the Mouriuri and Maruiwi stories. He showed conclusively that the Moriori were Polynesian, not Melanesian. He refuted the notion that they were a 'backward' or 'unintelligent' people. And he pointed out the inconsistencies and improbabilities of those parts of *The Lore of the Whare-Wananga* that purported to relate to the Chathams.

> It is necessary to speak plainly in this matter because the Maruiwi myth has taken firm hold on Maori history, and appears as the background of what may otherwise be regarded as definitive histories . . . not only has it been adopted in New Zealand, but it has influenced the work of well-known writers overseas. Further, the demonstration that one part of *The Lore of the Whare-Wananga* is unreliable must affect our judgement as to the reliability of the rest of that work.

Oddly, this call went unheeded. A smattering of scholars read and accepted the validity of Skinner's findings. The vast mass of New Zealanders, and many people outside New Zealand, remained trapped in the unreliable but more attractive features of the Maruiwi story.

There was another surprise in Skinner's book *The Morioris of the Chatham Islands*, which appeared in 1923. He announced that 'Dr Buck [Te Rangi Hiroa, the Maori ethnologist who would later head the Bishop Museum in Honolulu] discovered a full-blooded Moriori living among the Nga-Puhi at Dargaville . . . he came to New Zealand with Ngati-Mutunga as a child and is now over 70 years of age. I have Dr Buck to thank for photographs of the man.' Those photographs show a middle-aged Polynesian with a greying beard, and with eyes that look narrower than those of most Maori. His name is not given. The pictures were taken in Dargaville, apparently between 1920 and 1923.

Exhaustive enquiries in the Dargaville district and at the Bishop Museum in 1988 and 1989 failed to establish beyond doubt who the 'Dargaville Moriori' was. But one tradition* claimed that his name was Matene Totara Te Retimana, that his mother's name was Hine-Uru, and that she had been taken to Taranaki as a slave in the 1850s. This man had descendants, including a son also called Totara Te Retimana (who died in 1950); but they were divided over whether the account of his Moriori origins was accurate.

One other person has left a record of Buck's Moriori. Auckland poet Kendrick Smithyman believes he had the man pointed out to him when he was a child (he was born on Kaipara Harbour). In his poem 'The Last Moriori' he wrote:*

---

* From Hemi Hape, a Moriori descendant living in New Zealand.

** Smithyman wrote this poem from his childhood memory and without knowledge of the publicity given Buck's discovery.

Reputedly last of his kind,
quite surely one of the last
not crossbred but (as They said) pure
as pure goes, a Chatham Island Moriori
taken for a slave when a boy, taken
again in some other raiding, passed
from band to band, from place to place
until he washed up on the River . . .

. . . A tatty topcoat, bowler hat,
blanket which seemed to look your way
without seeing you from the stoop of a hut
at the Pa. A few weak hungers,
he survived. He endured,
already myth, beyond legends of his kind,
a poor fact. But the fact was, and the myth
was, and they endure together . . .

Henry Skinner was to return to the Chathams in 1924 as part of an even larger expedition (eleven men, including geologists, botanists, marine biologists, zoologists and magnetic surveyors). But he found no need to modify substantially the conclusions of his first study. When a revised edition of his book came out in 1928, *The Morioris*, under a joint H. D. Skinner/William Baucke byline, it largely confirmed the conclusions of the 1923 book: the Moriori were Polynesian and the probable source of their immediate migration to the Chathams was New Zealand. A large quantity of new material was contributed by Baucke, drawn from his memory and from his earlier articles for the *Taranaki Herald* and *New Zealand Herald*. It showed his characteristic blend of fact, imagination and prejudice; and it was written when he had been absent from the Chathams for more than fifty years. But many of his first-hand observations, about such things as Moriori fishing, birding and burial customs, were invaluable and available from no other source.

While accepting the Baucke manuscript for joint publication, Skinner felt compelled to warn readers:

It is . . . of uneven value . . . Baucke's account of Moriori physical anthropology is in conflict with all other accounts. Further, his estimate of Moriori intelligence, while true, doubtless, of the remnant that survived after the fifties, is certainly contradicted by the workmanship illustrated here . . . Moriori work in stone and bone need fear nothing in comparison with that of Samoa, and stands on an equal footing, say with that of the Society Islands, thus affording decisive evidence of Moriori intelligence in pre-European times . . .

One of the most interesting pieces of new information registered in the 1928 volume is its confirmation that Tommy Solomon was now the sole living 'full-blooded' Moriori. Paranihia Heta had died by 1928; so too had the Moriori whom Peter Buck had found in Dargaville but not identified.

Tommy Solomon knew little and (according to the evidence of his family) cared less about the debate that had raged on the mainland over the nature and origin of Moriori culture. Skinner had been the only one of the main protagonists to come and see him. And that was probably largely in the nature of a courtesy

This unnamed Moriori (left), found near Dargaville in the early 1920s, is clutched by Peter Buck as if he were a wildlife specimen that might take flight.

Auckland Institute & Museum

Skinner's party camped at
Te Roto, Chatham Island.

Hocken Library

call: he was no Hirawanu Tapu or Minarapa Tamahiwaka; he was not even a
Rangitapua Horomona Rehe. He had little specific information to offer
researchers about Moriori traditions. While he remained proudly Moriori in
identity, he was culturally Maori, since those among whom he lived and moved
and felt most at home were Maori. Like his father before him, he had seen no
future for Moriori culture distinct from Maori culture; so he had let many of its
vestiges fall away from him.

He did, however, sing Moriori waiata at island tangihanga (Jane Hough
remembered him doing so after Makarini Dix died). And he stressed to his
children that Moriori antecedents were something in which they should take
pride. In particular he emphasised the virtue of Nunuku's law over that of other
peoples and nations ('only fight till you draw blood, then stop'); and the signs that
were associated with death — strange animals appearing on the foreshore and
pods of stranded blackfish. He stressed, too, the need to remove fish and shellfish
from the shoreline before they were prepared for eating. Whenever the children
discovered skulls on the farm or on the burial ground at Manukau Point, they
were made to take them back and bury them immediately; Tommy respected the
presence of his ancestors.*

The other respect in which Tommy showed himself to be Moriori was in his
patronage of other people of Moriori descent. By the 1920s, those with Moriori
antecedents, Joe Mapu, Rakete Tipene ('Old Lockett') and his son Arthur
Lockett, Tamihana Heta, Joe Ashton, the Riwais, Bill Davis — all gathered
frequently at the Solomon homestead with their families for meals, card games,
or both; and all looked to Tommy as their leader, even though he was a younger
member of the group. This was not because of any suggestion of hereditary
chiefly status; it was an acknowledgement of Tommy's confidence and natural
leadership qualities, of the resources for entertainment that a successful farm
allowed him, and perhaps of the fact that he did have this almost mystical quality
that the others lacked — 'pure Moriori'.

---

* Skinner and others did urge Tommy to write his autobiography, and his eldest son says he toyed with the
idea. But in the end he doubted that he had sufficient material to interest anyone beyond the family.

Arthur Lockett of Te One,
half-Moriori.

Maui Solomon

Whenever visitors came to the island to investigate Moriori culture or simply to meet a Moriori, they were always directed to Tommy at Manukau; just as their predecessors had been sent to Hirawanu Tapu thirty or forty years before. Tommy may not have been able to *tell* them a great deal. But he always made them welcome and their visit memorable.

A small number of people resented Tommy's status and growing fame as a Moriori. One was Maui Pomare, son of Wi Naera, who had spent part of his youth on Chatham Island before being educated at Te Aute College and at the Seventh Day Adventist College in Michigan. He returned to New Zealand as the first Maori doctor, and subsequently entered Parliament as member for Western Maori in 1911. In 1912 he became Minister of Health in the conservative Reform Government, where he was more popular among his Pakeha colleagues than he was among the other Maori members.

In 1919, anticipating the visit to New Zealand of the Prince of Wales, Tommy Solomon organised a petition to Parliament asking the Government to provide special transport to allow the islanders to see the prince on the mainland. He forwarded it to Pomare and nothing further was heard of it. When Henry Hough visited the minister shortly afterwards and asked why the petition had not been presented, Pomare found the document and showed it to him. 'Just fancy,' he said, 'just fancy you letting that Moriori slave put his name at the top of the list ahead of your own people.' Hough was upset by this outburst but spoke quietly to his Ngati Mutunga relation. 'Maui,' he said, 'those things are forgotten now. We don't live that way. We're all one people and Tommy is one of us.'

At this period in island life, a curious reversal of previous Maori-Moriori positions was apparent (and this may have had some bearing on the attitudes of people such as Maui Pomare). Whereas in the mid-nineteenth century the Maori had control of major resources and the Moriori were deprived and wretched, in the 1920s the two most successful non-Pakeha families on the island were

Moriori: the Solomons and the Tamihana Hetas. Tamihana had remarried and lived in a large homestead on 120 hectares at Wairua. While the Mapus and the Locketts were not as affluent, they, too, were farming successfully and lived in what were — by the standards of the day — well-equipped homes. Most Maori families on the Chathams, totalling about 250 people, were not doing so well. Their good land was on lease to Europeans. They lived in overcrowded huts, and many of them suffered from physical and social diseases. A succession of doctors and police constables complained to the authorities about Maori living conditions without conspicuous success; and the doctors in particular had a high rate of turnover, because they found working on the Chathams strenuous, thankless and unproductive.

For Tommy Solomon, the early 1920s represented the years of his prime. In spite of increasing stoutness, he was still fit and strong. The Manukau property continued to provide him and his dependents with a comfortable living and his stock was better cared for than almost anybody else's on the island. He would travel to Christchurch each year to organise farm business and purchase new equipment, staying at the People's Palace, hiring taxis for days at a time, and cutting a memorable figure in his dark suit and homburg hat.

On Chatham Island he had been elected to the Owenga School Committee (by a largely Pakeha constituency) and took a close interest in his children's educational progress. He coached the Owenga rugby team, which each winter played in competition with the other settlements. His horses continued to win the Chatham Islands Cup, though he no longer rode them himself.

The role in which most islanders remember him at this time is that of master of ceremonies at dances in Owenga and Waitangi. Again, he would be dressed immaculately: black suit, white shirt, bow tie, white gloves and dancing pumps. He would announce the dances with a welter of blarney and jokes (lancers, schottische, quadrilles, military two-step, waltz); and he would call the figures in the ones that required it. His genius was to ensure that partners changed frequently so that everybody mixed; and to keep the participants laughing all evening. Those who had trouble with the steps found him down among them, helping them. People who were adolescents or young adults at this time recalled him as a man of fun and generosity, a person who deftly smoothed the way for their courtships and transition to adulthood.

Tommy was equally generous in other ways. He was still careless with money, only now he had it to spend. Anyone who was short of cash had only to ask him and he would pass it over without hesitation. Some of these 'loans' were repaid; most were not. When some of the Owenga fishermen with large families got into financial difficulties and finished up owing him more than £100 each for meat, Tommy wiped their accounts from the books and said they could start new ones. When he bought a sausage machine in Christchurch (and sent away for a butcher's recipe), he attached it to his shearing-shed engine and made pork and beef sausages for his family and friends and gave away dozens more in Owenga.

At home he entertained frequently, having other Moriori families, Maori friends like the Tuutas or Pakeha neighbours for dinner. He spoke English or Maori, depending on the company. Then he would put music on the gramophone, produce a bottle of square gin and lay out the cards for an evening of poker. One player recalled him taking on the local Indian storekeeper, a Mr Din, and cleaning him out because the man sitting all evening behind Din and singing

Roger Riwai at Owenga with one of his stepdaughters.

Canterbury Museum

179

Tommy Solomon taking part in the pistol-shooting competition at the annual Owenga sports day.

Pat Prendeville

softly in Maori was in fact calling out the cards that the storekeeper held. Tommy enjoyed the joke immensely and returned Din's money at the end of the session.

Those who were close to Tommy at this time — Moriori, Maori and Pakeha — were more than fond of him. They *loved* him, his spontaneity, his generosity, his sense of fun. And they turned sharply on a minority of Pakeha islanders who bad-mouthed him. Some spread the rumour that one of his grandparents was Chinese; others resented his success with the farm and could not believe it was achieved without duplicity of some kind; others were scathing about his appetite and his growing weight — all these criticisms seemed to stem from the fact that the perpetrators had been brought up to believe that the Moriori were an inferior 'race' and — despite the results of Skinner's research — they could not accept clear evidence to the contrary.

The high regard in which Tommy Solomon was generally held, on the Chathams and on the New Zealand mainland, was revealed in 1924 when he went with Rakete Tipene — 'Old Lockett' — to collect his mail from the Waitangi Post Office. Among the envelopes passed to him was a large one, registered, from Wanganui. He showed it to Lockett. 'Do you know anyone in Wanganui?' the old Moriori asked. 'No,' said Tommy, 'I don't think so.' 'Then let's go somewhere private to read it.'

When they opened it, the letter turned out to be a lengthy document from Tahupotiki Wiremu Ratana, the prophet and faith-healer who had established a religious movement at what came to be called Ratana Pa, south of Wanganui. Six years earlier, when he was forty-five years old and recovering from the great influenza epidemic, Ratana had seen a small cloud rise from the sea near his home and hover over his house. From the cloud Ratana heard the voice of God telling him that He had selected the Maori as the new Chosen People, and that Ratana's task would be to unite them and turn them to God.

Ratana's letter to Tommy explained the origin of his vision and recounted the successes Ratana had had in faith-healing and in politics (in 1922 his son had come within 800 votes of unseating Maui Pomare). It asked Tommy to call a meeting of Maori on the island to explain the Ratana mission and to recruit converts to the movement. It ended with a quote from Isaiah: 'A son will be born, and the Kingdom will be upon his shoulders.'*

The meeting was duly held, at Arthur Lockett's house at Te One, and a large number of Maori joined the Moriori to debate Ratana's request. Most were swept along by the vitality of the prophet's message, and by the fact that the death of Te Whiti O Rongomai in 1907 had left Te Ati Awa in a religious vacuum. Over the next five years almost all the Maori families on the island embraced the Ratana faith (often while retaining simultaneous allegiance to the Anglican Church) and T. W. Ratana sent them a minister, the Reverend Paniora Te Arahu. Tommy Solomon declined overtures to assume leadership of the movement on the island, but he remained a Ratana advocate until his death.

In 1925 the Chatham Islands County Council was established and Tommy elected as a foundation member, representing the eastern riding. Its purpose was to collect rates on land and spend these to provide amenities on the Chathams,

Opposite: Tommy Solomon photographed outside a shipping office in Christchurch on one of his last trips to New Zealand.

Canterbury Museum

---

* Before he died, Te Whiti had used the same text to anticipate the leader who would follow him. Some thought that it referred to Maui Pomare; others to Ratana. Its use in Ratana's letter to Solomon was enough to convince some islanders that Tommy was being identified as the instrument of God's will. (Interview Jane Hough.)

especially roads, and to take over most aspects of public administration. This exercise was not at first a success. Most Maori (and Moriori) could not be persuaded to pay rates — on the ground that they had never done so before and many lived at a subsistence level and were not part of a cash economy — and at one time the council was forced to close down for two years because it could not clear its overdraft.* When the second council was elected in 1928, Tommy was declared ineligible for membership because of non-payment of rates.

He was also involved in a further experiment in local government. In 1928 he was appointed by the Government a member of the first Wharekauri Maori Council, which was to take special responsibility for Maori health and social conditions on the island. Other members included Piritaka Pomare (son of Wi Naera and half-brother of the Minister of Health, Sir Maui Pomare), Reta Brown, who had survived drowning on the albatross expedition with Tommy in 1900, George Tuuta, who was Tommy's closest Maori friend, and Constable Ryan Holmes (appointed resident magistrate two years later).

The Department of Health, which had pressed for the establishment of the committee, soon learned about Chatham Islands inertia. In spite of repeated prodding from Wellington, the Wharekauri Maori Committee met only once in four years: to elect a chairman (Piri Pomare). After this it lapsed into unremitting inactivity. Ryan Holmes wrote to the Director-General of Health:

> No meetings have been held and no interest has . . . been exhibited by any of the members . . . There is a lack of cohesion amongst the Islanders as well as an indifferent attitude to anything in the way of progress. As a rule there is seldom sufficient interest long enough maintained in anything taken up to complete it or carry it into effect, and even if started it would only mean trouble for the promoters and failure for a certainty in the end . . .

When the first council's term of office expired in December 1932, still without another meeting being held, all former members were reappointed except Tommy Solomon. He was by now too ill to leave home.

Throughout the latter half of the 1920s Tommy was caught in the grip of his vast appetite and his body progressed from stoutness to gross obesity. Eventually he could only mount a horse by either stepping off a small cliff face next to the animal or climbing a ladder. More often he rode in and out of Waitangi in a horse-drawn sledge, with an armchair bolted to the floor. He would take a boy with him, usually Mannie, to open and close gates. By the end of the decade he was reputed to weigh more than 190 kilograms and had become as famous for his bulk — on the island and in New Zealand — as for his status as the 'last Moriori'.

Various theories have been put forward to explain Solomon's size. There may have been a hereditary factor. Both his parents, but especially his mother, were overweight by the time they died. Some alleged that the absence of fat in the traditional Moriori diet had left Tommy with a genetic craving for that substance. Others suggested that compulsive eating was a depressive reaction to constant reiteration that he was the last Moriori and that his doomed people would die out with his passing.

Whatever lay behind it, the island hummed with stories about his capacity for eating. His children remembered that he reserved the fattiest parts of the roast joints for himself, and consumed mutton birds in large quantity when they were

---

* To get around this problem, and the fact that many Chatham residents were not landowners, the council began rating goods that came across the wharf from 1936.

available. Bessie Clough recalled him eating tomatoes by the case. And James Fahey, who worked on the farm, remembered Tommy cooking him a midday dinner when the rest of the family were away. He had prepared roast meat and potatoes and two plum puddings. Both men had a large helping of meat and potatoes, then Tommy put half a plum pudding on each plate. Fahey cut his half in half, and put one piece back on the dish. He had to struggle to finish his quarter. Tommy meanwhile ate his half-pudding, plus Fahey's rejected quarter, and then the entire second pudding — all in one sitting and without difficulty.

Eventually his legs were unable to sustain the weight of his body. He could still walk, but only with the aid of crutches. He supervised farm work from the sledge. Outwardly, he remained his usual cheerful self, however, and Noel Cox received a spirited letter from him in August 1930: 'We had a good season this year. Sheep are looking well and my Hoggetts [sic] in good condition. But my cobber Mr Sim [a neighbour on Owenga Station], his Hoggetts are dying like flies . . . twenty and forty in one place. He [is] supposed to be a smart man. Only talk I think.'

Bessie Clough, a Pakeha, arrived at Owenga at about this time and received an invitation to visit the Solomons.

> Mrs Solomon had seen me approaching so she came down the hill to welcome me. Although I'd been told Tommy was outsize, I wasn't prepared to see such a large man . . . as I approached what was then his usual resting place, the kitchen couch, he looked up from his game of patience. I found myself looking into a pair of friendly brown eyes. Tommy had a pleasant face and dark skin. His hair was black and straight . . . I felt at once I had met a friend, though I could feel him summing me up as we chatted . . .
>
> Over the next three years I never saw him on his feet. He was either sitting on his couch at the back of the kitchen table or doing the rounds of the farm on a sledge pulled by two horses . . . He was still an excellent farmer and Manukau was in good order. He

Tommy uses a ladder to mount Jessie, his favourite horse, at Manukau.

Alexander Turnbull Library

Tommy and his family in the dray at Owenga. Rene Solomon is behind him, and at right, are Bu, Flora and Eric Solomon. Jack Martin stands alongside the dray and Cyril Black at right.

Pat Prendeville

knew how to handle men and generally got the best out of them. The farm then carried 4,500 sheep and 100 head of cattle.

The homestead was on a rise facing north, with a fantastic view of the Pacific Ocean . . . It was large and squarish with a verandah around the north and west sides, and was supplied with its own electricity. The inside was furnished comfortably with gadgets any New Zealand housewife would have been proud to own. The living room had a cabinet gramophone with piles of the latest records, a pianola and the latest radio. Everything Tommy bought was the best, and he did it to make the isolated life on the island more comfortable for Rene and the family.

Rene employed an island girl for home help by this time, and everything was always spic and span. It was no easy task coping with a house that size, a sick husband, five young children and four or five farmhands, all needing to be fed. The kitchen was large with a double-oven stove. The long white table along the centre of the room groaned with food. It was scrubbed every morning. Rene turned out bread and buns as good as those from any city bakery . . . outside there was a fine miniature butcher shop, with large meat hooks, a block and a brine tub. Like the rest of the homestead, it was spotless.

Despite his good humour and goodwill, Tommy's health was worsening. He found breathing increasingly difficult and his leg joints developed painful rheumatism. When Mannie left school, he was assigned the job of looking after his father: he remained with him all day to fetch things, he helped him wash and bathe, he took him to the toilet, and he rubbed his legs when they were painful.

Sometime in 1931 the island's medical officer, Dr H. V. Drew, told Tommy that his heart was damaged by his size and that if he did not lose weight rapidly he would die. Then began the most painful time his family would remember. Rene reduced the quantity of his meals drastically and cut all fat off his helpings of meat.

He did lose three or four stone over the next two years. But it was not easy for him nor for those around him. Bessie Clough remembers him sitting at the table angry because Rene refused to make him some dish he had asked for. 'He got his knife and fork and banged them on the table. He just went mad. Another day there was something else he wanted and she wouldn't give it to him — because she loved him and didn't want to lose him. So he got to his feet, grabbed the white tablecloth and yanked it sharply off the table. All the food and utensils went all over everybody and onto the floor. Rene started to cry and went out of the room. I followed her and said, "You have to understand what it's like for him. He's starving." '

Tommy's last appearance at Waitangi was on race day, December 1931. For those who witnessed his arrival at the course, the occasion was unforgettable. Jane Hough was there.

> Tommy came in the sledge with Mannie, who was always with him by this time. As the horse swung the vehicle off the Owenga road into the sports ground, my aunt, Betty Urutahi, got to her feet and began to karanga. Something that had never happened there before. Everybody was suddenly quiet and turned to see what was going on.
>
> She called out in Maori to Tommy, to his father and mother, and to all those other Moriori old people she had known, who were now dead. And she called out to the tipua Moriori — the spirits that the Moriori had been able to raise in the days when they ruled the island. She must have had some sort of premonition about Tommy. It was her way of saluting him and farewelling him, and of acknowledging that his people were the first people of the island.
>
> Tommy didn't say anything. He just stopped the sledge and listened to her, with his head bowed. The tears were rolling down his cheeks. The next time my aunt saw him he was dead.

Despite Tommy's waning health, visitors continued to come to him for information about the Moriori and island life. In February 1933 A. W. B. Powell of the

The last photo: Tommy Solomon's coffin is pushed and pulled to the waiting grave. The men in the centre are James Fahey (left) and George Tuuta.

Pat Prendeville

The Solomon homestead at Manukau, 1988.

Michael King

Auckland Museum called at Manukau, to ask about Chathams shells and seafood items in the Moriori diet. He was received warmly and went away with happy memories of Manukau hospitality and Tommy's sense of humour. He promised to return.

The following month, however, Tommy caught pneumonia, a serious illness in one his size (he was now a little under 190 kilograms, but still obese). A registered nurse who lived at Owenga, Aletha Clough, had moved into the house to help Rene look after him. For the first five days he was severely ill and unable to leave his bed. Then the crisis passed and he was able to get up for part of each day.

On the morning of 19 March he was sitting in his wide cane chair in the lounge, trying not to let Rene see that he was struggling for breath. Then he called the nurse and tried to say something to her, but she could not understand him. He was obviously in considerable discomfort. She in turn called Rene and asked her to feel his pulse, which was fading: but it was too much for the wife who had been dreading such a scene for years, and she left the room. Shortly afterwards his heart, enlarged and strained by a decade of overwork, simply stopped, as Dr Drew had warned him that it might. He was forty-eight years old.

The following day a Press Association message was filed to New Zealand in Morse code from the Chathams radio station. It recorded

the death of Tame Horomona or Tommy Solomon, the last pure-blooded survivor of the ancient Moriori race. In this unique position . . . Tommy Solomon has been a centre of much interest for many years past. He was recognised as a great authority on the history and traditions of his people, and it was customary for all visitors to the Chathams to seek him . . . His passing will be widely regretted, not only on account of the strange and tragic story of his people, thus brought to a close, but because of the kindly and genial qualities of the man that left pleasant memories with all who met him.

EPILOGUE

Renaissance

WITH TOMMY SOLOMON'S DEATH, MOST NEW ZEALANDERS accepted the claims of newspaper obituaries that the Moriori were now extinct. Others who could have provided an alternative focus for Moriori identity on Chatham Island — Rakete Tipene, Joe Mapu, Joe Ashton — had predeceased Solomon; and Tamihana Heta, scarred survivor of so many battles for Moriori rights, died in 1934, still trying to secure title to some of the land which he farmed. Many of the descendants of these people, who might have been expected to take a lead in island affairs, had not survived young adulthood. Nuku Davis, grandson of Ani Wi Hoeta, had shot himself in 1925 because of unrequited love for Edith Painter. Four members of Moriori families — three of Tamihana Heta's sons and one Ashton — were lost from a boat off Kaingaroa in July 1931 on their way to a rugby match at Owenga; the bodies were never found.

Rene Solomon tried to keep her family at Manukau, but she had never been happy there. With Tommy gone it became unbearable, particularly after she began to quarrel with the farm manager's wife. Before the end of the decade she had taken the children (except Flora, who had died in 1935) back to Temuka. Bill Davis, too, the man most able to assume leadership of Moriori descendants, abandoned the island, during the Second World War. Another of Joe Ashton's sons, Mana, was killed in that war. The one surviving went to live in New Zealand.

The 'most Moriori' person remaining on the island was Arthur Lockett, executor for Tommy Solomon's estate, who farmed at Te One. His father had been 'half-Moriori', his mother 'full'. He too regarded himself as Moriori but did not advertise the fact and did not become the magnet for Chathams visitors that Tommy had been. He was happy to talk about Moriori history and traditions with anyone who was interested, however, such as Bill Burt from the radio station. Lockett died childless in 1957.

The other family recognised as a Moriori clan, and who were, like Lockett, 'three-quarters' Moriori, were the children of Riwai Te Ropiha living at Owenga. But they too were discreet about their background. Roger Riwai, a retiring man, married an English nurse, inherited her four children from a previous marriage, and died in 1943. Ngaria Riwai, who had grown up with Tommy Solomon, married a South Island Maori fisherman, Jack Martin, raised a family at Owenga and died there in 1951. And Riria married Charlie Preece, who worked at the fish freezer, and produced six children who were 'three-eighths Moriori'; one of them, Alfred or 'Bunty', became chairman of the Chatham Islands County Council in 1973; another, Riwai, eventually became the island's Anglican pastor. Riria died in 1942.

It was not until Bully Solomon, Tommy's second son, brought his family back to the Chathams in 1950 and began to manage the Manukau farm that the island again had a strong Moriori presence. Although he was 'half-Moriori' in genetic terms, Bully identified completely with that side of his heritage and so did his sons. Through him, the Solomons resumed their role as the Moriori 'first family' at a time when other people with a comparable degree of Moriori inheritance, such as the Preeces, did not activate or draw attention to that part of their background.

In New Zealand, the contours of Elsdon Best's Maruiwi myth ran like a ridge through the national consciousness, overshadowing the forgotten work of Shand and Skinner. Book after book repeated the lie that the Moriori were a separate race who had been defeated by the Maori and taken refuge in the Chathams, and that they had been dark-skinned, repulsive-looking and shifty — all the images of European race-fear concentrated into one metaphor. The picture was further confused by amateur historians such as Herries Beattie writing about the earliest South Island Maori tribes as 'Moriori', confirming in the public mind that they too were remnants of the defeated pre-Maori people. These myths were propagated widely through schools, where several generations of New Zealand children were taught to look down on the Moriori as an 'inferior race'. Letters to the editor kept these negative images alive and insisted that Maori had disqualified themselves from special assistance or consideration from the majority culture because of their savage treatment of the Moriori in prehistoric New Zealand.

The unending barrage of negative and confusing propaganda had a powerful effect on Moriori descendants. Hundreds of them, especially those who lived on the New Zealand mainland, came to believe that it was a matter of shame to be Moriori; or that life was easier for them if they did not mention the fact. For three decades many of them concealed Moriori origins and — if asked — spoke of themselves as Maori; some who could pass as European did so.

A turning point for these people was reached in 1980, when Television New Zealand screened a documentary on the Moriori, written and produced by Bill Saunders (one of Samuel Deighton's descendants). This programme discredited the myths and emphasised important facts about Moriori: they were not a separate race; they were the most Polynesian of Polynesians; they had not been defeated and driven to the Chathams by the Maori; they were not a backward people with an inert culture; they had adapted superbly to their environment; their decline had been caused mainly by the introduction of disease and the effects of Maori conquest and colonisation in the nineteenth century.

In addition to provoking a reassessment of the value of their antecedents among Moriori descendants in general, the programme led to the first reunion of the Solomon family, at Temuka in 1983. Three of Tommy's children were still alive at this time; they in turn had thirty-four children among them and a growing number of grandchildren. After this hui, Bully Solomon stressed to the press that Moriori descendants *were* Moriori, if that was what they chose to be; and that it was a matter of pride to be so identified. The family as a whole agreed to collect money to raise a statue of Tommy Solomon at Manukau: so that he would be remembered, and to act as a memorial to all Moriori people. They also decided to use the project as a means of re-establishing Moriori in the public mind as tchakat henu of the Chathams, trying to sweep away the negative residue of the Maruiwi myths, and making membership of the Moriori iwi a matter of mana rather than a source of shame.

The public appeal for funds for the statue and an unveiling hui produced some unexpected reactions. The old myths about Moriori origins were aired in letters to the editor columns and on talkback radio. The new element was an apparent Maori campaign to deny the existence of the Moriori. A professor of Maori alleged that mention of the Moriori was designed to justify what Pakeha had done to Maori and to embarrass Maoridom, while a Tainui leader called the statue project 'a fraud against Maoridom'.

> It is a fraud because Tamehana [*sic*] Solomon was no more Moriori than I am. Its purpose is to permanently place my ancestors in the same category as Hitler and Eichmann when they exterminated millions of Jewish people . . . The psychological poison in that statue must be 'killed' before it is erected for the sake of our tupunas (ancestors) and all people who have Maori blood running in their veins.

Another Maori correspondent to an Auckland paper commented: 'Let us get one thing straight: there were no such people as the Moriori . . . Maori people are wounded every time ignorant talk about the Moriori arises. Please let us have no more of it.'

The Moriori presence persists after Tommy Solomon: Bully Solomon (his son) and Arthur Lockett (Tommy's executor) in front of the Te One church in 1951.

Alexander Turnbull Library

A pendulum had swung wildly from one side of the argument to the other. From being reviled as a degenerate race, Chatham Islands Moriori were now being told they did not exist and never had. Maui Solomon, a Wellington lawyer and son of Mannie, had taken over leadership of the statue campaign after his Uncle Bully died in 1985. He replied that the purpose of the project was to gain official recognition from Maori and Pakeha that the Moriori were not a myth, that they were tchakat henu of the Chathams and a component of New Zealand history as a whole.

> Mr Maniapoto talks of Maori people being wounded every time ignorant talk about the Moriori arises . . . the only 'wound' evident is that inflicted upon the Moriori by two hundred years of persecution, prejudice and neglect. The healing process has now begun but much has yet to be achieved before the great wrongs perpetrated against the Moriori can begin to be addressed . . . The truth about the Moriori must be told if the healing process is ever to be complete.

The life-size cement fondue statue of Tommy Solomon was unveiled at Manukau in December 1986 by the New Zealand Prime Minister, David Lange. He told the accompanying hui (the largest crowd assembled in one place in the Chathams since the Moriori council at Te Awapatiki in 1835) that New Zealanders as a whole had a duty to see that the Moriori, having lost all else, did not lose their place in history. 'They were not a myth. They were in these islands a real people. We cannot make them live again, but we can tell the truth about what happened to them.'

Taking up this theme, Maui Solomon pleaded for Moriori to be given their fair place in the history taught in New Zealand schools. 'Until then, the untruths and commonly held misconceptions about our people will continue. Before anything more is taught, however, that history must be carefully researched to compile a clear and accurate record from the vast amount of evidence scattered throughout New Zealand and the Chatham Islands.'

Only one of Tommy Solomon's children, Mannie, the eldest, lived to see the statue erected (he was to die in 1997). Bully and Bu had died during the fund-raising period. Eric had died the year the television documentary was shown, in 1980; and their mother Rene in 1968.

A Moriori revival spread from the statue unveiling and the publicity that accompanied it. Further individuals and families 'came out' and declared their Moriori ancestry and their interest in reclaiming their Moriori heritage. The Preece family (Riwai descendants) joined the Solomons in 1988 to set up a Rekohu Claims Committee 'to regain control of the resources of Rekohu for the benefits of the residents of Rekohu'. Specifically, the committee was to make a case for island ownership of the Chathams fishery; and eventually to consider land claims in compensation for Moriori losses in the nineteenth century. More than money and land was at stake, however. The committee's general objective was recognition of the Moriori as the indigenous owners and spiritual guardians of Rekohu.

In that same year a meeting was held at the islands' marae, Whakamaharatanga, to form a runanga to represent the interests of all indigenous peoples on the Chathams. Moriori and Maori attended. But then the organisers of the hui announced that, because Ngati Mutunga had taken mana whenua from the Moriori in the 1835 invasion, the only people entitled to speak at the meeting or on the marae were those with a whakapapa link to Ngati Mutunga — something almost all Moriori lacked. Further, the runanga was to be called

Te Runanga O Wharekauri, because that was the Maori name for Chatham Island, and it would have sole right to distribute funds for iwi welfare and activities that were being devolved at that time by central government.

The conduct of this hui had wide-ranging consequences. One was that Moriori, excluded from participation in the runanga and facing an absolute denial of their tangata whenua status, formed their own runanga, the Tchakat Henu Association (from the Moriori words for tangata whenua). Another was that most Chatham Island Maori recognised that an injustice had been done to Moriori. One Ngati Mutunga elder, Sunday Hough, sent a 'householder' letter to all islanders saying that he acknowledged Moriori, not Maori, as tangata whenua. Another, nonagenarian Jane Hough, announced that in her youth, the 'old people' had always regarded Tommy Solomon's whanau as 'first people' of the islands. Even islanders who were neither Maori nor Moriori could see the injustice, indeed, the ludicrousness, of saying that the people who had lived on the Chathams for six or seven hundred years had no rights; while the people who had been the third group to arrive on the islands, after both Moriori and Pakeha, were to be regarded as sole tangata whenua.

For a New Zealand mainlander, the whole historical equation on the Chathams turned stereotypes upside down. On the mainland, the settlement sequence had been Maori, then Pakeha, and the former had been colonised by the latter. On the Chathams the sequence had been Moriori, Pakeha (living on the islands from 1827) and then Maori; and it was Maori who had colonised the Moriori. In colonising them, they had never recognised Moriori status as tangata whenua, and they had done their best to annihilate Moriori culture. By the 1980s Ngati Mutunga spokespersons on the Chathams were saying that Moriori had no status, no rights, no identity, and they were to be excluded from all government funding of iwi activities and from all indigenous claims to land, birding or fisheries resources. Everything that Maori sought on the mainland as tangata whenua, Moriori sought on the Chathams; only on the Chathams, it was Maori who tried to withhold the access.

Bill Davis in army uniform. He became chairman of the Chatham Island County Council and leader of the Moriori on the island after Tommy Solomon's death.

Wilford Davis

The first edition of this book was published in 1989 and became itself another factor that gave momentum to the renaissance of Moriori culture and identity. It was not until the following year, however, that the most important cache of evidence of Moriori experience came to light. In the course of research, I had devoted considerable time trying, unsuccessfully, to discover what had become of Bill Davis. Davis, Moriori on his mother's side, had grown up in the 1890s and early 1900s at Hawaruwaru. As the last of the Moriori elders there sickened and died, they bequeathed their papers to him, believing he would carry what was left of Moriori history and culture into the modern world. They were right about identifying Davis as a man of ability and integrity. He had enlisted as a private in World War One and came home a second lieutenant. By 1940 he was a successful farmer and chairman of the county council. Then he left Chatham Island and nobody there had heard of him since.

In January 1990 I took a telephone call from a man who told me that I would not know him, but that his name was Wilford Davis. I did not know him, but I knew who he was: Bill Davis's surviving son. He told me that he had 'a few papers that might interest you.' Bill Davis turned out to have died at Laingholm, near Auckland, in 1962. After his death the son had found a box of fragile papers, written in pencil and ink and wrapped in newspapers in an effort to prevent their disintegration. Wilf Davis glanced at them, saw that they appeared to be written in Maori, which he did not read or speak, and then simply stored them away. Twenty-two years later, reading *Moriori*, he realised their potential significance and contacted me.

It was a moving experience for both of us to sort through these papers. Here were whakapapa, waiata, stories, information on Moriori tribal boundaries, navigation instructions, copies of letters to people in the government and public service, and much more. All had been painstakingly — and in some cases painfully — written by elderly men in smoky ponga huts in the latter years of the nineteenth century. Some pages still smelt of peat smoke and tobacco. They had survived miraculously. Collectively they amounted to a treasure trove of cultural and historical information, significant and enduring messages that Moriori ancestors had sent to their descendants and to posterity. I would, of course, have been grateful for knowledge of the Davis material while I was writing the book. As it turned out, there was nothing there that contradicted the evidence of other sources; the Davis papers extended and elaborated the Moriori story rather than recast it. They were a major plank in the Moriori case argued before the Waitangi Tribunal four years later.

That case, of course, was against the Crown, not Ngati Mutunga. It sought compensation for the Crown's failure to protect Moriori safety and interests after the Chathams became part of New Zealand in 1842; for the Native Land Court's decision to judge Chatham cases on the basis of Maori rather than Moriori custom; and for the 'group defamation' of Moriori perpetrated by the Crown through such official publications as the *School Journal* — a defamation, as one witness said, unparalleled in New Zealand, and equalled elsewhere only by the kinds of savage myths generated by anti-Semitism.

The hearing, in May 1994, was an intensely affecting experience for all who participated in it or adjudicated on it. It began in an open circle in the midst of an old kopi forest on the Te Awapatiki peninsula. This spot was significant for several reasons. It was the alpha point at which Stephenson Percy Smith began the first survey of the Chatham Islands in 1868. More importantly, it was the marae where Moriori had traditionally congregated over centuries to discuss island-wide initiatives and problems. It was here that they gathered to debate the Moriori response to the Maori invasion of 1835; and here that the elders collected and collated the evidence of their travail which they sent as a petition to George Grey in 1862. After that petition was despatched, the intention was to call the iwi together there again, either when the Governor replied to the petition, or when the Native Land Court ruled favourably on Moriori claims. Neither outcome occurred. And in the 132 years between the Grey petition and the Waitangi Tribunal hearing, the Moriori iwi had had no further reason to gather at Te Awapatiki, in hope or in celebration. The 1994 congregation was full of hope. The celebration was a long time coming, however. Six years after the hearing there was still no sign of a decision. As they always had been, Moriori turned out again to be low on the mainland order of priorities.

While the Moriori ethos awoke and stirred and grew among people with Chatham Islands antecedents, however, evidence of the material culture of the Moriori was disappearing at an accelerated rate. A New Zealand Historic Places Trust report warned in 1986 that erosion on Chatham Island was proceeding at a pace that would soon obliterate coastal middens and burial sites; and that

Moriori rock drawings and tree carvings could be gone altogether within a generation.

The petroglyphs on the western shore of Te Whanga lagoon were weathering from a combination of sunlight, wind and water. At Te Ana a Nunuku, where a vast wall of seal carvings had seemed to shiver with life several decades before, climbing their way up the rockface, half the carvings had worn away and the remainder were becoming so faint as to lose the vitality that had made the site so arresting in appearance and a source of spiritual fertility.

The dendroglyph groves, too, were dwindling and disappearing. The thousands of kopi that had formerly carried Moriori bark carvings were reduced to dozens by the late 1980s, most of the remaining ones in three protected stands. The kopi in unfenced areas had died as a result of damage by wind and stock; the carvings that survived on healthy trees were becoming distorted and obscure as the bark continued to grow.

And yet it was possible still to stand in these groves, particularly at Hapupu, surrounded by mute but recognisable faces; and to feel that those faces were watching the observer down a corridor of time. They said nothing, and they conveyed nothing except a presence. But that presence is powerful and still pervades the forest remnant. Because the trees live, the figures on them live, so long as they remain recognisable. To be in such a place, heavy with psychic residue, is to feel close to nature, close to the spiritual qualities of which nature is emblematic, and close to the people who carved the trees and then departed forever.

The opening of the Moriori Waitangi Tribunal claim at Te Awapatiki, May 1994. This was the first use of the traditional Moriori marae there for 134 years. The visible speakers are (from right): Gary Solomon, Charles Preece and Tommy Solomon.

Michael King

APPENDICES

1.   A Moriori vocabulary

This Moriori vocabulary — the only one gathered while some Moriori speakers were still alive — was compiled by Samuel Deighton, Resident Magistrate on the Chathams from 1873 to 1891. His main informant was Hirawanu Tapu of Manukau. Writing to the Under-Secretary of the Native Department in September 1887, Deighton notes:

'You will observe that, though many of the words are the same in writing as the Maori, the pronunciation is different; the letter "t" being pronounced "tch," as tamaiti (Maori), timiti tchimitchi (Moriori), the final i being hardly sounded: in fact, in the greater proportion of the words the

final vowel is almost dropped, or rather clipped off. I know of no other way of describing this peculiarity. There is also a more guttural pronunciation than is shown in the Maori language. The "tch" is more marked in some words than in others, a great many being precisely the same as in Maori. I find it difficult to put in writing the peculiar pronunciation, but my explanation will probably give you an idea of my meaning.'

The vocabulary appeared in the *Appendices to the Journal of the House of Representatives* in 1889 and has not been published since.

	Moriori	Maori
Abandon	Hokorere	Whakarere, *v.*
Abate	Maheiki-marie	Mahaki, *v.*
Abbreviate	Hokopoto	Whakapoto, *v.*
Abdomen	Takapu	Takapu, *s.*
Abhor	Kino	Kino, *v.*
Abhor	Hokino, hokotei	Whakakino
Abide	Noho	Noho, *v.*
Ability	Kaha	Kaha, *s.* (strength)
Abode	Kainga	Kainga, *s.*
Abolish	Hokorekore	Whakakore, *v.*
Abominable	Hokotae, hokote	Whakarihariha, *a.*
Above	Nui eti	Tera atu, *prep. in number*
Abound	Hu	Hua, *v.*
About (near to)	Tata ani ki tangata	Tata ana ki te tangata
Abridge	Hokopoto	Whakapoto, *v.*
Abscess	Whewhe	Whewhe, *s.*
Absent, to be	Ngaro	Ngaro, *v.*
Absorbed, to be	Miti	Mimiti, *v.*
Abstain, from food	Mokiau	Nohopuku, *v.*
Absurd	Kuare	Kuare, *a.*
Abyss	Rere kararo	Torere, *s.*
Accelerate	Hokohikohi	Whakahohoro, *v.*
Accept	Tango	Tango, *v.*
Access, to have	Tata	Tata, *v.*
Accident	Mate	Mate, *s.*
Accompany	Kehere tahe taua	Me haere tahi taua
Accomplished, to be	Taea	Taea, *v.*
Account, narration	Korero	Korere, *v.*
Accurate	Tika	Tika, *v.*
Accuse	Hokaia, hokotuaki	Whakapae, *v.*
Accustomed, to be	Taunga	Taunga, *v.*
Ache	E mae	Mamae, *s.*

	Moriori	Maori
Acid	Kawa	Kawa, *a.*
Acquire	Whiwhi	Whiwhi, *v.*
Acquired	Ku ai ka taonga (or miheke) ka riri ia i	He nui nga taonga ka riro ia ia
Action	Mahi	Mahi, *s.*
Active	Kohi	Hohoro, *a.*
Acute	Koi titio	Koi, *a.*
Add	Iapita	Apiti, *v.*
Adept	Tohonga	Tohunga, *a.*
Adhere	Piri	Piri, *v.*
Admire	Mihi	Miharo, *v.*
Admit	Tuku	Tuku, *v.*
Admonish	Hokaako	Whakaako, *v.*
Adorn	Tawhete	Whakapaipai, *v.*
Advance, go	Here, hunatu, here ra	Haere, *v.* Whanatu, *v.*
Advantage	Tie etiki anohi	Huhuatanga, *s.*
Adversity	Mate	Mate, *s.*
Adult	Tuwhatu, tangata matua	Kaumatua, *s.*
Adulterer	Tangata maka	Tangata puremu, *s.*
Adze	Komanga	Kapu, *s.*
Afar	Tiwheatu	Tawhiti, *adv.*
Affect	Mae	Mamae, *v.* (Ekore a e mamae)
Affection	Iaroha	Aroha, *s.*
Affirm	Hokoiana	Whakaae, *v.*
Affray	Rangataua	Whawhai, *s.*
Affright	Hokomataku	Whakamataku, *v.*
Afloat	Ka rewi i tawai	Rewa (te waka), *v.*
After	Murieneti i tena	Muri iho i tena, *prep.*
Afterbirth	Rauru	Whenua, *s.*

195

	Moriori	Maori		Moriori	Maori
Against	Ti taha	Ki te taha, *prep.*	Assemblage	Huinga	Huihuinga, *s.*
Aground, to be	Ka eke	Ka eke, *v.*	Assent	Hokotika	Whakaae, *v.*
Ahead	Imu	Imua, *v.*	Assimilate	Hokorite	Whakarite, *v.*
Alas	E taukiri	Aue, *int.*	Assist	Awina	Awhina, *v.*
Alike, to be	Penaeneti	Rite tahi, *v.*	Assume	Tango	Tango, *v.*
Alive	Ora	Ora, *v.*	Astray, to be	Mararake, mawaiwai	Marara, *a.*
All	Ka mai a nake	Katoa, *a.*	Athirst	Matewai	Matewai, *a.*
Allow	Tuku	Tuku, *v.*	Atone	Hokoririha	Whakaea, *v.*
Ally	Hokoauru	Whakauru, *s.*	Attempt	Hokomatau	Whakamatau, *v.*
Almost	Pene toke	Wahi iti, *adv.*	Attend	Rongo	Rongo, *v.*
Aloft	Ku runga	Ki runga, *adv.*	Avarice	Hopo	Kaiponu, *s.*
Alone	Enake	Anake, *adv.*	Avenge	Hiki i te(*che*) hara	Rapu utu, *v.*
Aloof, to be	Tu ke	Tu ke, *v.*	Avert	Pana, Pare	Whakanihinihi, *v.*
Aloud, speak	Kia nu te re	Kia nui te reo, *adv.*	Avoid	Hokore	Whakarere, *v.*
Also	Hoki	Hoki, *adv.*	Author (of evil)	Te a putake o te a kino	Te putake o te kino
Alter	Ka hiti ke i toho	Wakaahua ke, *v.*			
Although	Ihakoa	Ahakoa, *adv.*	Authority	Ihi	Mana, *s.*
Always	I tena wahi	I nga waha katoa, *adv.*	Awake, to	Aro korunga	Ara, *v.*
			Awe, to feel	Kapo	Hopohopo, *v.*
Ambush	Tangata huna Hokomoko	Haupapa, *s.*	Aye, yes	E	Ae, *adv.*
Amidst	Ti roto	Kei roto, *prep.*	Baby	Timi(*chi*), metoke	Potiki, *s.*
Amputate	Koti	Kokoti, *v.*	Bachelor	Tuma	Ropa, *s.*
Ancestor	Tupuna (singular) Karapuna (plural)	Tupuna, *s.*	Back	Kumuru	Ki muri, *adv.*
			Back	Tura	Tuara, *s.*
Ancient	Tuapoi	Tuarangi, *s.*	Back of a house	Turango	Tuaroa o te whare
Anger	Riri	Riri, *s.*	Backbone	Te imi o tura	Iwi tuaroa, *s.*
Ankle	Pona	Pona, *s.*	Backwards	Hokomuri	Whakamuri, *adv.*
Annihilate	Hokongaro	Whakangaro, *v.*	Bad	Wahike	Kino, *a.*
Annoyance	Torohe-kaupeke	Nganakia, Whakatakariri, *s.*	Bad weather	Oparo	Ori, *s.*
			Bait	Poa	Poapoa, *s.*
Another	I tera ngata atu	Tetahi atu, *a.*	Bake food	Tunu kei	Tunu kai, *v.*
Answer	Hoki ho kupu	Whaka hoki kupu, *v.*	Bald	Pakira	Pakira, *a.*
Antagonist	Horiri	Hoariri, *s.*	Baler	Tiheru	Tiheru, *s.*
Anus	Wenewene, Kaimiorokaokao	Tou, *s.*	Ballast	Hokotoimaha	Whakataimaha, *s.*
			Band	Ruku	Ruruku, *s.*
Anxious, to be	Maiharahara	Awangawanga, *v.*	Bandage	Takai, nunanga	Takai, *s.*
Apart	Ki pahaki	Ki tahaki, *adv.*	Banish	Pana	Pana, *v.*
Appear	Ka puta	Ka puta, *v.*	Bank (of the river)	Tahatu	Tahataha, *s.*
Appease	Hokomari	Whakamarie, *v.*	Banter	Hokorere	Whakangako, *v.*
Appetite	Tupa te manau, manau kore	Hiakai, *s.*	Bark	Kiri	Kiri, tapeha, *s.*
			Barren	Pakako	Pakoko, *a.*
Appoint	Hokorite	Whakarite, *v.*	Barricade	Arai	Arai, *s.*
Approach	Hokotata	Whakatata, *v.*	Basket	Kete	Kete, *s.*
Argue	Hokotiko	Tau tohe, *v.*	Basket (fish)	Punga	Hinaki, punga, *s.*
Arise	Maranga	Maranga, *v.*	Bastard	Wairangi	Poriro, *s.*
Arm (hand)	Ririma	Ringaringa, *s.*	Bathe	Kau	Kaukau, *v.*
Arm	Pakau	Ringaringa, *s.*	Battle	Rangataua	Parekura, *s.*
Armpit	Keke	Keke, *s.*	Bawl	Hamama	Parare, *v.*
Aromatic	Kara	Kakara, *a.*	Bay	Ngake	Kokorutanga, *s.*
Around	Ki te taha ki te taha	Ki tetahi taha ki tetahi taha	Beach	One	Takutai, *s.*
			Beak	Ngutu	Ngutu, *s.*
Arouse	Okohomauri, okohomori	Whakaoho, *v.*	Bear	Kawe	Kawe, *v.*
			Bear up (under pain)	Mananui	Manawanui, *v.*
Arrange	Hokotikitika	Whakatikatika, *v.*	Bear fruit	Hua, ngana	Hua, *v.*
Artery	Uau	Uaua, *s.*	Beard	Kumukumu	Pahau, *s.*
Ascend	Kake	Piki, *v.*	Beauty	Porotu, Humari	Ataahua, *s.*
Ashamed, to be	Hokomaha	Whakama, *v.*	Because	No re me	No te mea, *conj.*
Ashes	Purungehu	Pungarehu, *s.*	Beckon	Tawhiri	Tawhiri, *v.*
Ashore	Uta	Uta, *adv.*	Bed	Moenga, totaranga	Moenga, *s.*
Ask	Ui	Patai, *v.*	Beg	Maka kai, makari kei	Pinono kai, *v.*
Asleep, to be	Moe	Moe, *v.*			
Assault	Rere	Tau, Rere, *v.*	Begin	Timata, tutanga	Timata, *v.*

	Moriori	*Maori*		*Moriori*	*Maori*
Beguile	Taureia	Patipati, *v.*	Brim	Ngutu, tapa ngutu	Ngutu, *s.*
Behold	Na, E ti(*chi*) ra ko	Na, nana, rere, *int.*	Brittle	Papa	Papa noa, *a.*
Behold	E ti(*chi*) ra	Titiro, *v.*	Broil	Tunu	Tunu, *v.*
Belch	Toko mauru	Pupa, *v.*	Broken, to be	Ngawha	Pakaru, *v.*
Belief	Hokotika	Whakapono, *s.*	Brood, to	Kupapa	Tapapa, *v.*
Belly	Takapu	Kopu, *s.*	Brother of a sister	Hunau, timiriki	Tungane, *s.*
Belt	Tatu	Tatua, *s.*		maro	
Bend	Hokopiko	Whakapiko, *v.*	Brother, elder	Tukana, hunau	Tuakana, *s.*
Bend (of the arm)	Hokopeke	Whatianga, *s.*		tongihiki	
Benumbed	Pepeke	Korongenge, *v.*	Brother, younger	Hunau potiki	Teina, *s.*
Beseech	Tono	Inoi, *v.*	Brother-in-law	Pani	Taokete, *s.*
Besmear	Pani	Pani, paru, *v.*	Brow of hill	Taumata, tieki	Taumata, *s.*
Best	(Mea) Porotu,	Pai rawa, *a.*	Bruised, to be	Maru	Maru, *v.*
	(mea) humari		Build	Hanga	Hanga, *v.*
Betray	Tuku	Tuku, *v.*	Bump	Puku	Puku, *s.*
Betrothed	Hokomo	Taumau, *v.*	Bunch	Tautau	Tautau, *s.*
Better (rather)	Koi nana	Engari	Butterfly	Purehurehu	Purehurehu (moth),
Between	Ki wanganui o rawa	Ki waenga, *prep.*			*s.*
Bewitch	Kupu	Makutu, *v.*	Cajole	Makutu	Maminga, *v.*
Big	Rahi, me hara	Rahi, *a.*	Calculate	Tau	Tatau, *v.*
Bind	Nungana	Herehere, *v.*	Calf of leg	Hikari	Ateatenga, *s.*
Bird	Manu	Manu, *s.*	Calm	Kupe, he umu	Marino, *s.*
Bird's nest	Kuhanga	Kowhanga, *s.*	Canoe	Waka	Waka, *s.*
Birth	Whanautanga	Whanautanga, *s.*	Canoe, large	Paihihi	Pahi
Bit	I te Hunu, i te	Maramara, *s.*	Cape	Matarae, ihu	Rae, *s.*
	maramara, i te pito		Careful	Kia toho	Tupato, *a.*
Bite	Ngahu	Ngau, *v.*	Carry away by	Kahaki	Kawhaki, *v.*
Black	Pango	Pango, *a.*	stealth		
Bladder	Tongamimi	Tongamimi, *s.*	Carry to, as a child	Hiki (timiriki)	Hiki (tamariki), *v.*
Bladebone	Papamatu	Papaahuahua, *s.*	Carry on the back	Pikau, koenga	Pikau, *v.*
Blaze	Mura	Mura, *v.*	Carry on a pole	Amo, tukuwaru	Tauteka, *v.*
Bleed	Toto, parapara	Toto, *v.*	Carve	Hokoairo	Whakairo, *v.*
Blind	Pupura	Pura, *a.*	Cast, to	Pange, hokorere etu	Panga, *v.*
Blink	Momoe, tungehu	Momoe, *v.*	Cataract	Taheke	Taheke, *s.*
Blister	Kopuku	Koputa, *v.*	Catch	Hopu, kapo	Hopu, kapo, *v*
Block of wood	Poro-rakau	Poro-rakau, *s.*	Catch one's breath	Tokomauru	Huatare, *v.*
Blocked up	Puni, tutaki	Puni, *a*	Cave	Ana	Ana, *s.*
Blossom	Pu-rakau	Pua, *s.*	Causeless	Tipakore, takekore	Pokanoa, *a.*
Blow, to strike a	Moto	Moto	Cease, to make to	Hokoti	Whakaoti, *v.*
Blow	Puhi	Pupuhi, *v.*	Centre	Waenganui	Waenganui, *s.*
Blunt	Puhiku	Puhuki, *a.*	Channel, river	Awa	Awa, *s.*
Bluster	Hokorerehe	Rupahu, *v.*	Charcoal	Ngarehu	Ngarehu, *s.*
Body	Tino	Tinana, *s.*	Chase	Aruaru	Whai, *v.*
Bog (swamp)	Karupuru	Repo, *s.*	Chasm	Matatata, toha	Torere, *s.*
Boil	Koropupu	Koropupu, *v.*	Cheek	Paparinga	Paparinga, *s.*
Boil	Whewhe	Whewhe, *s.*	Chequered	Hokopanapana	Kotingotingo, *a.*
Bold	Toa	Toa, *a.*	Chew	Ngau	Ngau, *v.*
Bone	Imi	Iwi, *s.*	Chief	Ieriki-ieriki	Rangatira, ariki, *s.*
Border (of mat)	Taniko	Taniko, *s.*	Child	Timiti	Tamaiti
Bosom	Tarauma	Tarauma, *s.*	Chin	Kaue	Kauae, *s.*
Bough	Manga	Manga, peka, *s.*	Chip	Maramara	Maramara, *s.*
Boundary	Rohe	Rohe, *s.*	Chisel	Whao	Whao, *s.*
Bowels	Ngakau	Ngakau, *s.*	Chop, to	Koti	Koti (to cut)
Boy (child)	Timiti tane,	Tamaiti, *s.*	Chrysalis	Tunga	Tungoungou, *s.*
Breadth	Whanui	Whanui, *s.*	Circle	Potakataka	Porowhita, *s.*
Break of day	Ateata, maruapo	Atatu, *s.*	Circuitous	Awhio, pokai	Awhiowhio, *s.*
Break off	Whati	Whati, *v.*	Clandestinely	Me huna	Momote, *adv.*
Break on top of	Atea	Tuatea, *s.*	Clap	Pake	Papaki, *v.*
wave			Clean white, red,	Me ma, me panga,	Mea ma, whero,
Breast	U	U, *s.*	black	me whero	pango
Breath	Manawa	Manawa, *s.*	Clear, to be	Watea	Watea, *v.*
Breech	Papa, hope	Papa, *s.*	Cleave, to	Watoahi	Wawahi, *v.*
Bright	Kanape	Kanapa, *a.*			

English	Moriori	Maori
Cliff	Pari, panaunga	Pari, s.
Cling	Puri	Pupuri, v.
Clinch the hand	Kuku	Kuku, v.
Close, to	Piri	Piri, v.
Clot (of blood)	Tepetoto	Tepetepe, s.
Cloud	Kupe, he ao	Ao, s.
Cloudy	Pororo	Paroro, a.
Cluster	Tautau	Tautau, s.
Coast	Takutai	Takutai, s.
Cockle	Tupere	Pipi, s.
Codfish	Hakoma	Hapuku, s.
Coil	Pokai	Koromeke, s.
Cold	Matao	Matao, s.
Collarbone	He aha	Paemanu, s.
Collect	Apo	Apo
Come	Haramai	Haeremai, v.
Companion	He ho	Hoa, s.
Company	Tere	Tere, s.
Compare	Hokorite	Whakarite, v.
Compassion, love	Aroha	Aroha, v.
Concave, to be	Kokohu	Kokohu, v.
Conceal	Huna	Huna, v.
Condemn	Hokohe	Whakahe, v.
Concubine	He ho	Hoahoa, s.
Conduct	Iarataki	Arataki, v.
Confess	Hokotakorero	Whaki, v.
Confuse	Hokoraru	Whakararu, v.
Confused	Hokotanukunuku Makaha	Nanu, v. Poauau, a.
Connexion	Hokotaupiki	Whakatarunatanga, s.
Conscience	Hirangaro	Hinengaro, s.
Consideration	Hokoaro	Whakaaro, s.
Consolation	Hokomari kaoro te ngakau	Whakamarietanga, s.
Conspiracy	Tauangakau, patu huna	Kohuru, s.
Constant, to be	Pumau, kamau	Pumau, v.
Contend	Maro, hokotikatu, hokotikamau	Tautohe, v.
Contentious	Tupa tupe	Whakatenatena, a.
Continue	Kei iri, kurunga iai a enei	Tiwai tonu, v.
Cook	Tunu, tao	Tao, tunu, v.
Cool	Puhanuhanu, hau	Hauhau, a.
Cord	Tau	Taura, s.
Corpse	Tupapaku	Tupapaku, s.
Correct	Tikane	Tika, a.
Corrupt	Parau	Parau, a.
Cough	Mare	Mare, s.
Countenance	Paparinga	Paparinga (cheek), s.
Forehead	Rae	Rae
Nose	Purangaihu	Ihu
Eyes	Konehi	Kanohi, konohi
Eye-lash	Kemo	Kamo
Eyebrows	Tikamata, korokonei	Tukemata
Lips	Ngutu	Ngutu
Teeth	Niho	Niho
Tongue	Warero	Arero
Hair	Huruhuru	Huruhuru (hair on the body)
Head	Upoko	Upoko
Ears	Tiringa	Taringa
Neck	Kaki	Kaki
Country	Whenua, puwhenu	Whenua, s.
Cover	Poki	Taupoki, v.
Covet	Hopo	Kaiponu, v.
Crab	Pakapaka	Papaka, s.
Crafty	Makutu	Koroke
Crave	Moto	Hiahia, v.
Crawl	Totoro, toro	Ngaoki, toro, v.
Crayfish	Koura	Koura, s.
Crime	Hara	Hara, s.
Crimson	Whero	Whero, a.
Cripple	Mokai	Turingongengonge, s.
Crookback	Puku tura	Hake, s.
Crumple	Hutoi	Humene, v.
Crushed	Tutuku	Koparu, v.
Cry	Tangi	Tangi, v.
Cumbersome	Hirawerawe	Hirawerawe, a.
Curved	Koperu	Tiwhana, a.
Curse, to	Kupukupu	Kanga, v.
Custom	Toho	Ritenga, s.
Cut hair	Kokoti i ka uru	Tarotaro
Cuttle-fish	Wheke	Wheke, s.
Damp	Kumaku	Maku, v.
Dance (Native)	Motiha	Kani, s.
Dandle	Poipoi popo	Poipoi, v.
Dangle	Tata	Tawheta, v.
Dark	Pokerekere	Pouri, v. (pokere, in the dark)
Dark skin	Parauiri	Parauri
Daughter	Timiti mahine	Tamahine, s.
Daughter-in-law	Hunungo	Hunaonga, s.
Dawn	Atapangopango	Atatu, s.
Day	Ao	Ao, s.
Daybreak	Ataoheia	Atatu, s.
Daylight	Ohinata ohinawatea	Awatea, s.
Deaf	Turi, tai turi	Turi, v.
Death	Matenga	Matenga, s.
Deceitful	Makutu	Hangarau, a.
Decide	Hokorite	Whakarite, v.
Declare	Hokopuaki	Whakapuaki, v.
Decrease	A te(che) here	Iti haere, v.
Deep	Hohonu	Hohonu, v.
Delay	Hokoro	Whakaroa, v.
Delighted	Akureki	Ahuareka, v.
Deny	Hokorekore, tute	Whakakorekore, v.
Departure	Herenga	Haerenga, s.
Destroy	Hokongaro	Whakangaro, v.
Detest	Hokotae	Whakakino, v.
Devour	Kai, kei	Kai, v.
Dew	Haurangi	Haunui, s.
Diarrhoea	Pi, Pia	Tarahi, s. (pi, to flow)
Difficult	Uau	Uaua, a.
Difficulty, to be in	Hokoraru	Raruraru, v.
Dig	Keri	Keri, v.
Dilatory	Hokoro	Whakaroa, a.
Diligent	Morimahi	Ahuwhenua, a.
Dim	Hautomaru	Haumarumaru, v.
Diminished	Tauohorihori	Ahuahu, v.
Directly	Awaienei	Aianei, adv.
Dirt	Karupuru	Paru

	Moriori	*Maori*		*Moriori*	*Maori*
Disagreeable	Harengerenge	Whakarihariha, *a.*	Entice	Hokotipatipe	Whakapatipati, *v.*
Disappear	Poremi	Toremi, *v.*	Entrails	Ngakau	Ngakau, *s.*
Disbelieve	Haku	Whakateka, *v.*	Envy	Manau puku	Hae, *v.*
Disclose	Hokopuaki	Puaki, *v.*	Equity	Tikanga	Tikanga, *s.*
Disease of the skin	Waihekeheke	Waihakihaki	Erect	Tu	Tu tonu, *a.*
Disembowel	Tuaki	Tuaki, *a.*	Evaporate	Miti	Mimiti, *v.*
Disinclined	Ngakaukore	Ngakaukore	Evening star	Kopiriango	Rereahiahi, *s.*
Disobedient	Hokoteke	Tutu, *a.*	Everlasting	Ora e neti	Ora tonu, *a.*
Dispirited	Marohi	Marohirohi, *a.*	Examine	Etiro	Titiro, *v.*
Dispute	Tauhokotiko	Tautohetohe, *v.*	Excavate	Hekaruru	Whakakorua, *v.*
Distant	No paorangi	Tawhiti, *a.*	Exceed	Hipa	Hipa, *v.*
Ditch	Tawhakere	Awakeri, *s.*	Excite	Tareo	Whakahauhau, *v.*
Dive	Ruku tupo	Ruku, *v.*	Excoriated	Mehare	Mahore, *a.*
Dizzy	Ngaruru, taka te whenua	Anini, *v.*	Expand	Roha	Roha, *v.*
			Explode	Ka tangi, pa	Papa, *v.*
Drag	Kume	Kukume, *v.*	Extended	Mohoro	Mahora, *a.*
Dread	Wehi	Wehi, *v.*	Exult	Hokotama tama	Whakakake, *v.*
Dream	Momoea	Moemoea, *s.*			
Drink	Inu	Inu, *v.*	Fall	Hingi	Hinga, *v.*
Drip	Turu	Tuturu, *v.*	False	Hiwa, hewa	Hewa, *a.*
Drizzle	Punehu	Konehunehu, *v.*	Famine	Iri wa kai kore	Onge, *s.*
Drowned	Kamate ko ro te wai	Paremo, *v.*	Famish	Manawa kore	Hemo kai, *v.*
			Farewell	Wanatu ra, tau atu ra	Hei konei ra, *int.*
Drowsy	Hiama	Hinamoe			
Dry	Moroke	Maroke, *v.*	Fasten	Hokau, hokou	Whakau, *v.*
Duck	Perere	Parera, *s.*	Fasting	Mohokiau	Nohopuku, *a.*
Dumb	Pukiho	Wahangu, *a.*	Fat	Ihara	Momona, *a.*
Durable	Marote	Maro, *a.*	Father	Papa	Papa, *s.*
Dust	Pawa	Nehu, *s.* (paoa, smoke)	Father-in-law	Mati hongoi	Hungawai, *s.*
			Fatigued	Oeha, Ngenge	Ngenge, *a.*
Dwarf	Tupepe	Hakahaka, *s.*	Feather	Piki	Piki (plume)
			Feeble	Oeha	Ngoikore, *a.*
Ear, lobe of	Popoi	Hoi, toke, *s.*	Feed	Whangai	Whangai, *v.*
Earthquake	Ru whenu	Ru, *s.*	Fence	Pa	Taepa, *s.*
East	Rat(*ch*)akimai	Rawhiti, *s.*	Fern leaves	Rauruhe	Rauaruhe, *s.*
East wind	Hau marangei	Marangai, *s.*	Fern root	Aruhe	Aruhe, *s.*
Easy	Ngawari	Ngawari, *a.*	Fever	Kiri wera	Kirika, *s.*
Eat ravenously	Tianga	Horomiti, *v.*	Finger	To	Matihao, *s.*
Eat raw	Kai mata	Kaimata, *v.*	Thumb	To nui	Konui
Ebb	Tai miti	Timu, *v.*	1st finger	To roa	To roa
Eddy	Iauripo	Ripo, *s.*	2nd finger	To e hau	Manawa
Eel	Tuna	Tuna, *s.*	3rd finger	To pere	Mapere
Egg	Hu manu	Hua, *s.*	4th finger	To iti	To iti
Eight	Tewaru	Waru, *a.*	Finger nail	Maikuku	Maikuku, *s.*
Elbow	Tukutuke	Tuketuke, *s.*	Fire	Ahi, ehi	Ahi, *s.*
Elder person	Tangata matua	Kaumatua, *s.*	Firewood	Wahi, kohia	Wahie, *s.*
Emaciated	Tangata kiko kore	Kiko kore, *a.*	Firmament	Ko ri kiko o te rangi	Kikorangi, *s.*
Embark	Kanu waka	Eke, *v.*			
Embers	Momotu	Motumotu, *s.*	Fish	Ika	Ika, *s.*
Embrace	Awhi	Awhi, *v.*	Fish, to	Hi	Hi, *v.*
Encampment	Kainga	Puni, *s.*	Fish hook	Matau	Matau, *s.*
Encircle	Pokaiamio	Pukoro, *v.*	Five	Terima	Rima, *a.*
Encumber	Hokowehewehe	Whakawheru, *v.*	Flame	Mura ahi	Muramura, *s.*
End, to	Hokomutu	Whakamutu, *v.*	Flank	Kaokao	Kaokao, *s.*
Endeavour	Hokotiko	Tohe, *v.*	Flatter	Hokotipatipa	Whakapatipati, *v.*
Endless	Mutunga kore	Mutunga kore, *a.*	Flax	Harapepe	Harakeke, *s.*
Enemy	Horiri	Hoariri, *s.*	Flay	Kai hore	Hore, *v.*
Enlarge	Hokonui	Whakanui, *v.*	Flea	Kutu-porenga	Kutu (louse), *s.*
Enlighten	Hokomarama	Whakamarama, *v.*	Flesh	Kiko	Kiko, *s.*
Enquire	Ui	Ui, *v.*	Flint	Tutekiore	Kiripaka, *s.*
Ensnare	Mehanga	Mahanga, *v.*	Flood	Waipuke	Waipuke, *s.*
Entangle	Whiwhi	Whiwhi, *v.*	Flood tide	Tai puiha	Tai pari, *s.*
Entertainment	Iaoreka	Atawhaitanga, *s.*	Flower	Pua	Pua, *s.*

	Moriori	Maori
Fog	Kohu	Kohu, *s.*
Foot	Wawae	Waewae, *s.*
Foreigner	Ko re kau o paorangi	Pakeha, *s.*
Forest	Ngaherehere	Ngaherehere, *s.*
Forget	Ka-na waina	Wareware, *v.*
Forgive	Ho rongo	Hohou te rongo, *v.*
Forgotten	Ngaro	Ngaro, *v.*
Fork of a tree	Peka, manga	Peka, *s.*
Form	Iahu	Ahua, *s.*
Formerly	Imata, Imu	Inamata, imua, *adv.*
Fornication	Maka	Puremu, *s.*
Forsake	Hokore	Whakarere, *v.*
Four	Tewha	Wha, *a.*
Fracture, bone	Imi whati	Whati, *s.*
Fragile	Kimiaha	Papanoa, *a.*
Frost	Huka tongeheupapa	Huka haupapa, *s.*
Fruit	Ngana, hua	Hua, *s.*
Fungus	Popoi i ngaherehere	Harore, *s.*
Gale	Koparo	Tupuhi, *s.*
Gape	Hamama	Kowhera, *v.*
Garment	Kakahu	Kakahu, *s.*
Genealogy	Korero tupuna	Kawai, korero tahu, *s.*
Ghost	Wairu	Wairua, *s.*
Giddy	Amimio	Amiomio, *v.*
Gift	Homai e neti, hoatu e neti	Mea homai noa, *s.*
Gills of a fish	Puhea	Puha, *s.*
Girl	Tamahine	Tamahine (daughter), *s.*
Glad	Ka ko	Koa, *a.*
Glutton	Tanga teanga, horo tatakau	Kaihoro, *s.*
God	Tetua	Atua, *s.*
Good	Humaria	Humarire (beautiful), *a.*
Grandchild	Mokopuna	Mokopuna, *s.*
Grandfather	Tipuna-tane	Tipuna, *s.*
Grandmother	Tipuna-wahine	Tipuna-wahine, *s.*
Grass	Taru	Tarutaru, *s.*
Gravel	Kiri pohatu	Kirikiri, *s.*
Grease	Hinu	Hinu, *s.*
Grey	Hina	Hina (grey hair), *a.*
Halo	Tihangeera	Pukoro, *s.*
Handle	Kau	Kakau
Hang	Tarewa	Tarona, *v.*
Harangue	Whaikorero	Whaikorero, *s.*
Hard	Maro t(*cth*)enga	Maro, *a.*
Hasten	Kohi	Hohoro, *v.*
Head	Upoko, uraki, uru	Upoko, uru, *s.*
Heart	Hiringaro, hirengaro	Hingengaro, mauri, *s.*
Heat	Pawerewere	Pawera, *s.*
Heavy	Taumaha	Rorotu, *a.*
Heel	Rekereke	Rekereke, *s.*
Height	Tikitiki	Tiketike, *s.*
Hesitates, the man	Kahewa te tangata	Ruarua, pohehe, *v.*
Hiccough	Tokomoru	Tokohana, *s.*
Hide	Huna	Huna, *v.*
High	Tikitiki	Tiketike

	Moriori	Maori
Hindermost thing	E hiku	Hiku, *s.*
Hips	Papae-hope	Hope, *s.*
Hip bone	Papa hepe	Humu, *s.*
Hole	Rua, puta	Poka, puta, *s.*
Hook	Matau	Matau, *s.*
House	Waiau whare	Whare, *s.*
How many	Ewhi, tokohia	Ewhia, tokohia
Hundred	Tahi te rau	Rau, *a.*
Hunger	Manaukore, tapa te manau	Hemokai, *s.*
Hurry	Okoikoi	Taruketanga, *s.*
Husband	Tane	Tane, *s.*
Hush	Ta karo ra	Maniania, *int.*
Idle	Mangere	Mangere, *a.*
Idol	(No word)	Whakapakoko, *s.*
Ignorance	Kuaretanga	Kuraretanga, *s.*
Impetuous	Tangata kaha	Tai kaha, *a.*
Incite	Tupetupe	Whakahauhau, *v.*
Infant	Potiki, timiti	Potiki, *s.*
Insect	Ngarara, koruatawhito	Ngarara, *s.*
Insert	Komo	Kokomo, *v.*
Inside	Koro	Roto, *adv.*
Instruct	Hokoako	Whakaako, *v.*
Inward	Hokoroto	Whakaroto, *a.*
Irregular	Hokopihipiha	Whakahipahipa, *a.*
Island	Whatu	Motu, mautere, *s.*
Itch	Waihakihaki	Waihakihaki, *s.*
Jabber	Umuumu korerorero	Hautete, *v.*
Jaded	Ngenge	Ngenge, *a.*
Jaw	Kaue	Kauae, *s.*
Jealous	Kiato	Tupato, hae, *v.*
Jerk	Kai iemo	Takiri, *v.*
Join	Apiti	Apiti, *v.*
Joint	Ponopono	Pona, *s.*
Joist	Pae	Kurupae, *s.*
Jump	Hupeke, poi	Tupeke, *v.*
Keel	Hua	Takere, *s.*
Kick	Takehi	Whana, *v.*
Kidney	Iara kihi	Takihi, *s.*
Kill	Patu	Patu, whakamate, *v.*
Kindle by rubbing sticks	Kaunaki	Hika, *v.*
Kindle a fire	Tau e te ehi	Tahuna te ahi
Kindred	Whanaunga	Whanaunga, *s.*
Knee	Turi	Turi, *s.*
Kneel	Kaparu, kapiko	Koropiko, *v.*
Knob	Puku	Puku, *s.*
Knock	Kurukuri, patoto	Patoto
Knowledge	Totohungatanga	Matauranga, *s.*
Ladder	Tira	Arawhata, *s.*
Lake	Roto	Roto, *s.*
Lame	Mokai	Ngongengonge, *a.*
Lament	Aue	Aue, *v.*
Land	Whenua	Whenua, *s.*
Landing-place	Tauranga, ekenga	Tauranga, *s.*
Landslip	Horopari	Horo, *s.*
Language	Reo	Reo, *s.*

	Moriori	*Maori*		*Moriori*	*Maori*
Languid	Ngoi, oeha	Ngoikore, *a.*	Misgive	Manukanuka	Manukanuka, *v.*
Large	Hara, nuitewai	Nui (hara, excess), *a.*	Mist	Kohu	Kohu, *a.*
Lash (to fasten)	Hohou	Hohou, *v.*	Mix	Pokepoke	Pokepoke, *v.*
Last night	Iripo, irupo	Inapo	Moan	Auta	Aurere, *v.*
Laugh	Kata	Kata, *v.*	Moon	Marama	Marama, *s.*
Launch (canoe)	Hokoputa, kokiri	Kokiri, *v.*	Moonlight	Iatamarama	Atamarama, *s.*
Lay	Hokototoranga	Whakatakoto, *v.*	Morning star	Wa nui	Tawera, *s.*
Lazy	Mangere	Mangere, *a.*	Morrow	Apo	Apopo, *adv.*
Lead	Iarataki	Arataki, *v.*	Mosquito	Namu	Waeroa, *s.*
Leaf	Pa rakau	Rau, *s.*	Moth	Kapukapuai	Punehunehu
Leak	Turu	Tuturu, *v.*			(Kapowai,
Leap	Peke, poi	Tupeke, *v.*			dragon-fly)
Left, to be	Mahue	Mahue, *v.*	Mother	Matehine	Whaea, matua-
Left-handed	Ririma maui	Maui, *a.*			wahine, *s.*
Legend	Kauho	Kauwhau, *s.*	Mother-in-law	Mati-hongoi-	Hungawai, *s.*
Leisure	Atetanga	Ateatanga, *s.*		mahine	
Length	Roanga	Roanga, *s.*	Motion	Korikoringa	Korikoringa, *s.*
Level	Tika marie	Tika tonu, *a.*	Move swiftly	Rere	Omaki, *v.*
Liar	Tangata hiwa	Tangata teka, *s.*	Move up and down	Pipui	Piupiu, *v.*
Lick	Mitimiti	Mitimiti, *v.*	Move the lips	Kewa ka ngutu	Komekome, *v.*
Lie	Hiwa	Horihori, teka, *s.*	Mountain	Maunga	Maunga, *s.*
Life	Ioranga	Oranga, *s.*	Mourn	Tangi	Tangi, *v.*
Lift up	Hapai	Hapai, *v.*	Mouth	Waha	Waha, *s.*
Light (not heavy)	Mama	Mama, *a.*	Mouth of river	Ngutuawa	Ngutuawa, *s.*
Lightning	Uira, rauira	Uira, *s.*	Mud	Karipuru	Paru, *s.*
Liken	Hokorite	Whakarite, *v.*	Murmur	Maukewa	Kowhetewhete, *v.*
Limp	Toti	Totitoti, *v.*			
Line, string	Tau	Aho, nape, *s.*	Naked	Kiritoanga	Takakore, *a.*
Lip	Ngutu	Ngutu, *s.*	Name	Ingoa	Ingoa, *s.*
Little	Me toke	Nohinohi, *a.*	Navel	Pito	Pito, *s.*
	(little thing)		Neap tide	Tai hokopu	Tai ririki, *s.*
Liver	Ate	Ate, *s.*	Neck	Kaki	Kaki, *s.*
Lizard	Ngarara	Ngarara, *s.*	Nephew	Whairamutu,	Iramutu, *s.*
Load	Koenga	Kawenga, *s.*		Kahutoto	
Loathsome	Hokotae	Whakarihariha, *a.*	Net	Kupenga	Kupenga, *s.*
Loll	Hokorinaki	Whakawhirinaki, *v.*	Nine	Teiwa	Iwa, *a.*
Longlegs	Wewe roro	Tokoroa, *s.*	Nip	Kini	Kikini, *v.*
Loose	Korokoro	Korokoro, *v.*	Noose	Mehanga	Tawhiti, *s.*
Lost	Ngaro	Ngaro, *v.*	North	Whakuru	Raki, *v.*
Lump of earth	Pokepoke oneone	Pokurukuru, *s.*	N.E. wind	Haupawhakuru	Pawhakarua, *s.*
Lungs	Pukupuka	Pukapuka, *s.*	N.W. wind	Ti(ch)u maro,	Kotiu, *s.*
				tiu makehu	(North wind)
Mad	Tangata-maka	Porangi, *a.*	Nose	Purunga ihu	Ihu, *s.*
	(maniac)		Notch	Kokoti	Whakakarikari, *v.*
Maggot	Iro	Iroiro, *s.*			(Koti, to cut)
Maimed	Maru	Kero, *a.*	Numerous	Kuahi	Hira, *s.*
Mainland	Tuwhenu	Tuawhenua, *s.*	Nurse a child, to	Hiki tamariki, timiti	Hiki, *v.*
Malice	Hokomomohara	Mauahara, *s.*			
Man's sister	Whanau-Timiriki-	Tuahine, *s.*	Obey	Rongo	Rongo, *v.*
	mahine		Obstinate	Hokotiko, maro	Whakakeke, *a.*
Marrow	Hinu imi	Mongamonga, *s.*	Obtain	Whiwhi	Whiwhi, *v.*
Marshy	Tapatupatu	Tapokopoko, *a.*	Ocean	Moana	Moana, *s.*
Mat	Tukohu	Kaitaka, *s.*	Odour	Mea kara	Kakara, *s.*
Mellow	Ngawari	Maoa, *a.*	Offensive	Mataku	Anuanu, *v.*
Melt	Rewa	Rewa, *v.*	Offering	Oatu	Hoatu, *s.*
Membrum virile	Ure, Tino, Tawhito	Ure, *s.*	Offspring	Uri	Uri, whanau, *s.*
Memory	Mehara	Mahara, *s.*	Old	Tawhito	Tawhito, *a.*
Mesh	Mokoru	Kanakana, *s.*	One	Tehi	Tahi, *a.*
Messenger	Kerere	Karere, *s.*	Oppress	Hokorutu	Whakawhiu, *v.*
Meteor	Kokirikiri	Kotiri, *s.*	Origin	Tutanga	Timatanga, *s.*
Middle	Waenganui	Waenganui, *s.*	Orphan	Pani	Pani, *s.*
Midnight	Turuhea	Turuapo	Oven	Umu	Hangi, *s.*
Mildew	Heka	Hekaheka, *s.*	Overhang	Taumarumaru	Tauwharewhare, *v.*

	Moriori	Maori		Moriori	Maori
Overtaken	Potaietu	Rokohanga, *a.*	Ridgepole	Tahuhu	Tahuhu
Ourselves	Tatau, matau	Tatou, *pron.*	Roast	Tunu	Tunu, *v.*
Outside	Ko waho	Waho, *s.*	Rock	Pohatu	Pohatu, *s.*
Oyster	Karauria	Tio, *s.*	Roe of fish	Hu	Hua
			Roof	Tapatu	Tuanui, *s.*
Paddle	Hiwa	Hoe, *s.*	Roof of mouth	Arere	Pikiarero, *s.*
Pain	Mae	Mamae, *s.*	Root	Purakau-timu	Paiaka
Palatable	Reka	Reka, *a.*	Rough	Tatarame	Ongaonga, taratara, *a*
Pare	Hore	Hore, *v.*	Rough, as the sea	Karekare	Karekare (surf), *a.*
Passage	Aranui	Ara (aranui, highway)	Round	Potaka	Porotaka, *a.*
			Round about	Pokaikai	Awhiowhio, *adv.*
Patch	Koropanga	Papaki, *s.*	Rumbling noise	Heruru	Haruru, *v.*
Patient	Manawanui	Manawanui, *a.*	Run	Rere	Rere (as water), *v.*
Pause	Okioki	Okioki, *v.*	Rustle	Kakit(*ch*)ia	Ngahehe, *v.*
Peacemaker	Tangata hou rongo	Kaihohou rongo, *s.*			
Pedigree	Kawei	Kawai, *s.*	Sacred	Tapu	Tapu, *a.*
Perch	Tau	Pae, *s.*	Saliva	Ware	Ware, *s.*
Permanent	Turu	Tuturu, *a.*	Salt	Marurua	Mataitai, *a.*
Persecute	Hokoteke	Whakatoi, *v.*	Sand	One	Onepu, *s.*
Perspiration	Werewere	Kakawa, *s.*	Satisfaction	Manawareka	Manawareka, *s.*
Pigeon	Parea	Kereru, *s.*	Scoop	Tikaro	Tikaro, *s.*
Pillow	Urunga	Urunga, *s.*	Scorch	Inaina, tamahana	Rangirangi, *v.*
Pimple	Tona	Kiritona, *s.*	Scrape	Raku	Rakuraku, *v.*
Placenta	Rauru	Whenua, *s.*	Scrape flax	Haro	Haro, *v.*
Plait	Ranga	Raranga, *v.*	Sea coast	Tatatei	Tatahi, *s.*
Play	Hokorereto	Takaro, *v.*	Sea urchin	Kina	Kina, *s.*
Pluck	Huiti	Whawhaki, *v.*	Seal	Puhina, mimiha	Kekeno, *s.*
Plunder	Eoho	Muru, *v.*	Seaweed	Rimu	Rimurimu, *s.*
Polish	Hokonape	Whakanapanapa, *v.*	Seven	Tewhitu	Whitu, *a.*
Porch	Kotare	Whakamahau, *s.*	Shake	Ruru	Rurerure, *v.*
Porpoise	Iakauta	Tupoupou, *s.*	Shake in the wind	Hokaangi	Kopekope, *v.*
Post	Pou	Pou, *s.*	Shake, as the ground	Ngaere	Ngaere, *v.*
Posteriors	Toino	Tou (anus), *s.*	Shake, as a line by fish	Tongi, ruru	Tongi, *v.*
Precipice	Pari, panaunga	Pari, *s.*	Shallow	Papaku	Papaku, *a.*
Pregnant	Hapu	Hapu, *a.*	Shame	Hokoma	Whakama, *s.*
Press	Tamira	Tami, pehi, *v.*	Shark	Mango, ngu, tatere, Huanga, mangoruake	Mango, *s.*
Prickly	Taramu	Taratara, *v.*			
Pride	Hokotaingahiwa	Whakapehapeha, *s.*			
Propitiate	Tapore, porepore	Whakaporepore, *v.*	Sharpen	Hokotara, hokoikoi	Whakakoi, *v.*
Proverb	Hokotauki	Whakatauki, *s.*	Shell	Ngaruru, mitimiti	Pupu, *s.*
Pull the hair	Huiti, uti	Tauhutihutu, *v.*	Sheltered	Ruru	Maru, *a.*
Pumice	Pungatei	Pungapunga	Shine	Kanape	Kanapa, *v.*
Pungency	Pukaukau	Pukawa, *s.*	Ship	Poro, wharau	Kaipuke, *s.*
Pupil of the eye	Honehu pango	Karupango, *s.*	Short	Poto	Poto, *a.*
Put out the tongue	Hokotetero	Whatero te arero	Side	Kaokao	Kaokao, *s.*
			Sing	Karamiha	Waiata, *v.*
Quicksand	Tapatupatu	Powharuwharu, *s.*	Singe	Murumuru	Hunuhunu, *v.*
			Six	Teono	Ono, *a.*
Raft	Whata	Kahupapa, *s.*	Skeleton	Tinani	Koiwi, *s.*
Rafter	Oko	Heke, *s.*	Skin	Kiri	Kiri, *s.*
Rainbow	Aniniwa	Aniwaniwa, *s.*	Slippery	Mania	Mania, *a.*
Rat	Kiore	Kiore, *s.*	Smoke	Auahi	Auahi, *s.*
Ray, fish	Whai, tarawai	Whai, *s.*	Smooth	Maene	Maeneene, *a.*
Reason	Take	Putake, *s.*	Sneeze	Tihe	Tihe, *v.*
Reel	Iawangarua	Hukeke, *s.*	Snore	Tangipurunga iho	Ngongoro, *v.*
Refuse	Hokotaingahiwa	Whakananau, *v.*	Snow	Haware	Huka
Regret	Manapa	Manawapa, *v.*	Snuffle	Whengu	Whenguwhengu, *v.*
Relax	Hokokoro	Whakakorokoro, *v.*	Sob	Pukumauri	Hota, *v.*
Remains of food	Toe kai	Toenga kai, *s.*	Sole of foot	Arowa, tapue	Kapukapu, *s.*
Respect	Manawa reka, hokotuiho	Manaaki, *v.*	Solitary	He ohokore	Mokemoke, *a.*
Restless	Hokioki	Okeoke, *a.*	Soot	Iawe	Awe, *s.*
Revenge	Hiku i t(*ch*)e hara	Rapu utu, *v.*	Soothe	Hokomarie, Hongona	Whakamarie, *v.*

202

	Moriori	*Maori*
Sore	Mae	Mamae, *a.*
Sore throat	Kateruku, tupuki	Katirehe, *s.*
Sorrow	Ka tau te-po	Ketekete, *s.*
Sour, to be	Kawa	Kawa, *v.*
South wind	Tonga	Tonga, *s.*
South-east	Marangai, matonga	Putonga, marangai, *s.*
South-west	Urumatonga	Tongakotaratara, *s.*
Spark	Korakoru	Korakora, *s.*
Spear	Tuparipari	Tao, *s.*
Spider	Purehe	Pungawerewere, *s.*
Spilled	Maringi	Maringi, *a.*
Spin	Hokowhenu	Miromiro, *v.*
Splash	Tupopo	Pohutuhutu, *v.*
Splinter	Maramara	Maramara, *s.*
Sponge	Puhongo	Pungorungoru, *s.*
Spotted	Hokopanapana, kotingotingo	Kotingotingo, *a.*
Sprawl	Maka	Takawhetawheta, *v.*
Spread	Takapo	Whariki, *v.*
Squall	Poahau	Pokaka, *v.*
Squeak	Hinamoko	Kotokoto, *v.*
Squeeze	Romi	Roromi, *v.*
Squint	Rewa	Tiwa, *v.*
Staff	Totoko	Tokotoko, *s.*
Stagger	Turorirori, ingainga	Turori
Star	Whetu	Whetu, *s.*
Start	Homauri	Ohomauri
Starve	Hokotiki	Whakatiki, *v.*
Steal	Kaiaha	Kaia
Stone	Pohatu	Pohatu, *v.*
Strange tribe	Kai imi, tua imi	Tauiwi, *s.*
Strange land	Whenua a rangi, te ikara	Tauwhenua, *s.*
Stranger	Manuwiri, mata hore	Manuhiri, *s.*
Strangle	Kuku iripuki	Nonoti, *v.*
Stubborn	Maro	Maro, *a.*
Stupid	Kuare	Kuare, *a.*
Suck	Momomi	Momi, *v.*
Summer	Raumati	Raumati, *s.*
Sun	Ra	Ra, *s.*
Surf	Huka tei	Huka tai, *s.*
Surrender	Tuku	Tuku, *v.*
Surround	Pokai	Mui, *v.*
Survivors	Morehu	Morehu, *s.*
Swallow	Horo	Horo, *v.*
Swell of sea	Huru	Huamo, *s.*
Swelling	Puku	Puku, *s.*
Swim	Rewa	Kau, *v.* (rewa, to float)
Swoon	Hokomohemo	Hemo, *v.*
Tail	Hiore	Hiore
Tame	Piri	Rarata, *a.*
Tear	Reimata	Roimata, *s.*
Tear	Heihei	Haehae, *v.*
Ten	Meangauru, tearauru, ngauru	Ngahuru, *a.*

	Moriori	*Maori*
Thick	Matotoru	Matotoru, *a.*
Thigh	Kuwha	Kuwha, *s.*
Thin	Mea tae	Tupuhi, *a.*
Thistle	Puwha	Puwha, *s.*
Three	Toru	Toru, *a.*
Throb	Kapakapa	Kapakapa, *v.*
Thunder	Whaitiri	Whatitiri, *s.*
Tickle	Hokoi	Whakakoekoe, *v.*
Tie, to	Nape	Nape (to weave)
Tight	Whaiti	Kiki, *a.*
Toothache	Nihotu	Nihotunga, *s.*
Tradition	Tukuiho	Tukunga iho, *s.*
Tree	Rakau	Rakau, *s.*
Tribe	Tua imi	Iwi, *s.*
Turn, to	Huri	Huri, *v.*
Twilight	Korikoko	Rikoriko, *a.*
Twins	Maihanga	Mahanga, *s.*
Twinkle	Hokopanopano	Kotamutumu, *v.*
Two	Teru	Rua, *a.*
Ugly	Tangatae	Ahua kino, *s.*
Ulcerated	Kotungutungu	Kikohunga, *a.*
Uncle	Matu ke	Matua keke, *s.*
Unite	Hokotei	Whakakotahi, *v.*
Unseasoned, as timber	Maimai	Torouka, *a.*
Urine	Mimi	Mimi, *s.*
Uvula	Koropuku o ro puanga	Tohetohe, *s.*
Vomit	Ruaki	Ruaki, *v.*
Waist	Hope	Hope, *s.*
Waste	Hokomau	Maumau, *a.*
Waterfall	Taheke	Taheke, *s.*
Wearisome	Oha	Hoha, *a.*
Whale	Rongomoana	Tohora, *s.*
Whirlpool	Ripo, koripo	Riporipo, *s.*
Whisper	Kotamutumu	Kohumuhumu, *v.*
Who?	Kuai	Ko wai, *p.*
Widow	Maetauaro	Pouaru, *s.*
Wind	Hau, matangi	Hau, matangi, *s.*
Wind (rainy)	Tawa	Hau ua, *s.*
Wing	Pakau	Pakau, *s.*
Wink	Kamo	Kamokamo, *v.*
Woman	Wahine, mahine	Wahine, *s.*
Womb	Teewe	Ewe (placenta), *s.*
Worm	Tunga	Toke, *s.*
Wriggle	Korikore, kewa	Korikori, *v.*
Wrinkle	Mingo	Mingomingo, *s.*
Yawn	Amama	Kohera, *v.*
Young	Kuo	Kuao, *a.*
Younger relative	Muri tae	Muringa, teina, *s.*
Youngest child	Potiki	Whakaotinga, potiki, *s.*
Yours	Na katou	Na koutou
Youth	Ropa tamiriki, ropa koropourangi	Taitamariki, *s.*

2. *List of Moriori living in 1861*

This census was compiled by Maori leaders on Chatham Island in October 1861 for William Seed, a government landing surveyor and former secretary to Sir George Grey, Governor. It is not entirely satisfactory inasmuch as some Moriori (like Maori) were known by more than one name; some names are misspelt; and it may not include all Moriori of mixed Moriori-Maori blood. The names are arranged according to districts. Note the small number of children in proportion to adults. The list was first published in the *New Zealand Gazette*, 1862.

KAINGAROA

Men:

Minarapa	Kirapu	Waiti
Horomona	Turukehu	Hori
Noa Tiki	Apakuku	Poki
Ranga	Tuhariu	Numi
Manahi		

Boys:

Henere	Poki	Rama

Women:

Ngaria	Mateo	Whero
Awaawaroa	Onepu	Pureti
Motu	Ngamiko	Tiomanu
Ngohiturua	Amiria	Emiri
Weko	Rako	Hariata
Reuma		

Girls:

Hema	

OUENGA (OWENGA)

Men:

Torea	Rutapu	Tume
Maikona	Ngarito	Makora
Puha	Tumutangi	Te Teira
Pewa	Tame	Popotai
Tamihape	Tapu	

Boys:

Horomona	

Women:

Moanarua	Wairanga	Tini
Ngapine	Paranihi	Patehou
Akahu	Hiwa	Panga
Wharekohu	Miru	Paranihi
Nuka	Apia	

Girls:

Katarau	Paranihi	Ngahine

TUPUANGI AND TE RAKI

Men:

Potini	Rongo	Matataia
Poea	Mairu	Moko

Women:

Pinarepe	Hariata

WAITEKE (WAITANGI)

Men:

Ngira	Taituha	Turi
Rangi	Pawa	Tamakohao
Pahitoa	Tunanga	Eparaima
Ngori	Ngamunanga	Mawete
Hape	Tara	Tatana
Tatahi	Rau	Tiemi
Horomona	Tamahuaru	Hange
Te Koro	Pewa	Tamotoke
Toro	Pohatu	Tiori
Pukerua	Pumipi	Kakau
Paru	Ngamaia	Wiri
Iwikorekaha	Rawiri	Waiorua
Ngoingoi	Horomona	Paraki
Puru	Tame	

Boys:

Apiata	Hapurono

Women:

Hinetoa	Tururu	Hinekapiti
Tepuku	Ngarua	Makuku
Hiko	Papaki	Piaro
Taramea	Manukau	Tauteke
Tukahau	Makutu	Rititia
Hiteke	Whano	Te Puku
Mangape	Mihi	Toa
Matiti	Kino	Hara
Kahoki	Remu	Ko-oke
Para	Turangamu	
Turi	Tahouhou	

Girls:

Papa	

WHAREKAURI

Men:

Maitahuri	Tame	Arohitu
Tarahina	Tunu	Pokare
Mokai	Tiemi	
Maitakawa	Tiemi	

Boys:

Mangu	

Women:

Paana	Urukapu

3.   Moriori migration traditions

The following traditions accounting for the Moriori presence in the Chatham Islands and the sequence of settlement there is reprinted from Alexander Shand's *The Moriori People of the Chatham Islands*, Memoir of the Polynesian Society, volume II, Wellington, 1911, pp. 100–119.

The first canoe of which the Morioris have any tradition was Kahu's (*Ko ro waka a Kahu*), and of this story there are two versions. The people of the north end of the island hold that Kahu arrived first at Kaingaroa Harbour, where he planted his fern-root (*aruhe*) at a place named Tongariro. This was called Kahu's fern-root, and was known as such until after the arrival of the Maoris in 1836, when it was destroyed by pigs. Another name for fern-root was 'Kahu's root' (*Te aka a Kahu*), a simile. There was a difference between his fern-root, it is said, and the ordinary kind. That of Kahu had a very light fibre (*kaka*), and when the outside rind was scraped off, was white and soft; it was evidently a finer variety, not having the strong yellow fibre of the ordinary kind.

He brought with him his god — Kikokiko — also named Kahu, which he secreted at Rangikapua, the point on the western side of Kaingaroa Harbour. He also brought the *kumara* (sweet potato), which he planted on the island, but it would not grow. This was the *karakia* (incantation):

> Kumara no Aropawa[1] i ko
> Kumara na rau toro, tinaku[2] e.
> Homai e i ahu ai o wahine[3] ti.
> E kaha, takina[4] na rau toro, tinaku e.

Kumara from distant Aropawa,
Kumara of the spreading leaves, increase (or grow deep);
Come, be heaped up by the (your) junior wives,
Be strong, spring up the spreading leaves, increase.

By this recital, which is a very ancient one, it will be seen that the Morioris preserved the knowledge of the *kumara* plant in their isolation. Beyond the fact of its having been brought here, they knew nothing more, until told of it by the Maoris on their arrival in 1836. Prior to this, on seeing potatoes brought to the island by the early ships, they said they were *kumara*; also called *pakamara*. It would appear from this that both Moriori and Maori carried their seed *kumara*, &c., with them on their journeys, and they must have had canoes (or perhaps vessels) constructed so as to keep them safe from sea water, which would have rotted them. The Morioris fix the date of Kahu's arrival in the time of their autochthone ancestors Kahuti and Te Akaroroa, who lived at Kaingaroa; of Maripane, who lived at Matarakau; of Tamakautara, who lived at Te Awapatiki; of Karangatai and Karangatua, who lived at Whangaroa; and of Tapeneke and Taponi, who lived at Waitangi. The name of the canoe was said to be 'Tane,' and the crew were *hokoru(a)* (forty in number). Some of the old men appeared to be in doubt as to the name, and referred to it generally as Kahu's canoe — *Ko ro waka a Kahu*. On arrival, Kahu found the island in an unsettled state — *kauteretere* (floating) — and he joined together some places, and separated others.

According to another story, his canoe arrived first at Tuku, as it is called — the name in full being Tuku-a-Tamate(a), who was one of the crew of Kahu's canoe, and apparently a man of distinction. Leaving the canoe there, Kahu proceeded round the island by way of the cliffs of the south coast to Ouenga, and afterwards to Te Awapatiki on the east coast, where he slept, and the place was called by his name, Kahu. There were many places on his journey where he could not sleep. Proceeding on his journey, he went by the north coast as far as Waitaha (where he found the sea breaking through from coast to coast) and into Whangamoe in Petre Bay, thus making a separate island of the north-west corner of the island, so that he could not go to Maunganui. From Waitaha he went across to Whangamoe, where he signalled by fire for his canoe to come to him from Tuku. The crew complied, and came across to Ohuru or Tei-kohuru (calm sea), another name for Whangaroa Harbour. Previously to this, however, he had joined together the gaping waterway, presumably to get across to his canoe at Tei-kohuru.

What the origin of this part of the story is, would be very difficult to conceive. At present there is nothing whatever in the configuration of this part of the island to suggest a passage of the sea from the north coast across to Whangamoe. None of the Morioris could throw any light on the subject, or say what was meant.

After rejoining his canoe at Whangaroa, Kahu then sailed across to Waitangi, and planted his *kumaras* at a place called Okahu, at Mongoutu, with the result that they would not grow. After staying there for some short time, he departed, saying that the land was a *whenua rei* (a wet land), and returned to Aropawa and Hawaiki, as shown by the *karakia* called 'Kahu's Tides' (*Ka Tai-a-Kahu*):

> Ko tai miti, ko tai whano,
> Miti tai ki Aotea,
> Whano tai ki Hawaiki.

'Tis the ebbing tide, 'tis the departing tide.
Ebb, O tide! to Aotea,
Depart, O tide! to Hawaiki.

> Paonga, e miti[5] ka tai o Aotea,
> Paonga, e miti ka tai o Aropawa,
> Paonga, e miti, Paonga e horo.
> Whakarongo ki tai nei,
> Ka ki te pai o Pehanga-riki,
> Ka pa te tai ki Tauwaehoro.
> Ko tai mitikia e Kahu,
> Ooi! ko tai rere ki Hawaiki.

Paonga, lick up[6] the tides of Aotea;
Paonga, lick up the tides of Aropawa.
Paonga, lick up, Paonga, devour.[7]
Listen to the (this) tide.
The tide sounds at Pehanga-riki,
The tide beats on Tauwaehoro.
'Tis the tide swallowed up by Kahu,
Ooi! 'tis the tide which flows to Hawaiki.

The story of Kahu's canoe staying at Tuku appears doubtful, as it is only a boat-harbour, and unsuitable for a canoe to stay at in certain winds, and more so for a vessel such as this must have been to have come even from Aotea (New Zealand), not to speak of Hawaiki. However, the story appears so far circumstantial in the lighting of a fire-signal for the canoe to come to Whangaroa, and it is given as related.

RANGIHOUA AND RANGIMATA CANOES

The next canoes to arrive at the island were Rangihoua and Rangimata. The cause of this migration, they say, was fighting in Hawaiki. There appear to have been various *take* (causes) of disturbance. First, the troubles of Manaia; second, the killing of Rakei; third, the burning of Ta-Uru-o-Monono or Manono. The last trouble, which caused the immediate departure of these canoes, arose through one Tama-te-kohuruhuru, son of Tu-moana, who killed his wife or sweetheart, Papa, in a fit or rage, because she accused him of impotency.

Tu-moana's tribe was named Wheteina, and it is evident from the story that they lived in pretty close proximity to the Rauru tribe, to which Papa, or Tahu, and her father Horopapa belonged. It would appear that, although said to be of different tribes, they both were evidently of the same stock, and related to one another, as Tu-moana called Papa his son's sister (no doubt a cousin of some kind or other), and Horopapa he speaks of as his uncle. On discovering the murder of his daughter, Horopapa and his people surrounded the house of Tu-moana, his son, and people at night, and killed them all, with the exception of Tu-moana, who escaped into 'his thickets' (*hitiki*), and hid there for some time. Tira, his brother-in-law connived at his escape. (Tira was a younger brother of Horopapa, and married Tu-moana's sisters — a Ra Puhi rau ko Ro Pua — Te Puhi and Te Pua.) Tu-moana, after this, gathered his people and commenced fighting with the Rauru tribe. One of the Wheteina, Koro-wahia, lying in ambush in the hollow of a *totara* tree (*Podocarpus totara*), killed Tira, which added fuel to the fire. Horopapa then sent to fetch his elder brother Hapa-kiore (all three were sons of Tchura-huruhuru = Maori Tuara-huruhuru), who gathered all their tribe, the Rauru-motchihere, or -motuhake — the true Rauru — to fight with the Wheteina and their allies. The battle took place on the sand-beach of Whanga-patiki (said by the old men to have been a short one, not more than half a mile in length). One of the headlands was called Tauranga, the other Tapuika. The Rauru occupied the Tauranga, and Tu-moana, with his allies, the Tapuika end of

the beach. The latter people were exceedingly numerous, covering the beach, hence Horopapa's proverb — 'Tapuika is dark, Tauranga is light' (*Ka po Tapuika, ka ao Tauranga*), in allusion to the multitude of Tu-moana's people, and the few of the Rauru. The names of the tribes who assisted Tu-moana were Ruarangi, Muturangi, Wheteina, Harua, Tch-Eitara, Makao-a-uha, Makao-a-to(a), Matanga, Poutama, Tch-Eituhi, Tch-Etikoke and Tch-Etiao or Etiaw'(a). They fought, it is said, until the sea on the shore was red with blood, and in the end the Rauru defeated Tu-moana and his people. The account is vague as to how long the fighting was going on previous to the battle; but during that period the canoes Rangihoua and Rangimata were being built, and they put to sea during the fight. Rangihoua was not properly completed when she was launched, though Rangimata was. To this fact they attribute the former's ill-luck in getting ultimately wrecked, and in consequence very little is known about her people, of whom only a few were saved. All the legends and *karakias* concentrate around Rangimata and her arrival at the island. Although it is said Tu-moana and his tribal allies were defeated, it does not appear from a further part of the account that they were so completely. When Rangimata was afloat with Rangihoua, before setting forth on her voyage, the Rangimata people recognised the voice of Kirika, elder sister of Tu-moana, reciting the incantation of girding the *marowhara* (*Pikinga i ri marowhara*) of her brother. After recording this, the story says, *Ka torikirikitii Ta Uru Manuka* ('Ta Uru Manuka became small in the distance').

Their home left, they 'set out to live or die' (*Pokai ta uru o te whenua, pokai ta uru o te moana*), to wander round the crown of the land, to wander round the crown (expanse) of the ocean, to arrive after all their wanderings at the Chatham Islands. It is evident from the accounts that they endured severe privations on the way, particularly in the case of the Rangihoua canoe, whose crews were dying from lack of food and water, and in their helpless condition were wrecked on the north coast of the island, at Okahu. Another canoe, called Pouariki, made at the same time as Rangimata and Rangihoua, was said to have left with them, but, beyond this statement, nothing more was heard of her after leaving. From the short account given of her, however, she appears to have been a double canoe of some kind, having a consort, 'Katoko' by name — *He whakapiri no Pouariki* ('An adjunct' — lie close together — 'of Pouariki'). As the Moriori raft-canoe was not in the least like this, of which the tradition alone is preserved, it is evident that the original canoes or vessels in which they came here from Hawaiki were entirely of a different character to any thing now in use either by Moriori or Maori. With Pouariki was another canoe, Poreitua, whose consort (*whakapiri*) was named Mano, which came likewise, but, as in the case of Pouariki, nothing further is known of her. There were also two other canoes, called Te Rangi-tu-makohakoha and Turore; these were canoes of witchcraft (*E waka makutu*). It does not appear if these were double or not, and nothing further was known of them by the narrator.

The canoe-launching chorus (*Tau to waka*) was as follows:

E Pouariki, Ooi!
Tokina mai au, E-ei, E-ei!
E ka ki ku rung' o Pouariki.
E kei, e ke ro.

O Pouariki, *Ooi!*
Drag me along, E-ei, E-ei!
It sounds (of dragging) on Pouariki,
She moves (or rises), she moves altogether.

The Rauru people are said to have had seven canoes which did not come with the others, but were left in Hawaiki. Their names were Tama-kororo, Tupu-ngaherehere, Mata-rangi, Tohoro-i-ongongo (waste of nettles), Hape, Karangatai, and the last, Tihauwea, was another canoe of witchcraft. The *karakias* (or prayers) only of these canoes were said to have been brought to the Chathams. Nothing further is known of Rangihoua after being dragged down to the water, followed by Rangimata in the darkness of the early morn (*tchi ata marua po*). They were launched silently, for fear of their enemies, and after a while their crews set out on their long voyage with anxious hearts. Rangihoua, after being buffeted about, her crew weak and dying with thirst, arrived on the north coast of the island, where the vessel, apparently out of control, was either beached or driven ashore among the breakers, and was rapidly smashed up; many of the crew being drowned, or dying on landing. The few known to have escaped, and whose names have been handed down, are Tunanga, Taupo and Tarere. The captain of Rangihoua, Te Raki-ro(a), apparently died, or was drowned. Many of them died on landing, through exposure, and from drinking water. This was the case with their *ariki* and priest, Honeke, who in his extreme thirst, forgetting that he was carrying his god, Rongomai-whiti, on his back, proceeded to drink. The god, in his anger at this desecration, killed him, the priest dying as he drank. It is reasonable to suppose that whatever rites and religious ceremonies were known to the Rangihoua people, were equally well known to those of the Rangimata, and would be preserved by them; but owing apparently to this wreck, and to the fact that all the old men of the north-west corner of the island were dead before these traditions were collected, such (if any ever existed) were lost with them. The account given by the others is, that the Rangihoua immigrants left no rites and ceremonies.

The season when these canoes arrived was *Te Whitu o Rongo* (the seventh of Rongo or July, sometimes including part of August), the stormiest weather about the island; so that, apart from the rough strong winds, the cold of these southern latitudes must have been most trying to the immigrants, accustomed as they were to milder climates.

To return, however, to Rangimata and her crew. Her captain or chief was Mihiti, whose wife was Kimi. The names of three of their sons were remembered; the eldest, Mawake, was said to be a bad man; the second, Tama-te-kahia, they are silent about; but the youngest, Mawete, was a good man. But how they showed these qualities is not recorded. Mawake, the eldest, was the husband of Wairaka,

who was a woman of rank, and of whom further mention will be made later on. The builder of Rangimata was Ru, of the Rauru clan; his wife's name was Pe, a niece (*timit'-a-kahu*) of Kahukura. Others who are remembered to have come in Rangimata were Nunuku, Pehe (a nephew of Kahukura), Mihi-toro, Tarewa (with Tokoraro, his wife, and their son Kauitia), with other passengers, Hapa and Kakatai. Maruroa and Kauanga were also of the crew, with Tchu-te-ngana and Matarangi, whose house was Whareama, as well as many others whose names are forgotten.

Maruroa and Kauanga were brothers, and it was they who are said to have gone to the land of Tahiri, Irea and Momori (prior to the migration), who told them of Rekohu, or the Chathams, and taught them many other things. The place they went to was called Hukurangi, from whence they assert they brought the *karaka* tree, the *kumara* or *pakamara*, with the *marautara*. It would appear therefore, if this statement is correct, that the Morioris knew of the island and its position before coming to it. At the same time, their case must have been urgent, to cause them to leave their homes at such a time of the year. There once existed a *karakia* called a *kenewaka* (*utanga waka* in Maori) which recited all the names of the crew and people of Rangimata, but unfortunately it could not be remembered by the old men, otherwise all her passengers would have been known. Before dragging the canoe into the water, they performed the ceremony of burning the chips from the place where Rangimata was made (*a ra kohanga o Rangimata*), and chanted the following *umere* (*awa-moana* in Maori):

Wera, wera te rangi[8] [*or ra*] tu-nuku, tu-rangi,
Ka pai a Nuku, ka pai a Rangi,
Kahukura[9] wahia te moana,
Tungia i Hhiawaiki [Hawaiki] 'a[10] wera,
Ka puta ki waho Tu-ta-wake,[11]
Hiko,[12] hi marua to, hiko ki marua to.
Wera, wera te ra tu-nuku, tu-rangi.
Ka pai a Nuku, ka pai a Rangi,
Kahukura wahia te moana,
Tungia i Hhiawaiki 'a wera,
Ka rapu Mataihawata, Tane,
Ka mahuta a Tu-tawake.
Hiko, hi marua to, hiko hi marua to,
Rere atu, rere mai, rere papa.
Kia tuia[13] te kohao,
Whakarere — Taki.
Hokoihoko[14] te manu ka turiki,
E rongo Kenowaka (= kenewaka).

Burn, burn, O sun, shining on earth, in heaven,
Nuku is propitious, Rangi is propitious (Earth and
  Heaven).
Kahukura, divide the sea!
Light up Hawaiki that it may consume.
Tutawake comes forth,
Remove, remove quickly. Remove, remove quickly.
Burn, burn, O sun, shining on earth, in heaven,
Nuku is propitious, Rangi is propitious.

Light up Hawaiki that it may burn
The weird ones Mataihawata, Tane.
Tu-tawake comes forth.
Remove, remove quickly. Remove, remove quickly.
Rush forward, rush hither, rush gliding along.
To fasten the connection (or seising).
Leave, start!
Let the fledgling bird flap its wings,
'Tis a sound of departure.

After this they recited the *kenewaka*, a fragment of which only is remembered, beginning:

1. Maruroa, Kauange e pa'[15] ki whea taua e?
   E pa' ki roto, ka pange ko roto, ka pange ko roto, e.
   E Haupapa, e Haupapa mo Tahiri[16] te rangi
   Ka pange ko roto, ka pange ko roto, e.

2. Maruroa, Kauanga e pa' ki whea?
   E pa' ko waho, ka pange ko waho, ka pange ko waho, e.
   E Haupapa, e Haupapa mo Tahiri te rangi
   Ka pange ko waho, ka pange ko waho, e.

1. Maruroa and Kauanga, where shall we two be placed?
   Be placed inside, be placed inside, *e*.
   O Haupapa, Haupapa! the day is Tahiri's —
   Place him in, place him in.

2. Maruroa and Kauanga, where shall (they) be placed?
   Throw them out, throw them outside, *e*.
   O Haupapa, Haupapa! the day is Tahiri's (Mangatea) —
   Throw them out, throw them outside, *e*.

And in this manner all Rangimata's crew were recited, verse after verse. It seems not improbable, however, that this was composed after the event, by way of commemoration, and to prevent the names of the crew being forgotten.

When the above ceremonies were over, the morn began to break (*Ka pa tch ata o Heia*), and the canoes moved out to sea, about which time, probably, the incident occurred of Kirika reciting the *maro* of her brother Tu-moana, which was as follows:

1. Ko Tu, ko Rongo te maro ka mehori, Tane, Tangaroa.
   Pera hoki e tapu, taputapu,[17]
   Te maro o ti Ariki,[18] te maro o Waiorangi.
   Tangohia i tih'(i) o Ro Maka,[19]
   E taua ki Whiti, taua ki Tonga, taua ki Whiti te wawa,[20]
   Eke tu mai runga,
   Rawea mai ke whiti makorapa,
   No wai te maro ka mehori?

2. Ko Uru, Ngangana, Aiorangi,
   Ko Tahu, ko Moko, ko Maroro, ko Wakehau
   te maro ka mehori,

Pera hoki ra e tapu, taputapu,
Te maro o ti Ariki, te maro o Waiorangi,
Tangohia i tih'(i) o Ro Maka,
E taua ki Whiti, taua ki Tonga, taua ki Whiti te wawa,
Eke tu mai runga,
Rawe ake whiti makorapa,
No wai te maro ka mehori?

1. 'Tis Tu, 'tis Rongo the outspread *maro*, Tane and Tangaroa,
   As also the sacred ends,
   The *maro* of the Lord, the *maro* of Waiorangi.
   Seize the crown of the Maka,
   Fight to the east, fight to the west, fight to the distant east,
   Rise, stand up!
   Gird that it may encircle.
   Whose is the *maro* which is outspread?

2. Uru, Ngangana, Aiorangi,
   Tahu, Moko, Maroro and Wakehau is the outspread *maro*,
   As also the sacred ends,
   The *maro* of the Lord, the *maro* of Waiorangi.
   Seize the crown of the Maka,
   Fight to the east, fight to the west, fight to the distant east,
   Rise, stand up!
   Gird that it may encircle.
   Whose is the *maro* which is outspread?

This, as regards the Rangimata migrants, was the last they heard or saw of their Hawaiki home (if such it was), where these incidents took place, until some considerable time after, when Moe, one of the Rauru adversaries, came to the island with his people in the Oropuke canoe. It is at this stage that *Ko Matangi-ao* ends, and all later stories of their voyage to the Chathams, and their subsequent war with Moe and his people, are called *Hokorong'(o) tiring' (a)* ('Hearing of the ears'), in opposition to the former 'dawn of existence.'

The *karakias* in connection with their voyage show that they must have suffered considerable hardships, presumably from contrary and baffling winds, as well as lack of food and water. Hence their voyage is referred to as *kimi* (the searching) and *waipu* (immensity of water, ocean only). It is highly probable that these *karakias* were based on, or were the original ones used in their Polynesian voyages, but subsequently modified and brought more into accord with their surroundings. They still bear the strong impress of the troubles the people passed through. Thus in the story of '*Waipu*,' the first *karakia* is called *Ta Upoko Hauta* (*hau-ta*) ('Slaying the heads of the wind'), in which are recited the names of the gods, together with the 'Heaven-born.' Apparently in all these cases they are invoked to give effect to the *karakia* —

TA UPOKO HAU-TA

1. Ko Tu, ko Rongo, Tane, Tangaroa,
   Ka tuakina[21] ki te rakau hanga[22] mua,
   Ka tuakina ki te rakau hanga roto,
   Ka tuakina ki ta uru o Mahuta,[23]
   Ka tuakina ki ta uru no Mahuta, a.

2. Ko Uru, Ngangana, Aiorangi,
   Ka tuakina ki te rakau hanga mua,
   Ka tuakina ki te rakau hanga roto,
   Ka tuakina ki ta uru o Mahuta,
   Ka tuakina ki ta uru no Mahuta, a.

3. Ko Tiki, ko Toi, Rauru, Whatonga, &c.

1. 'Tis Tu, Rongo, Tane and Tangaroa
   Who perform the *tua* with the first-made timber,
   Who perform the *tua* with the inner-made timber,
   Who perform the *tua* with the crown of Mahuta,
   Who perform the *tua* with the crown from Mahuta, a.

2. 'Tis Uru, Ngangana, Aiorangi,
   Who perform the *tua* with the first-made timber,
   Who perform the *tua* with the inner-made timber,
   Who perform the *tua* with the crown of Mahuta,
   Who perform the *tua* with the crown from Mahuta.

The third and remaining verses continue to recite the rest of the 'Heaven-born,' down to the last, Ro Tauira.

The next *karakia*, of which we give an example, is recited by the Morioris in this order, and is called *Ko e hau te kamakama* (Maori, *Ko hau te kamokamo*) — 'The light-puffing wind.'

1. Ko e hau te kamakama,[24]
   Kamakama i runga, kamakama i raro,
   Ka tu me re kamakama,
   Ko ro toki ai?
   Ko ro toki a uru,
   Ko ro toki ai?
   Ko ro toki a Ngana, hei whakarehua,
   Nganangana[25] i tche Nuku, nganangana i tche Rangi
   E Tchua.[26]
   Koe[27] ra ta mata mo Ruanuku[28]
   Kuai te mata mo Mauhika?
   Ko au ko Rawa[29]
   Hurauwa, hurauwa, hupaka, hupaka, hutoi te rangi.

2. Ko e hau te kamakama
   Kamakama i runga, kamakama i raro
   Ka tu me re kamakama
   Ko ro toki ai?
   Ko ro toki a Uru
   Ko ro toki a Ngana i te Nuku ai whakarehua
   Nganangana i tche Nuku, nganangana i tchia Rangi
   E Tchua.
   Koe ra te mata mo Ruanuku.
   Kuai ta mata o Mauhika?

Ko au ko Rawa.
Hurauwa, hurauwa, hupaka, hupaka, hutoi te rangi.

3. Tuakina i ta uru o tch Anini,[30] o tch Arohi
   Hiti ki roto hau te kamakama
   Ko ro toki ai?
   Ko ro toki i a Tiki, i a Toi, i a Rauru, i a Whatonga.
   Ko ro toki ai?
   Ko ro toki i a Rongomai, ia Kahukura.
   Ko ro toki ai?
   Ko ro toki i a Motuariki, i a Ruanuku, Tch Aomarama.
   Ko ro toki ai?
   Ko ro toki i a Tumare me Ta Ranganuku,
   Matirito, Wari ko Ro Tauira
   Ka tu me re kamakama
   E Hina[31] tae ake ru—u
   E Hina tae toro, e—.

1. 'Tis the light puffing wind:
   It puffs above, it puffs below,
   It comes with puffs.
   Whose is the axe?
   'Tis the axe of Uru.
   Whose is the axe?
   'Tis the axe of Ngana, with which to destroy.
   To fight in earth, to fight in heaven.
   Oh, 'tis a Tchua [= Tua].
   Thou art the face for Ruanuku [you are doomed
       to destruction].
   Whose is the face of Mauhika?
   'Tis I, 'tis Rawa.
   Be gathered, be gathered together, be roasted,
       be roasted [dried up].
   Let the heaven [or sky] be shrivelled up.

2. 'Tis the light puffing wind:
   It puffs above, it puffs below,
   It comes with puffs.
   Whose is the axe?
   'Tis the axe of Uru.
   Whose is the axe?
   'Tis the axe of Ngana with which to destroy.
   To fight in earth, to fight in heaven.
   O, 'tis a Tchua [= Tua].
   Thou art the face for Ruanuku:
   Whose is the face of Mauhika?
   'Tis I, 'tis Rawa.
   Be gathered, be gathered together, be roasted, be roasted,
   Let the heaven be shrivelled up.

3. Chop down the crown of the Anini [sensation],
       of the Arohi [shimmering all]
   Veer into the puffing wind.
   Whose is the axe?
   'Tis the axe of Tiki, Toi, Rauru, Whatonga.
   Whose is the axe?
   'Tis the axe of Rongomai and Kahukura.
   Whose is the axe?

'Tis the axe of Motuariki, Ruanuku Tch Aomarama.
Whose is the axe?
'Tis the axe of Tumare and Ranganuku,
Matirito, Wari, and Ro [te] Tauira.
It comes with puffs
O Hina! come forth there.
O Hina! come! *Toro, e—* [a song-ending].

The following *karakias* apparently show what straits the people were in owing to lack of water. There are three, called *Waihau o Waipu*, as well as *Ka Kapu hokaina o Waipu*, 'Drinking from the hollow of the hand, or from a wooden vessel.' The Morioris made drinking vessels of wood, called *hakana*, to hold water, with lids, and the same to keep ornaments in or to hide the relics of their gods, but generally on land they used *puwai*, *i.e.*, tightly laid up blades of green flax in a long funnel shape, which lasted until the flax shrivelled up and had to be renewed.

KA KAPU HOKAINUI O WAIPU

1. Tena e Tu, e Rongo, Kotia ta uru o Moti-hanga,[32]
   Taapa te hou ki te rangi ko whakataunarewa
   Ka utu au tau[33] kapu e
   Utu ki te rangi a Utua[34] ka roa koi toro, e.
2. Tena e Rongomai-whiti, e Rongomai-rau, kotia, &c.
3. Tena e Rongomai-mana, e Rongomai-ha, e
   Rongomai-tauira, kotia, &c.
4. Tena e Tiki [reciting all the 'Heaven-born'], kotia
   ta uru, &c.

THE DRINKING FROM THE HOLLOW OF THE HAND OF WAIPU

1. Then, O Tu! O Rongo! cut off the crown of
   Moti-hangai,
   Pierce direct into the high exalted heaven.
   I fill (or dip) the hollow of my hand,
   Dip to the heaven of utua, 'tis long indeed — *toro, e*.
2. Then, O Rongomai-whiti! Rongomai-rau! cut off
   the crown, &c.
3. Then, O Rongomai-mana! Rongomai-ha!
   Rongomai-tauira! cut off, &c.

There are a number more of verses reciting the 'Heaven-born,' but all commencing the same as the first verse. This incantation, with others, was used by the Morioris in dry summer to bring rain, when the water was dry in some parts of the island.

ANOTHER WAIHAU

This is evidently a more recent version of the above. The names mentioned are those of people who came to the island in the canoes, but, with that exception, the words are the same, and need not be translated.

1. Tena, e Mehoriki, e Patea, e Kahukura-hangaitorea,
   kotia ta uru o Moti-hangai,

Taapa te hou ki te rangi, ko whakataunarewa,
Ka utu au tau kapu, e.
Utu ki ta rangi a Utua ka roa, koi re,
Ka utu au tau kapu, e.
Utu ki ta rangi a Utua ka roa, koi toro.

2. Tena, e Maruhoanga, e Tutoake, kotia ta uru, &c.

3. Tena, e Rongomai-taihongo, e Tchuteme, kotia, &c.

WAIHAU O WAIPU

1. Hunake i raro nei ko wai pupu, ko wai whanake,
   Kia homai kia utuhia ki te mauru o Utihau,[35]
   Takina[36] e, takina, takina rangi, takina, e.

2. Hunake i ranga nei ko ua nui, ko ua roa, ko ua torikiriki,
   Ko ua topanapana, ko pata ua, ko pata awha
   Kia homai kia utuhia ki ri mauru o Utihau.
   Takina e, takina, takina rangi 'taina,[37] e takina,
   takina, rangi takina.

3. E whaoa rangi whao,
   E k' whakataka, whakataka, whakataka te kapu
   Whakatake e, 'taina, takina rangi 'taina.

1. Rise up from beneath, waters bubbling, waters
   ascending,
   That it may be given and dipped from the spirit
   of Utihau.
   Oh draw it, draw it, draw from heaven, oh draw it.

2. Come forth from above, the great rain, the long
   rain, the small rain,
   The pattering rain, the drops of rain, the tempest drops,
   That it may be given and dipped from the spirit
   of Utihau.
   Oh draw it, draw it, draw from heaven, fill it (the vessel),
   Oh draw it, draw from heaven, draw it.

3. Oh fill in heaven, fill,
   Oh pour down, pour down, pour down (into)
   the vessel,
   Oh pour down, fill in, draw from heaven, fill in
   (or lade it).

It will be seen by this last incantation, or it may be called a prayer, how much the Rangimata people must have suffered from lack of water. It was contended by some of the Morioris that the stories told under the head of *Waipu* did not belong to Rangimata, but referred to the Oropuke canoe. This does not, however, appear to be the case, as in the second *Waihau*, or *Kapu hokainu*, or *Whakainu*, the names of Maruhoanga and Tutoake appear, who were admittedly Rangimata people.

Another form of incantation, to beat down an unfavourable wind and obtain a fair one, also used by the migrants, was called an *Umu-toa-rangi* ('Oven to roast the heaven'), of which there were many, but only one example will be cited here, called *Ta Umu-o-Waipu* or *Tonga-minino* (otherwise *Tongamani*), strong south-east wind:

TONGAMININO

Taona ta umu, popokia atu ki te Marangai te Marepe,
    e Tongaminino!
Taona ta umu, popokia atu e Tongaminino!
    e Tongaminino!
Ko ta umu na Horohoro, e Tongaminino! e Tongaminino!
'Taina ta umu popokia atu te whakuru(a), tch Angaiho,
    e Tongaminino!
'Taina ta umu popokia atu ta Uru ro(a) ta Raki ro(a).
Popokia atu ta Uru ro, te Tonga ro e Tongaminino!
Ko ta umu na Horohoro, na Whaminino hoki, na
    Wawao, e.
E Tongaminino! e Tongaminino!
Taona ta umu popokia atu tch Anini,[39] tch Arohi, e
    Tongaminino! e Tongaminino, e!

Light the oven, press back the east and north-east
    wind, O Tongaminino!
Light the oven, press it back, O Tongaminino!
    O Tongaminino!
'Tis the oven of Horohoro, O Tongaminino!
    O Tongaminino!
Load up the oven, press back the north and north-
    north-west winds, O Tongaminino!
Load up the oven, press back the south-west and
    west winds,
Press back the south-west and south-east winds,
    O Tongaminino!
'Tis the oven of Horohoro, of Whakaminino also,
    of Wawao, e.
O Tongaminino! O Tongaminino!
Light the oven, press back the Anini, the Arohi,
    O Tongaminino! O Tongaminino!

There is also another incantation used, called 'The Basket of T' Whai Tokorau' (*Ko ro Kete o T' Whai Tokorau*). This Whai Tokorau was a son of Tahiri Mang-ate(a), the wind-god, or father of the winds, but this incantation was not used until that of 'The Axe of Heau-mapuna' (*Ko ro Toki o Heau-mapuna*), the swaying-wind, had first been recited, after which *Ro (te) Kete o T' Whai Tokorau* ('His Basket in which to confine the winds'). Then, to produce a calm, came *Ta Umu a Huirangi* ('The Oven of Huirangi'). These, with others, may appear at another time.

All these incantations, but especially those to allay tempests, were constantly used by the Morioris in their fishing excursions, or passages from one island of the group to another, when caught by strong winds. Their raft-canoes, being slow of progression, made it difficult to get home or into safety.

Rangimata, it is said, arrived at or made the land on the north coast of Chatham Island, and some of her crew landed and planted the *karaka*[40] tree, which they called *wairarapa*, at a place called Wairarapa, as well as the *marautara*[41] (a kind of convolvulus creeper), also at Wairarapa, on the coast near Te Ika-rewa, at Te Umumoki. It grew nowhere else on the island, hence possibly the especial note made of it by the Morioris.

Rangimata's next place of call was Te Whakuru(a), at the north-east part of the island, where she anchored, and there Maruroa, Kauanga, and others landed, finding, it is said, Rongopapa and his people (authochtones) at that place.

On their meeting, Rongopapa enquired, '*Wari ko tere?*' ('Who are the strangers — party?'). Answer, 'Maruroa and Kauanga'; who, in reply, asked, '*Wari ko hunua?*' ('Who are the people of the place — *tangata whenua?*'). Answer, 'Rongopapa.' Upon this, Maruroa and Kauanga enquired, 'What are those things which you are killing?' They replied, '*Hipuku* (sea-elephant), *puhina* (fur-seal), *mimiha* (hair-seal). The skins are our clothing, but what is your clothing?' They answered, '*Waruwaru* [*weruweru* in Maori]. *Ko te pere nui a Tawaru*' (a proverb). Rongopapa said, 'Your clothing is chilly and cold (*mataanu, makariri*), but this is the skin of our ancestor, Hhia Maitai,[42] and cannot be worn for its warmth.'

After this, Rangimata arrived at Okawa. Here Utangaroa landed and dwelt; although another says he landed at Mairangi and stayed there, his name being retained in the *Tokotoko-o-Utangaro(a)*. The canoe was nearly wrecked, however, at Okawa, on the sunken rock of Manapo, but she was luckily got off, on which occurrence Wairaka's voice was heard to exclaim, '*A, te rere mai i roto whaiti*' ('See, she sails in the channel, or passage'). By others it is alleged that Rangimata came from the south, and got on to or else into very close proximity to Kaira, a sunken wash about four miles off 'The Horns,' where Wairaka saved her by the incantation *Ko ro Tutaki a ra Waku* ('The closing of the *Waku*'), and added, when in safety, *Ka to ra manino* ('The clam prevails'). Whether either of these stories had any real foundation in fact appears to be questionable. Had Rangimata touched on Manapo Reef in fine weather she might have escaped, but Kaira is a wash on which a heavy surge constantly breaks, and from which, unless carried by, nothing could escape destruction. It seems not improbable that the story had its origin either in or on their way from Hawaiki, as the name Wairaka is common to the Maoris as well, and a very similar occurrence is said to have happened to the Mata-atua canoe after her arrival at Whakatane, in New Zealand, in which another woman named Wairaka took part.

After her escape from this danger, Rangimata sailed to Te Awapatiki, where she and her crew landed . . . and were opposed by the Kau Te Hamata (Hamata people), the autochthones of the place. Marupuku and his people, on seeing the migrants, put in a post in the sand with the image of their god, Heauoro. But the general account of Rangimata was, that on landing at Te Awapatiki, the Whanga Lagoon was full, and ready to burst out, as it does sometimes. In dragging the canoe up, it made a small channel, which the waters of Te Whanga entering, forthwith burst out and wrecked Rangimata. A small island of jagged limestone rocks in the Whanga Lagoon is fabled to represent Rangimata's crew. There appears very little reason to doubt that Rangimata was wrecked at the place, and in the manner stated. After this occurrence, it is said the crew went to Rangatira, and gave names to different places, such as Nukutaurua, Nukutaotao, Mana-aotea and Moreroa, with many others, and also to a plant called *arapuhi*, which grew at Hakepa (near the Red Bluff). This plant had twelve branches, representing the twelve months of the year. It was peculiar to the one place, and is now extinct. No one but the old men ever saw it. It was said to be in existence on the arrival of the Maoris; it has evidently been destroyed by the stock.

There was in connection with this plant, a belief or mythical story that its twelve branches were again sub-divided into twelve months. The names of the twelve years as first given were (1) Hitanuku, (2) Hitarangi, (3) Hitara, (4) Hitikaurereka, (5) Hitikaupeke, (6) Towhango-poroporo, (7) Towhanga-rei, (8) Muru-whenua, (9) Murutau, (10) Muru-koroki, (11) Murua-ngina, (12) Putihapa; but in another place the years (apparently a mistake for the months) are given as (1) Poapoarangi, (2) Nukutaotao, (3) Nukutaurua, (4) Meretaura, (5) Putchihapa, (6) Morero, (7) Merekohai, (8) Muruwhenu(a), (9) Murutoake, (10) Muruangina, (11) Wairarapa, (12) Mana-aotea.

It is not impossible that there was some old legend or story in connection with this, but, although the old men were carefully questioned on the subject, they could afford no further information, nor did these names appear to be in general use as far as could be discovered.

According to Tamahiwaka, from Rongopapa to himself (inclusive) are twenty-six generations, then since his time there are two adult and one more of children, say twenty-eight generations. Giving a period of twenty-five years to a generation, by this it would appear that 700 years have elapsed since Rangimata's arrival with the Moriois on the Chathams.

OROPUKE

Touching the arrival of this canoe, there is not any direct evidence of the way she arrived at the island, or where she touched first, but that she did arrive some years after Rangimata there appears very little reason to doubt. The chief of this canoe was Moe, a grandson of Horopapa, of the Rauru tribe, who, it will be remembered, was left fighting Tu-moana and his allies as Rangimata and Rangihoua left, at which date Moe was said to be a growing or nearly grown lad. Hopu was Moe's father, who, with his other sons and a daughter, came in Oropuke. Moe was a younger son, the cause of his prominence being that he was a valiant warrior and the most noted of Hopu's sons. What induced the Rauru people to migrate and come to the same place as their adversaries does not appear, nor could the Moriois assign any reason for it. There is, however, a tradition that, long before Moe left, peace had been established.

As before mentioned, Moe, when Rangimata left, was a lad. On arrival at the Chathams he was of mature age, and

was spoken of as recognisable by a bald patch on his head (not necessarily very old). This may form a slight basis on which to estimate the time which elapsed between the arrival of these canoes. The only suggestion that offers regarding Moe's leaving, although there is no mention of it handed down, is that Tu-moana and his allies, who were left fighting the Rauru, had ultimately vanquished them, causing them in turn to migrate from their home in Manukau. Before leaving, Moe went to see his grandfather Horopapa, who addressed him thus: 'Grandson, come and measure me' (*Mokopuna whanganga i au*), which he did, finding that he was *E whitu, e waru ki ri pata* (seven and a half stretches, or fathoms). Horopapa added, '*E tae koe ki ta ika, e uia mai ko, E hi to (a) o Manukau? E whitu, e waru ki ri pata*' (When you reach the land and you are asked, What length is the warrior of Manukau (say) Seven, eight with the half, or bit over — meaning seven and a half *whanganga*, or stretches). It is farther said that Horopapa admonished his grandson, on leaving, that on reaching '*ta ika*' (the land) they were to cease manslaying and live peaceably, which they did, until provoked by one of the Rangimata people, named Hangarua, who commenced the old troubles by killing Henga-mai-tawhiti, and ate part of him. Moe and his brothers then killed Hangarua, and fighting with man-eating began again. According to the story, many were killed, and after fighting for some time on the main island, Moe with his people crossed over to Pitt Island (Rangiauri), and, it is said, fought the Rangimata people there, killing and eating several. There is considerable conflict in the accounts regarding Moe at this period. The general story was that the Rangiauri people, the Matanga, and others, burnt him and his people in their huts at night, so ending the fighting. Another account says he returned to Hawaiki; and yet another states Oropuke was wrecked at the cliffs of Chatham Island, in Pitt's Strait, so giving the name to all that part of the cliffs and up to trig station L, about a mile inland. The crew landed in safety. As many of the Moriois claim descent from the Rauru people of Oropuke, this, coupled with the doubtfulness of the statement of her return to Hawaiki, makes it appear that not much reliance can be placed on these latter accounts, and in all probability the story of Moe's being burnt, as it was the one which received general acceptance, represents what actually took place. Further, had Moe lived, it seems hardly probable that the others would have preserved their independence, but would have been enslaved.

Be that as it may, at this time Nunuku-whenua, one of the autochthones, said to be a relative of Moe's (how does not appear), a man of great influence among his people, convened them, and made a law that henceforth man-slaying and man-eating were to cease for ever, and that in the case of quarrels, the first blood shed, no matter how trifling, even an abrasion of the skin, was to end the strife. In consequence of this *ture* (law), which was kept until the arrival in 1836 of 'Ka Kaupeke,' as they called the Maoris (the general meaning of which is wicked and mischievous people = *nanakia*), with one known exception, four generations after Moe, when the Rangitihi people, who had cherished their own grudge against the Rauru since Moe's time, came to Porua at Manukau and attacked the Rauru, who, with Tuteme, their chief, defeated them there, killed and roasted a number of them in an oven at Whakare, this was, as far as is known, the last occurrence of the kind. Through the cessation of war and man-slaying, the Morioris had no further use for their old weapons of offence, which thenceforth were laid aside, and the art of war ceased. Consequently the Maoris on their arrival found them an easy prey, being an inoffensive, harmless people, and forthwith enslaved them without resistance. The only weapon they retained (unless it was a subsequent invention) was the *tupurari*, a kind of long quarter-staff . . . With this they went to their *tanu* (*tauas*, so called), in which they kept up and recited all their old war ceremonies, as if in actual battle, but, beyond which, no harm was done.

Rangimata's crew were said to be *hokowha* (eighty), and Oropuke's the same. How far these numbers are reliable may be an open question. Probably they are correct, as the old Moriori could count by name about seventy of Rangimata's crew, and it appears reasonable to suppose that Oropuke's crew were fairly equal, or they would hardly have dared to make war with the former people as they did.

In the matter of the cessation of man-slaying, the Morioris appear to be the only section of the Polynesian race that established and kept such a law. One, Houmai-tawhiti, when taking farewell of his sons, attempted to impress on the original Arawa migrants to New Zealand the observance of this law. In the case of the Morioris, the same thing took place when Moe took leave of Horopapa, but the reality was subsequently established by Nunuku.

NOTES

1. The question suggests itself, whether by this name Aropawa, the ancient name of the north part of the Middle Island of New Zealand is intended, or whether the name was brought from Hawaiki.

2. *Tinaku.* Williams' Dictionary gives the meaning as 'Seed potatoes; a garden and cultivated ground'; evidently implying cultivation. The Moriori meaning is, to grow deep and strong, or increase.

3. *O wahine 'ti*; in Maori, *O wahine iti.* Junior wives. Presumably the senior one was exempt from work; but whether this is correct or not, the *wahine iti* were evidently assumed to do the hilling up of the Kumara.

4. *Takina*, draw forth, spring, shoot forth. *Ka taki i* [= te] *tupu*, the shoot comes forth.

5. There is a legend in which one Pupaonga or Paonga went to a certain island with a party of people, and there killed an ogress — *Tipu(a?* — called Tchurawhateitei, whose custom it was to entice and then devour all people landing at her place. Whether this is the same Paonga or not is uncertain, although, as e was one of the Moriori heroes, it appears not improbable.)

6. The word *miti* (lick), scarcely embodies the full meaning of the original, which here implies swallowing up, exhausting the tide.

7. Devour, bolt whole, leave no remnant.

8. Although *rangi* is also used, *ra* is preferable, not clashing with *Tu-rangi*.

9. Kahukura, a shark god, hence the invocation.

10. '*a* = *kia*. The *ki* left out because of the *ki* in Hawaiki.

11. *Ka puta* or *mahuta a Tutawake*; in Maori, *Ka puta te Waka-ariki*, ''Tis a war-party!'

12. *Hiko*, &c., might also be rendered, 'Stride, spring away.'

13. *Tuia*, sew, reeve the sennet lashings to bind the parts of the canoe together.

14. *Hokoihoko* (in Maori, *Hokahoka*) *te manu hauturuki.* 'Like a fledging bird they leave and take flight.'

15. *Pa* (= *panga*), to throw, place.

16. Tahiri-mangatea; committing themselves to the winds, represented by this god. Those favoured were thrown (placed) in Rangimata, those unfavoured were not.

17. Ends waving: ends of the *maro* at back and front of wearer.

18. Or senior chief.

19. *Tih' o Ro Maka.* Another variant of this is: *Kapihia* [= *Kapchia*] *i tchu o Ro Maka*, 'snatch it from beyond the Maka.' There is nothing to show who this Maka really is.

20. *Whiti te wawa. Wawa* also bears the meanings of 'scattered' and 'dispersed'. It appears to be a question whether this does not refer to a much farther off Whiti than the one they came from, especially as the recitation of the *Maro* referred to was alleged to have taken place in Hawaiki.

21. *Tuakina.* It suggests itself as a reasonable rendering of this word *Tua*, here used in the passive form, that it had originally in its first use, as well as in these incantations, the meaning of chopping down or felling, as a tree — symbolically, of course — to overcome the object, or to achieve the end desired, using at the same time in the ceremony sprigs of trees — *manuka* and others — as the visible medium of breaking (chopping down) the power fought against. The same idea is seen in ancient incantations, both Maori and Moriori, which speak of '*Taku toki whanatu ana e hahau i te takapu o te rangi*' (slightly altered in certain cases), 'my axe which proceeds to chop the belly of the sky,' *i.e.*, induce a calm. Sometimes the *Karakia* is compared to an *Umu*, oven, 'to roast the crown of the sky.'

22. *Te rakau hanga mua, roto*, &c., are evidently pieces of wood used in the construction of the keels (*Hua*) or stem-piece (*Koua*) of the canoe for which the fair wind is desired.

23. *Uru o Mahuta.* The hair of the crown of the head of Mahuta, one of their ancient ancestors. The head being the most sacred part of his body is used figuratively here as an agent to break down the adverse power. Mahuta also represents the woods, with their fragrance.

24. *Ko e hau te kamakama.* The Morioris have a peculiar manner of pronouncing the word *hau* (= wind), apparently in accordance with an undefined rule of sound; in other cases pronounced *heau* — *Ka heau*, the winds, all the vowels being sounded and blended. *Kamakama* appears to be the equivalent to the Maori, to bubble up, as water, with a slight variation in this case, light puffs of air, barely perceptible.

25. Nganangana is evidently a play upon the name Ngana (Maori Ngana and Ngangana), to contend, to strive — hence, in this case, to fight against Nuku and Rangi, to obtain the wind sought for.

26. *E Tchua.* ''Tis a *Tchua*' (= *Tua*) — an incantation to chop, fell, the evil power. This is really identical with the Maori *Tua*, to subdue the winds.

27, 28. *Koe ra te mata mo Ruanuku.* 'Thou art the face for Ruanuku' — under the symbol of Ruanuku, old age, shall die, &c.

29. He, Rawa, in assuming the face of Mahuika, *i.e.*, attributes of fire, will burn and crumple up the heaven, or the evil power of the wind.

30. Still with the simile of an axe to chop down or fell the sacred

crown of Tch Anini and Tch Arohi, classed as winds, but really having no compass bearings, meaning as in translation.

31. *E Hina tae ake ru — u(= ra)*. The Morioris are unable to explain who Hina may be, or what it refers to. From the construction of the sentence, Hina would appear to be a person, or, what is probable, the object desired — fair wind and weather personified. An old Maori incantation to subdue and change a wind may throw some light on the meaning: *Takataka to hau ki te Uru, whakataka to hau ki te Tonga, kia tu mahinahina i uta, kia tu marokeroke i tai*, &c. *Mahinahina* was explained as referring to the way the silver grey of the leaves turned with the wind appeared when a storm of wind and rain abated and the general appearance showed fine weather, which last is the object sought by the incantation.

32. Utihau, another name for the wind.

33. *Takina*, draw, induce, shoot forth.

34. *Taina* (= *utaina*), fill in, lade.

35. Motihangai is said to represent heaven or the sky; there is nothing to show any other meaning, and the above would appear to be in a figurative sense.

36. *Tau* (= *taku*). This pronunciation seems as if the Morioris had retained here the pronunciation of their Tahitian brethren.

37. Utua, figurative for heaven, where the water was supposed to be.

38. Tongaminino, the south or south-east wind. The additional word Minino is said to be derived from the story of Tawhaki's ascension to heaven, in which his foot slipped in ascending on the south-east wind. *Ko ro minitanga [maniatanga in Maori] o ro wewe o Tawhaki ku rung' i Tonga*, the slipping of Tawhaki's foot on the south-east wind.

39. Anini and Arohi, as remarked in a previous note, are merely mythical winds.

40. It appears strange how persistently this tradition of bringing the Karaka berry and planting it is held by both peoples, Maori and Moriori, separated as they each were for at least six hundred years. With the exception of the Kermadec Islands, to the north of New Zealand, the tree does not appear to be known elsewhere, and what has originated the legend?

41. *Marautara*, a kind of creeping plant of the convolvulus family, which one of the Ngati-tama Maoris recognized as growing over the old decayed huts at Poutama, White Cliffs, Taranaki, New Zealand: he called it *Popohue*. It is now extinct. From its close proximity to the sea, it seems not improbable that the seed was drifted here and thrown up by a gale to the place where it grew.

42. *Maitai* is an ancient word, both Maori and Moriori, denoting all kinds of fish, including seals; *hhia* is a particle, introduced for euphony — *Ko hhia Maitai*.

SOURCE NOTES

A major difficulty needs to be registered in relation to the first two chapters. The only relatively reliable evidence about the pre-European Moriori comes from the visit of the British naval vessel *Chatham* to the northern coast of Chatham Island in 1791; and from the activities of professional archaeologists. All else — including later accounts of Moriori traditions and European observations — is less sound, because it records information long after events took place. As Rhys Richards has pointed out, the major observers of early Moriori life — Frederick Hunt, Johannes Gottfried Engst, William Baucke and Alexander Shand — did not even arrive at the Chathams until thirty-five, thirty-seven, forty-three and fifty years respectively after regular contact between Moriori and European had begun. That is a considerable time lapse. Further, there are virtually no contemporary descriptions of the effects of the presence of sealers on Moriori life between 1805 and 1835, and much of what can be said about that period is speculation based on slender evidence.

As far as the rest of the nineteenth century is concerned, it is probable that no part of New Zealand has had so much unsubstantiated rubbish written about it as the Chatham Islands. I have read and discarded much from secondary sources that turned out to be either pure invention on the part of the writer, or the consequence of repeating earlier errors, or the result of the writer being subjected to practical jokes by Chatham Islanders. Hence there are no stories here about sailors from Callao, Peru, thrashing the Moriori, nor of early Portuguese colonising the islands before Broughton's arrival. I have tried wherever possible to work from primary sources, and primary sources that can be shown to be reliable. Where I have doubts about the value or validity of evidence, these are noted in the text or in the source notes that follow.

For the events of more recent years, I have relied more heavily on oral informants than I would normally for a book of this kind. This is partly to compensate for the paucity of other forms of documentation of Moriori life in the twentieth century. But it is also a recognition that oral communication and oral history are still strong forces in the Chathams, which (at the time of writing) lacked television to absorb family evenings. People still talk with one another there far more and far more often than they do on mainland New Zealand. Evening discussions in most homes are long and detailed, sometimes contentious, sometimes hilarious. A

man such as David Holmes of Waitangi absorbed and repeated stories he heard while working with Charlie Seymour in the 1920s; Seymour had arrived in the islands in 1866; David Holmes' stories, therefore, cover a combined period of more than 120 years of first- and second-hand experience, as do those of Rose Swann (née Ritchie), whose father landed on Chatham Island in 1864. Here too I have opted wherever possible for accounts of first-hand experience in preference to second, third, fourth or fifth; and I have depended most heavily on informants noted for their honesty and reliability.

I am grateful to the Chatham Islanders for their ability to talk; and for their willingness to do so to an outsider in the interests of giving history a more permanent form.

Prologue

The information about Manukau comes from the author's observation, and from the recollections of Mannie Solomon (Tommy Solomon's son), David Holmes and Pat Prendeville. The account of the funeral comes from some of those who were there — including Mannie Solomon, Jane Hough, Pat Prendeville and Bessie Hough — and from Simpson 1950, pp. 64–66. William Baucke's derogatory comments are from his 1922 series of articles for the *New Zealand Herald* (15/7/22 and 22/7/11); the others quoted are from Langdale-Hunt.

1. Tchakat Moriori

The myths cited about Kahu come from the Ritchie Papers in the Christchurch Public Library (information given to Thomas Ritchie by the Moriori elders Torea and Puanga); from an article in the Maori language newspaper *Te Korimako* by Horomona Rehe and Timoti Tara (1/4/1883); and from Shand 1911 (see Appendix Three). Information about other ancestors and canoes is also from *Te Korimako* 1883 and Shand 1911. The Pitt Island story about the Tuiti was told by Koche, a Moriori, in Ewing 1873. The 'public dreams' phrase is Joseph Campbell's.

For archaeological information about the Chathams, I am indebted to everything written and published by Douglas Sutton, and to information elicited in conversation with Sutton, Bruce McFadgen, Rhys Richards and David Simmons. Ross Clark and Ray Harlow gave invaluable advice on the characteristics of the Moriori language, and Phillip Houghton on the analysis of Moriori skeletal remains. I am grateful for such considerable assistance on matters outside my own expertise, but I stress that the conclusions I have drawn are my own, and that some of them may be disputed by my informants. One especially contentious issue is the likely date of the arrival in the Chathams of the ancestors of the Moriori. At the time of writing, archaeologists and prehistorians were divided between those who refused to accept a valid radio carbon date earlier than the sixteenth century; and those who argued that as the great East Polynesian voyages of exploration had resulted in the discovery and settlement of all East Polynesian islands and New Zealand by the ninth century, it was unlikely that the Chathams had escaped this colonising wave, and that communities recognised and dated as belonging to the sixteenth century are unlikely to have been the first on the Chathams.

Information about the evolution of Moriori cultural characteristics is drawn from the published work of Douglas Sutton; and that about pre-European Moriori life from Sutton, Shand, Baucke, Richards and Simmons. Earlier scholars have argued about the relative reliability of Shand and Baucke, whose conclusions are sometimes at variance. I am inclined to place more reliance on Shand: he is less overtly prejudiced about the Moriori than Baucke; and Baucke had inherited a family dislike for the Shands based on a nineteenth-century land dispute, which William Baucke's father lost in favour of Alex Shand's father. This may have been a factor in Baucke's determination to discredit some of Shand's writing on the Moriori.

The quoted section on p. 26 is from Skinner and Baucke 1928, p. 377; that on p. 28 from Sutton 1982, pp. 170–172; and that on p. 35 from Shand 1894, pp. 121–122 and 129, translated by and reproduced with the permission of Margaret Orbell, Canterbury University. For the explanation of the likely role of dendroglyphs in Moriori culture, I am indebted to discussions with David Simmons and Stuart Park of Auckland.

2. The Sun People

I was heavily reliant on three sources for the bulk of this chapter: journals from the voyage of the *Chatham*; Rhys Richards' immensely scholarly book *Whaling and Sealing at the Chatham Islands* (1982); and David Holmes of Waitangi.

The *Chatham* journals are quoted from McNab 1914, and Skinner 1923. The Moriori accounts of Broughton's visits are from the Ritchie Papers (36/3, 3/6), a letter from Alexander Shand to Dr Hocken (8/7/91), Hocken Papers; Stevenson Percy Smith's notebooks in the Auckland Institute and Museum Library; and Koche's comments in Ewing 1873.

Comments on the effects of sealers' presence in the Chathams between 1805 and 1835 have to be largely deduction and informed speculation, because so little evidence has survived from that period. I am grateful to Rhys Richards for permission to quote from his book (1982) and his thesis (1962).

The quote from Jacky Marmon, first published in 1881,

is from Richards 1982, p. 22; that from Captain John Biscoe from the same book, p. 40. The anonymous quote on p. 50 is from Richards 1952, p. 101.

3. The Gods are Dead

I leaned most heavily on three sources for information about the Ati Awa invasion of the Chathams: Shand's 1892 and 1893 articles in the *Journal of the Polynesian Society* were invaluable — so much so that the chapter could not have been written without them; also Koche's story in Ewing 1873; and the Native Land Court minutes for the Chatham Islands, 1870.

One must express some reservation about Koche's memoir. Parts of it are clearly influenced by Dieffenbach (1841 and 1843), and the writer, the American lawyer, Ewing, must have had access to those sources. But allowing for the removal of information derived from Dieffenbach, there is much in the article which is original and which is verifiable from other sources (the role of Matioro, for example).

Koche's account of Matioro's arrival and of his time in slavery are, as noted, from Ewing 1873. All the Maori-sourced information about events leading up to the Ati Awa invasion are from Shand 1892. The Moriori accounts of the same event and its aftermath are from GNZMS 144, a manuscript in the Sir George Grey Manuscript Collection in the Auckland Public Library (see further information about this material on pages 113 and 114); Horomona Rehe and Timoti Tara in *Korimako*, 1/4/83; Percy Smith's diary (1868) in the Auckland Institute and Museum Library; Halse 1867; Mair 1904; and from Mannie Solomon, oldest son of Tommy Solomon.

The quote on p. 61 is from Mair 1904, p. 161. Those on pp. 62 and 63 from Mair, p. 161; Native Land Court minutes, Chatham Islands, Book 1, p. 15, and Halse 1867, p. 6. That on p. 64 is from Dennison 1977, pp. 23–25. That from Rakatau is from the Native Land Court minutes, Chathams Islands, Book 1, p. 10. That from Dieffenbach 1841, p. 208.

The account of the *Jean Bart* incident is from Shand 1893, as is the information about the fighting at Waitangi in 1840. The Dieffenbach quotes on pages 71 and 72 are from Dieffenbach 1841, pp. 207–209. The final quote from the Maori elders at Te Awapatiki is from GMNZS 144.

4. The Mangahuka Experiment

Sources for the story of the Maori, Moriori and European invasion of the Auckland Islands were Shand 1893, pp. 78–86; Malone 1854; Mikaere 1986; Scadden 1988; Richards 1982; McLaren 1948; Records of the Governor, National Archives; Sir George Grey Manuscript Collection, Auckland Public Library; Native Land Court Minute Books for the Chatham Islands, and — for southern Maori traditions about the migration — correspondence with Syd Cormack of Tuatapere.

The list of Moriori names on p. 80 is from Shand 1893, p. 79. The additional names are from Chatham Islands Native Land Court minutes and correspondence with Mr J.

Eyles of Blenheim, a Moriori descendant. Rohana's references to her Auckland Island experiences are also in the minutes of the Native Land Court.

The quotations on p. 82 are from Shand 1893, p. 84 and Mikaere 1986; on p. 83 from Shand 1893, p. 85; on p. 85 from Malone 1854, p. 73; the letters from Matioro to Sir George Grey are held in the Grey Manuscript Collection, Auckland Public Library, and Records of the Governor, National Archives; the quotation on p. 86 is from Shand 1893, p. 82; and Archibald Shand's observations are from the Letter Book of Archibald Shand (National Archives, Christchurch). Information on the fate of Moriori who did not return to New Zealand is from the Native Land Court minutes, correspondence with Mr Eyles of Blenheim, and discussions with other Moriori descendants and Messrs David Holmes and Norman Thomas of Waitangi.

5. European Settlement

The major sources for the European colonisation of the Chathams were Richards 1962 and 1982, government reports in the *New Zealand Gazette* and *Appendices to the Journal of the House of Representatives*, Hunt 1866, the Thomas Ritchie Papers, E. R. Chudleigh's diary and interviews and correspondence with David Holmes.

The quotes from Hunt's book are taken from a typescript held by David Holmes; the Selwyn quotes on p. 92 from a letter to Hawkins, 30/8/48; the Shand quotes are from his letters held at National Archives, Christchurch: pp. 94, 22/11/55; pp. 96, 25/1/59. The estimate of population decline on p. 94 is from Richards 1962. William Seed's report is in the *New Zealand Gazette* of 1862, pp. 26–33.

Information on William Baucke comes from Skinner and Baucke 1928, Baucke 1922 and members of the Baucke family, especially David and Anita Baucke of Porirua and Elisabeth Jenkins of Karori, Wellington. The quotes are all from Baucke 1928: that on p. 98 from p. 356; those on pages 99 and 100 from pp. 381, 378, and 381; p. 100 from p. 372. Travers's report is from Travers 1868, pp. 121–123, and the Travers quote on p. 104 from pp. 120–121.

6. Moriori Voices

Moriori letters from the Ritchie Papers (Canterbury Public Library), and the George Grey Manuscript Collection in the Auckland Public Library, especially manuscripts in GNZMS 16 and GNZMS 144, and minutes of the Native Land Court sittings (Chatham Islands Books 1–4, Department of Maori Affairs, Christchurch), contributed most of the information for this chapter.

Individual quotations are from the following sources: The letters on p. 111 (16/9/70) and p. 111 (10/7/74) are from folder 2/7 of the Ritchie Papers, as is Hapurona Pawa's testimony on p. 111 and the Robert Ritchie letters cited. Translations are by (and by permission of) Lyndsay Head of Canterbury University's Maori Department, to whom I here express my immense gratitude. The Otonga manuscript is GNZMS 16 in the Sir George Grey Collection; and the Te Awapatiki petition and letters, GNZMS 144. The first

part of the Te Awapatiki petition quoted is from Mair 1904, and seems to be a summary of a version of GNZMS 144, but one that is not identical to that now deposited in the Auckland Public Library. Mair appears to have obtained his material from South Africa, where the manuscript originals were held at that time. Although his translation does not precisely match an existing manuscript, it is a fair summary of the spirit of GNZMS 144. The translation of the document on p. 117 is by Lyndsay Head. The pronouncement on land by Hirawanu Tapu on pages 117 and 118 is from the Burt Papers in the Alexander Turnbull Library, bundle one; as is the proclamation on animals. The Shand letters quoted, 18/3/62 and 3/4/62, are from the Shand Letters, National Archives, Christchurch. The Baucke story on p. 117 is from Skinner and Baucke 1928, p. 372. Henry Halse's report is from the *Appendices to the Journal of the House of Representatives*, 1867, A-4, pp. 3–8.

7. Judgment

Evidence from this chapter is drawn almost entirely from the minutes of the Native Land Court sittings at Waitangi in the Chathams from 16/6/70 to 26/6/70: Chatham Islands Minute Book 1, pp. 1–49, held in the Christchurch office of the Maori Land Court. Additional information on the outcome and Moriori settlements at the time comes from David Holmes and Jane Hough.

8. Fog Before the Sun

The chapter title is a quote from Johan Gottfried Engst, taken from (among other places) Natusch 1977, p. 111. The population figures on p. 135 are taken from: 1870 (Native Land Court minutes); 1883 (Census); 1889 (Tregear 1889); 1900 (Census).

The quote 'to save the ancient thought from silence' on p. 135 is from an unpublished paper on Thomas Ritchie by Lyndsay Head; and that likening Moriori petroglyphs to 'the walls of Sennacherib's Palace' from the *Otago Daily Times*, 10/6/72. Ritchie's observations about petroglyphs are from his diary, and his comment about the Moriori place in the 'scale' from an undated note in his papers. The Shand quotes on p. 136 are from Skinner 1922, pp. 35–36. Deighton's letter on p. 137, dated 19/10/73, is from the McLean Papers, Alexander Turnbull Library. Information on Riwai's marriage and Thomas Ritchie's letter to Kiti Clark's mother is from the Ritchie Papers (2/11), and from minutes of the Native Land Court. The letters to Thomas Ritchie are also from the Ritchie Papers, Folder 2/7. The Motuhara claim is covered in the minutes of the Native Land Court for 6/2/85, Chatham Islands Minute Book 1, Maori Land Court office, Christchurch; that for Kekerione in minutes for 16/2/94, Chatham Islands Minute Book 2; for Te Awapatiki in the minutes for 16/2/94 and 28/1/98; and that for Hirawanu Tapu's land in minutes for 14/2/06 and 19/3/07, Minute Book 4.

The Tregear quotes are from Tregear 1889, pp. 75–79; the Shand letters to Thomas Hocken in GNZMS 451, Hocken Library; the pouwa (giant bird) story is from Forbes

1893, p. 682; the Portuguese story quoted from the *Press* (Christchurch), 20/12/84, p. 13; information about the dog tax largely from the cited dates in Chudleigh's diary; and about Heta Namu's escape, from Gascoyne 1916, pp. 146–147.

Information about individual Moriori comes from David Holmes, Jane Hough, Chudleigh's diary and descendants of the people specified. The stories about the possible cause of Alexander Shand's death come from Stephen Barker and David Holmes.

9. And Then There was One?

Information about Tommy Solomon and the Rehe clan has come from those who knew Tommy: Mannie Solomon (his eldest and, at the time of writing, only surviving child), David Holmes, Jane Hough, Ani Kamo, Pat Prendeville, Bertha Wilson, Bessie Clough, Rose Swann (née Ritchie), and others. Noel Cox's unpublished manuscript in the Hocken Library was also of particular help. I am indebted to David Simmons for material on the Maruiwi myth, the Whatahoro manuscript and the name of the Dargaville Moriori. Tombstones and the Chatham Islands Register of births, deaths and marriages provided essential dates.

The Baucke quotes on birding are from his series of articles in the *New Zealand Herald* in 1922: 22/7/22 and 2/9/22. Information on the Tupuangi Beach boating accident was from Chudleigh's diary (28/8/1900) and David Holmes; that on Tommy's brushes with the law from Chudleigh (7/3/01) and Noel Cox's manuscript, pp. 8 and 44. The quote about Solomon being a spendthrift is from the Chatham Islands Native Land Court minutes, Book 4, 16/3/07. Material on Tommy's marriages came principally from Kera Brown, Neta Hopkinson, Bill Torepe and Rose Solomon of Temuka. Facts about the Owenga fishing operation are from David Holmes.

The quote from Skinner on p. 169 is from Skinner 1923, p. 3; that from Gilbert Mair from the *Transactions of the New Zealand Institute*, vol. 37 (1904), p. 604; MacMillan Brown from the Christchurch *Weekly Press*, 24/8/10; Elsdon Best on pp. 171–2 from Best 1915, pp. 435–437; Skinner on p. 173 from Skinner 1923, p. 4; on p. 174 from the same book, p. 37 and pp. 132–133 and on p. 175, p. 21; the quote about the Dargaville Moriori is from Skinner 1923, p. 38. Information on that man's likely identity was supplied by members of the Retimana and Totara families. Kendrick Smithyman's poem 'The Last Moriori' is quoted with his permission. The Baucke 1928 quote is from pp. 355–356.

The stories about Solomon's petition concerning the Prince of Wales and the introduction of the Ratana faith to Chatham Islands are from Jane Hough, who heard them from Henry Hough (her father-in-law) and Arthur Lockett.

Material on the Wharekauri Maori Committee and Ryan Holmes' letter to the Director-General of Health, are from the Health Department archives, National Archives, Series 121 B. 133 121/30. Tommy Solomon's letter on p. 183 is from the Cox manuscript p. 40; and the long quote from Bessie Clough from an interview in Christchurch on 1/11/87. The information on Solomon's death is from Mannie Solomon, and the Press Association quote from the Christchurch *Weekly Press*, 22/3/33.

Epilogue

The Epilogue is drawn from discussions with members of the Solomon family, Bunty, Riwai, Pat and Charlie Preece, David Holmes, Bill Burt, Norman Thomas and the author's personal observations. The professorial quote on p. 189 is from the *Evening Post* 12/9/85; the Tainui one from the *Waikato Times*, 26/10/84; and the other Maori correspondent from the *New Zealand Herald*, 22/9/87; Maui Solomon's reply is from the *New Zealand Herald*, 6/10/87. The quotes from the unveiling of the Tommy Solomon statue are recorded by the author.

BIBLIOGRAPHY

UNPUBLISHED

A. Interviews

Kera Brown, Bill Burt, Bessie Clough, Ross Clark, David Holmes, Neta Hopkinson, Jane Hough, Ani Kamo, Bruce McFadgen, Bunty Preece, Charlie Preece (senior), Charlie Preece (junior), Cissy Preece, Pat Preece, Riwai Preece, Pat Prendeville, Rhys Richards, David Simmons, Charles Solomon (senior), Gary Solomon, Maui Solomon, Rose Solomon, Tommy Solomon, Douglas Sutton, Rose Swann (née Ritchie), Norman Thomas, Bill Torepe and Bertha Wilson.

B. Private Papers

Aldred, J., 'Journal 1832–64', manuscript Alexander Turnbull Library, Wellington

Brodie, William (*c.* 1840), 'Visit to the Chatham Islands', McNab Miscellaneous Manuscripts 133, Alexander Turnbull Library, Wellington

Burt, Bill, manuscript papers in Alexander Turnbull Library, Wellington

Chudleigh, E. R., Diaries 1863–1921, Canterbury Museum Library, Christchurch

Cox, Noel, 'History and Life of Cox Family and Self', manuscript held at Hocken Library, Dunedin

Davis, Bill, manuscript papers in Alexander Turnbull Library, Wellington

Deighton, S. J. (1873), letters to Douglas McLean, McLean Papers, Alexander Turnbull Library, Wellington

Engst, J. G., manuscript in Florance Collection, Canterbury Museum Library, Christchurch

Florance, R. S., Collected Papers 1898–1904, Canterbury Museum Library, Christchurch

Grey, Sir George, manuscripts in the George Grey Maori Manuscript Collection, Auckland Public Library, Auckland; GNZMSS 16, history and genealogical tables compiled by Rakei Ora Tauro, Otonga, 22/4/59, 24 pp; GNZMSS 122, letters from Chathams to William Seed and Grey, 1862, 2 pp; GNZMSS 144, genealogies, traditions and letters to Grey from Moriori elders, 1862, 131 pp.

Hunt, Frederick (1866), 'Twenty-Five Years Experience in New Zealand and the Chathams', manuscript held by David Holmes, Waitangi

Jacobs, W., Diary 1922–1948, Alexander Turnbull Library, Wellington

Knight, H.H., 'Of One Blood, The Story of a New Zealand Moriori Family,' unpublished paper

McLean, Donald, manuscript papers, Alexander Turnbull Library, Wellington

Ritchie, Thomas William, manuscript papers in Christchurch Public Library, Christchurch

Seed, William (1873), letter to S. J. Deighton, 3/4/73, Burt Collection, Alexander Turnbull Library, Wellington

Shand, Alexander, letters to S. Percy Smith, 1868–1910, Alexander Turnbull Library, Wellington

Shand, Alexander, letters to Dr Hocken, 1885–1891, Hocken Library, Dunedin

Shand, Alexander (1889), letter to Sir James Hector, 2/10/1889, National Museum, Wellington

Smith, Stephenson Percy, Diary 1863–1912, and notebooks, Auckland Institute and Museum Library, Auckland

Smith, Stephenson Percy (1916), 'Reminiscences of a Pioneer Surveyor', typescript in Auckland Institute and Museum Library, Auckland

Sutton, Douglas G. (1994), 'The Moriori in the Chatham Islands', unpublished paper

Thomas, W. E., 'The Chatham Islands Official Yearbook', 5 August 1863–31 December 1864 (official records of Resident Magistrate), held by David Holmes, Waitangi

C. Official Papers

Minutes of the Native Land Court, Chatham Islands sittings, as identified in individual source notes; especially Chatham Islands Books 1–4, held in the Christchurch office of the Maori Land Court

Records of christenings and burials, Te One Anglican Church, Chatham Island

Records of the Departments of Native (Maori) Affairs, Health and Internal Affairs, National Archives, Wellington

Records of the Governor, National Archives, Wellington

Registry of births, deaths and marriages, Waitangi, Chatham Island

Shand, Archibald, Letterbook of Resident Magistrate, Chatham Islands, National Archives, Christchurch

Theses and Research Papers

Head, Lyndsay (n.d.), 'Friend Ritchie', unpublished manuscript held by author

Mills, S. M. (1933), 'A History of the Chatham Islands and their Inhabitants', unpublished M.A. thesis, Victoria University College

Richards, Rhys (1962), 'An Historical Geography of Chatham Islands', unpublished M.A. thesis, University of Canterbury

Seymour, Maude (1924), 'A History of the Chatham Islands', unpublished thesis towards an M.A. degree, University of New Zealand

Taylor, R. M. S. (1924), 'The Hard Palate of the Morioris', unpublished B.D.S. thesis, Otago Dental School

PUBLISHED

A. Books

Anderson, P. C. (1882), *The Chatham Islands, with Notes of a Visit There in the Months of July, August and September, 1882*, Turner, Christchurch

Arbuckle, G. A. (1971), *The Chatham Islands in Perspective*, Hicks Smith and Sons, Wellington

Baucke, William (1905), *Where the White Man Treads*, Wilson and Horton, Auckland

Baucke, William and Skinner, H. D. (1928), *The Morioris*, Bishop Museum, Honolulu

Beattie, Herries (1941), *The Morioris of the South Island*, Otago Daily Times, Dunedin

Bell, Gerda (1976), *Ernest Dieffenbach, Rebel and Humanist*, Dunmore, Palmerston North

Buck, Peter (Te Rangi Hiroa) (1950), *The Coming of the Maori*, Whitcombe and Tombs, Wellington

Dansey, H. D. B. (1947), *How the Maoris Came to Aotearoa*, Reed, Wellington

Davidson, Janet (1984), *The Prehistory of New Zealand*, Longman Paul, Auckland

Dieffenbach, E. (1843), *Travels in New Zealand*, Murray, London

Gasgoyne, F. J. W. (1916), *Soldiering in New Zealand*, Guildford, London

Heaphy, Charles (1842), *Narrative of a Residence in Various Parts of New Zealand*, Elder Smith, London

Holmes, David (1993), *My Seventy Years on the Chatham Islands*, Shoal Bay Press, Christchurch

Houghton, Philip (1980), *The First New Zealanders*, Hodder and Stoughton, Auckland

Hunt, Frederick (1866), *Twenty-five Years Experience in New Zealand and the Chathams* (John Amery editor), William Lyons, Wellington

King, Michael (1990), *A Land Apart, The Chatham Islands of New Zealand*, Random House, Auckland

Langdale-Hunt, Ernest (n.d.), *The Last Entail Male*, Adams, Christchurch

McDonald, Geoff (1985), *Shadows Over New Zealand*, Chaston, Christchurch

McDonald, Geoff (1986), *The Kiwis Fight Back*, Chaston, Christchurch

McLaren, F. B. (1948), *The Auckland Islands*, Whitcombe and Tombs, Wellington

McNab, Robert (1913), *Old Whaling Days*, Whitcombe and Tombs, Wellington

McNab, Robert (1914), *Historical Records of New Zealand*, Volume 2, Government Printer, Wellington

Malone, R. E. (1854), *Three Years Cruise in the Australasian Colonies*, Bentley, London

Natusch, Sheila (1977), *Hell and High Water, a German Occupation of the Chatham Islands 1843–1910*, Pegasus, Christchurch

Orange, Claudia (1987), *The Treaty of Waitangi*, Allen and Unwin /Port Nicholson Press, Wellington

Potts, T. H. (1882), *Out in the Open*, Lyttelton Times, Christchurch

Prickett, Nigel (ed) (1982), *The First Thousand Years, Regional Perspectives in New Zealand Archaeology*, Dunmore, Palmerston North

Richards, E. C. (1950), *Diary of E. R. Chudleigh 1862–1921, Chatham Islands*, Simpson and Williams, Christchurch

Richards, E. C. (1952), *The Chatham Islands: their Plants, Birds and People*, Simpson and Williams, Christchurch

Richards, Rhys (1982), *Whaling and Sealing at the Chatham Islands*, Roebuck Society, Canberra

Shand, Alexander (1911), *The Moriori People of the Chatham Islands, Their History and Traditions*, Polynesian Society, Wellington

Simmons, D. R. (1976), *The Great New Zealand Myth, a Study of the Discovery and Origin Traditions of the Maori*, Reed, Wellington

Simpson, Frank A. (1950), *Chatham Exiles*, Reed, Wellington

Skinner, H. D. (1923), *The Morioris of the Chatham Island*, Bishop Museum, Honolulu

Skinner, H. D. and Baucke, William (1928), *The Morioris*, Bishop Museum, Honolulu

Smith, Stephenson Percy (1915), *The Lore of the Whare-Wananga*, vol. 2, Polynesian Society, New Plymouth

Vancouver, G. (1792), *A Voyage of Discovery to the North Pacific and Round the World*, vol. 2, London

Weiss, B. (ed) (1901), *Mehr als Funfzig Jahre auf Chatham Inseln*, Deutscher Kolonial-Verlag, Berlin

Williams, John A. (1969), *The Politics of the New Zealand Maori*, Oxford University Press, Wellington

B. Articles, pamphlets

Barwell, J. S. (1931), 'Moriori People of the Chatham Islands', in *The Maori and Education*, pp. 393–420

Best, Elsdon (1916), 'Maori and Maruiwi', *Transactions of the New Zealand Institute*, vol. 48, pp. 435–47

Best, Elsdon (1928), 'Maori and Maruiwi', *Journal of the Polynesian Society*, vol. 37, pp. 175–225

Dendy, Arthur (1901), 'On Some Relics of the Moriori race', *Transactions of the New Zealand Institute*, vol. 34, pp. 123–34

Dennison, K. J. (1977), 'Early German Missionaries in the Chatham Islands', *Working Papers in Chatham Islands Archaeology*, Anthropology Department, University of Otago

Dieffenbach, E. (1841), 'An Account of the Chatham Islands', *Royal Geographical Society Journal*, vol. 2, pp. 195–215

Downes, W. (1933), 'Maruiwi Maori and Moriori', *Journal of the Polynesian Society*, vol. 42, pp. 156–66

Duckworth, W. L. H. (1900), 'On a Collection of Crania with Two Skeletons of the Mori-ori or Aborigines of the Chatham Islands', *Journal of the Anthropological Institute*, vol. 30, pp. 141–52

Ewing, C. (1873), 'Koche, King of Pitt', *Catholic World*, July, pp. 545–57

Forbes, Henry O. (1893), 'The Chatham Islands and Their Story', *Fortnightly Review*, no. 59, May, pp. 669–90

Harlow, R. B. (1979), 'Regional Variation in Maori', *New Zealand Journal of Archaeology*, vol. 1, pp. 123–38

Head, Lyndsay (1988), 'E Hoa, E Riti — Friend Ritchie', *Archifacts*, no. 2, pp. 21–27

Jefferson, Christina (1955), 'The dendroglyphs of the Chatham Islands', *Journal of the Polynesian Society*, vol. 64, pp. 367–441

Mair, Gilbert (1870), 'Notes on the Chatham Islands and their inhabitants', *Transactions of the New Zealand Institute*, vol. 3, pp. 311–13

Mair, Gilbert (1904), 'The Early History of the Moriories with an Abstract of a Moriori Narrative', *Transactions of the New Zealand Institute*, vol. 37 pp. 156–171

Mikaere, B. (1986), 'Maungahuka — the Nearest Maori Settlement to the South Pole', *Tu Tangata*, nos. 31 and 32

Park, G. S. (1976), 'The Dendroglyphs and Petroglyphs of the Chatham Islands', *Working Papers in Chatham Islands Archaeology*, Anthropology Department, University of Otago

Richards, Rhys (1972), 'A Tentative Population Distribution Map of the Moriories of Chatham Island, circa 1790', *Journal of the Polynesian Society*, vol. 81, pp. 350–374

Robertson, John A. (1890), 'Chatham Islands', in *Proceedings and Transactions of the Queensland Branch of the Royal Geographical Society of Australasia*, vol. 5, pp. 72–92

Scadden, Ken (1988), 'The Auckland Islands: Research in Progress', *Archifacts*, no. 1, pp. 2–15

Shand, Alexander (1892 and 1893), 'The Occupation of the Chatham Islands by the Maoris in 1834', *Journal of the Polynesian Society*, vol. 1, pp. 83–94; 154–63; 202–09; vol. 2 (1893), pp. 74–86

Shand, Alexander (1894), 'The Moriori People of the Chatham Islands, their Traditions and their History', *Journal of the Polynesian Society*, vols. 3–7; reprinted as Shand (1911) — see book list

Shand, Alexander (1904), 'The Early History of the Moriories', *Transactions of the New Zealand Institute*, vol. 37, pp. 144–56

Simmons, D. R. (1962), 'The Moriori of the Chatham Islands', *New Zealand Archaeological Association Newsletter*, vol. 5, pp. 238–44

Simmons, D. R. (1964), 'Chatham Island Archaeological Survey', *New Zealand Archaeological Association Newsletter*, vol. 6, pp. 51–69

Simmons, D. R. (1969), 'A New Zealand Myth, Kupe, Toi and the Fleet', *New Zealand Journal of History*, vol. 3, pp. 14–31

Simmons, D. R. (1979), 'Some Dendroglyph Styles in the Chatham Islands', *Records of the Auckland Institute and Museum*, vol. 17, pp. 49–63

Smith, Stephenson Percy (1918), 'Discovery of the Chatham Islands', *Church Gazette*, Auckland Diocese, 1 January, p. 5

Sutton, Douglas (1980), 'A Culture History of the Chatham Islands', *Journal of the Polynesian Society*, vol. 89, pp. 67–93

Sutton, Douglas (1982), 'Chatham Islands' in *The First Thousand Years* (ed. Nigel Prickett), Dunmore, Palmerston North, pp. 160–78

Sutton, Douglas (1986), 'Maori Demographic Change, 1769–1840: the Inner Workings of a Picturesque but Illogical Simile', *Journal of the Polynesian Society*, vol. 95, pp. 291–339

Travers, H. H. (1868), 'On the Chatham Islands', *Transactions and Proceedings of the New Zealand Institute*, vol. 1, pp. 119–27

Travers, W. T. L. (1871), 'Notes on the Chatham Islands' (extracted from letters from H. H. Travers), *Transactions of the New Zealand Institute*, vol. 4, pp. 63–66

Travers, W. T. L. (1876), 'Notes on the Traditions and Manners and Customs of the Mori-oris', *Transactions of the New Zealand Institute*, vol. 9, pp. 15–27

Tregear, Edward (1889), 'The Moriori', *Transactions of the New Zealand Institute*, vol. 22, pp. 75–79

Walters, Muru (1977), 'An Examination of Literary Evidence for the Existence of Discrete Groups of Moriori in the Chatham Islands in the 19th Century', *Working Papers in Chatham Islands Archaeology*, Anthropology Department, University of Otago

Weiss, B. (1975), 'More than Fifty Years on Chatham Island' (translated by K. J. Dennison), *Working Papers in Chatham Islands Archaeology*, Anthropology Department, University of Otago

Welch, E. A. (1870), 'An Account of the Chatham Islands', *Journal of the Anthropological Institute*, vol. 8, pp. xcvii–cviii

Williams, H. W. (1919), 'Some Notes on the Language of the Chatham Islands', *Transactions of the New Zealand Institute*, vol. 51, pp. 415–22

Williams, H. W. (1937), 'The Maruiwi Myth', *Journal of the Polynesian Society*, vol. 46, pp. 105–22

C. Official Papers

Deighton, S. J. (1889), 'A Moriori Vocabulary', *Appendices to the Journal of the House of Representatives*, G.5, pp. 1–7

Florance, R. S. (1900), 'The Chatham Islands', *New Zealand Official Yearbook*, Wellington, pp. 531–39

Halse, Henry (1867), 'Report on the Chatham Islands', *Appendices to the Journal of the House of Representatives*, A.4, pp. 3–8

Seed, William (1862), 'Report on the Chatham Islands', *New Zealand Gazette*, no. 4, pp. 26–32

D. Newspapers

Baucke, William (1922), 'An Extinct Race, Moriories of the Chathams', *New Zealand Herald*, 8/7/22, 15/7/22, 22/7/22, 29/2/22, 5/8/22, 12/8/22, 19/8/22, 26/8/22, 2/9/22, 9/9/22, 23/9/22, 14/10/22

Relevant issues of the *Listener*, *New Zealand Woman's Weekly*, *Otago Witness*, *Otago Daily Times*, *The Press* (Christchurch), *Lyttelton Times*, *Christchurch Star*, *Evening Post* (Wellington), *Waikato Times*, *New Zealand Herald* and *Auckland Star*, and other publications, all identified in individual source notes

INDEX

In cases where nineteenth-century Moriori or Maori have no identifiable surname, they are listed according to the name by which they were best known (which often became a surname for their descendants). References in illustration captions are indicated in *italics*; and in footnotes by the letter n.

WRESTLING WITH THE

Angel

a *life* of janet frame

MICHAEL KING

Janet Frame, born in 1924, is New Zealand's most celebrated and least public author. Her early life in small South Island towns seemed, at times, engulfed in a tide of doom: one brother still-born, another epileptic; two sisters dead of heart failure while swimming; Frame herself committed to mental hospitals for the best part of a decade. Later, her surviving sister was temporarily felled in adulthood by a stroke, an uncle cut his throat and a cousin shot his lover, his lover's parents and then himself.

All this propelled Frame into a territory resembling that 'where the dying spend their time before death'. Those who return alive from such a place, she would say, bring a point of view 'equal in its rapture and chilling exposure [to] the neighbourhood of the gods and goddesses'.

This, then, is an inspiring biography of a woman who climbed out of an abyss of unhappiness to take control of her life and become one of the great writers of her time. And to enable her biographer to write this book scrupulously and honestly, Janet Frame spoke for the first time about her *whole* life. She also made available her personal papers and directed her family and friends to be equally communicative.

The result is a biography of astonishing intimacy and frankness. Just as Frame's own writing takes readers to the boundaries of the knowable, so this book penetrates deeply into the mind and character of its subject. The fact that Frame has previously been known above all else for her reticence makes this achievement all the more remarkable.

'Michael King has succeeded magnificently. The comprehensiveness and intelligence of his treatment are highly rewarding . . . [This] book is a remarkable exception to the rule that biographers cannot write about living subjects.'

Michael Holroyd

TOMORROW
COMES THE SONG

A LIFE OF PETER FRASER

Michael Bassett with Michael King

Peter Fraser was a New Zealand Labour Prime Minister and Commonwealth statesman of great stature whose life and career spanned the early and mid-twentieth century.

Born into poverty and discontent in the Highlands of Scotland, Peter Fraser came to New Zealand in his twenties. He moved rapidly through the ranks of union and Labour leaders. He organised strikes and he was twice jailed in New Zealand in the First World War for opposing conscription.

At the end of the war, not long out of prison, Fraser was elected to Parliament, and became a leading architect of Labour's path to power in the 1920s and early 1930s. In the first Labour Government in 1935 he was a senior figure, serving as deputy Prime Minister to Michael Joseph Savage. He was an outstanding Minister of Education and Health.

He became Prime Minister on Savage's death in 1940 and steered the country through the Second World War, a performance that led Winston Churchill to say that New Zealand 'never put a foot wrong'. More than anything else, perhaps, he is known for this role.

During the war and the early years of peace, Fraser was a courageous voice on behalf of smaller nations at Commonwealth conferences and he also played a significant world role in the setting up of the United Nations Organisation.

This major book, in the tradition of Keith Sinclair's *Walter Nash* biography, is written by two leading historians, Michael King and Michael Bassett. While it covers the whole of Fraser's life, it concentrates especially on the decade 1940 to 1950 when, as the authors note, he *was* the Labour Party in New Zealand.

Tomorrow comes the Song will be published by Penguin Books in early 2001.

FRANK SARGESON
─── A LIFE ───

Michael King

Frank Sargeson (1903–82) was the first major New Zealand writer to remain in New Zealand. From the 1930s, he turned New Zealand writing in a new direction, publishing short stories that 'moulded the language and rhythm of everyday New Zealand speech into a literary form' and won acclaim throughout the English-speaking world.

Born in Hamilton, where his father was a leader in the Methodist Church, Sargeson qualified as a solicitor, travelled to Britain and Europe, then spent nearly two years on an uncle's King Country farm before establishing himself as a writer on Auckland's North Shore in 1931. Sargeson lived in Takapuna for the next fifty years. There, in a primitive family bach and later in an asbestos cottage that still stands, he wrote the stories which earned him a world-wide reputation for their compression and power. Later he wrote plays, then novels that escaped the severe boundaries he had imposed on his stories.

Sargeson was a man of contradictions. While rejecting the puritanism of his youth, he was puritan in his total commitment to his calling as a writer. In genuinely poor health much of his life, he was also a hypochondriac. At times quarrelsome and even malicious, he was generous and deeply compassionate as a mentor to younger writers, notably Janet Frame, and in caring for social derelicts. He was unflinchingly honest about most things, yet every aspect of his life and writing was touched by the need to conceal his homosexuality and a traumatic court case which arose from it.

All this is is brought out in this masterly biography by Michael King. Like its subject it is alternately illuminating, entertaining, and affecting.

BEING PAKEHA NOW

*Reflections and Recollections
of a White Native*

Michael King

When *Being Pakeha* appeared in 1985 it was acclaimed as a seminal book: the first serious analysis of what it meant to be a non-Maori New Zealander. This book continues the story.

Now, more than a decade later, that original text has been re-thought, rewritten and expanded considerably to include the author's sometimes bruising encounters with Maori and Moriori, his interaction with other New Zealand writers, and his engagement with his own culture of origin, that of Catholic Ireland.

In *Being Pakeha Now*, Michael King carries the cultural debate forward. While recognising and respecting the place of Maori in New Zealand, he argues that Pakeha too belong inescapably to this country and have no other home. Just as imported East Polynesian ingredients were eventually transmuted into Maori culture, so the attitudes and values carried by Europeans have been transformed here in interaction with forest, mountain and sea, and with Maori. They have coalesced into a second indigenous culture, that of Pakeha New Zealanders. The wooden church and the macrocarpa, King asserts, are as much part of the spiritual and physical landscape of Aotearoa/ New Zealand as the meeting house and the cabbage tree.

Being Pakeha Now is part memoir, part apologia and part celebration of a country and its people. It is an exciting journey into the hinterland of the national psyche by New Zealand's most respected writer of history and biography.

MAKING PEOPLES

A History of the New Zealanders

*From Polynesian Settlement
to the End of the Nineteenth Century*

JAMES BELICH

This book reshapes our understanding of New Zealand history. It challenges traditional views on many fronts and asks questions that have not been asked before.

Making Peoples is the first book in a major two-volume work by James Belich. It covers the period from Polynesian settlement to the end of the nineteenth century.

Making Peoples examines Maori and Pakeha backgrounds, Maori settlement and pre-contact history. It re-interprets Maori-European relations from 1642 to the early 1900s, suggesting a new 'living' version of the Treaty of Waitangi. It traces European settlement, and unravels the myths and realities which drove the colonisation process. Finally, it presents a new picture of the colonial economy and society, and re-examines the origins of Pakeha.

A recurring theme is the construction of peoples, Maori and Pakeha: the response of each to the great shift from extractive to sustainable economics; their relationship with their Hawaikis, with each other, and with myth.

This immensely readable book, full of drama and humour as well as scholarship, is a watershed in the writing of New Zealand history. In making many new assertions and challenging many historical myths it seeks to reinterpret our approach to the past. It is essential reading for everyone interested in New Zealand history, and in the history of new societies in general.

The second volume in the series, *Paradise Reforged*, will be published by Penguin Books in late 2001.

THE
NEW ZEALAND
WARS

and the
Victorian Interpretation of Racial Conflict

James Belich

This trail-blazing book rewrites our understanding of the wars between Maori and Pakeha, and of colonial warfare in general. It is the inspiration for the five-part television documentary series of the same name which is written and presented by James Belich.

'James Belich's book is a tour de force. In a brilliant new analysis, he demolishes the received version of the course and outcome of the New Zealand Wars . . . explains how we came by the version and why it is all wrong, and substitutes his own interpretation. . . . It is a vigorous and splendidly stylish contribution to our historiography.'

Dr Ann Parsonson, *NZ Listener*

'A splendid book, fascinating, provocative and superbly researched . . . in a class of its own.'

Angela Sherlock, *Race and Class*

'As complete and as brilliant a re-examination as one could imagine.'
Dr Bruce Collins, *Times Higher Education Supplement*

'This is not just a good book. It is a remarkable book.'
Professor Keith Sinclair

The New Zealand Wars has won three book awards, including the international Trevor Reese Memorial Prize in 1988 for the most 'outstanding work of scholarship published in the field of imperial and Commonwealth history in the preceding two years'.

Struggle Without End
Ka Whawhai Tonu Matou

Ranginui Walker

'For 150 years the Maori has struggled . . .'

This respected and long-selling book is a new history of Aotearoa, New Zealand, recounted from a Maori perspective.

For Dr Ranginui Walker the past 150 years have been an endless struggle by Maori for social justice, equality and self-determination. His book provides a uniquely Maori view, not only of the events of 1990 and the past 150 years but also of the entire period of human settlement – and even beyond to the very origins of the Maori people. It deserves to be read by every Maori and every Pakeha.

First published over a decade ago, *Struggle With End, Ka Whawhai Tonu Matou*, has become the accepted version of the Maori view of New Zealand since first settlement.